Fountains of the Deep

Fountains of the Deep

BY STEVEN L. ROSS

SISTERS, OREGON

Fountains of the Deep

© 2010 by Steven L. Ross

Scripture verses are from the King James Version of the Bible unless otherwise stated.

Transliterated Pronounceable Bible™,
© 1988 by International Bible Translators, Inc.
© 1988 Electronic Work Project.
Ellis Enterprises, Inc.
4205 McAuley Blvd. #385
Oklahoma City OK 73120

Morris' Literal Translation Linked to Strong's Numbers
© 1988 by International Bible Translators, Inc.
© 1988 Ellis Enterprises, Inc.
Ellis Enterprises, Inc.
4205 McAuley Blvd. #385
Oklahoma City OK 73120

Published by
Deep River Books
Sisters, Oregon
http://www.deepriverbooks.com

ISBN 10: 1-935265-33-4
ISBN 13: 978-1-935265-33-7

Library of Congress Control Number: 2010931138

Printed in the USA

Cover design by Robin Black, www.blackbirdcreative.biz

CONTENTS

Section One:

A Science Teacher's Commentary on the Creation Story

Beginning at the Beginning

Introductions

Often people start off by asking me, "What kind of creationist book is this?" This tells me that they have already put some time into studying the various systems and simply want to know whether they already agree with me or not. So, with deep reluctance, I take a deep breath and let them know that they can place this book in the pigeonhole labeled "Old-earth Creationism."

I really, really don't like that.

The secular college student who opposes any kind of creationist position will assume that I am some kind of crank who thinks Darwin was the devil and that I will engage in sneaky word games and crackpot science to try to shove my dubious religion down their throats.

"Young-earth" creationists will automatically assume that I am a semi-heathen who enjoys trampling all over the Word of God, ignoring what it plainly says.

1

"Old-earth" creationists will think they already know everything I have to say, and then wonder why they should bother to read the text.

This means I have to introduce this book while standing in the crossfire between three bitterly feuding groups—all three made up of people who deserve my respect. So, here goes.

FIRST—TO THE SECULAR COLLEGE STUDENT: That you have this book in your hand at all tells me that you at least have some curiosity about this issue. While primarily a Bible study, this book sticks strictly to mainstream science, or at least it tries to. If I do stray from mainstream scientific thought, it is simply a mistake on my part; I have no intention of proposing my own astounding scientific theories. I have no scientific axes to grind. You can find all of this book's science in any current encyclopedia.

Also, I did teach high school science for twenty years. While this hardly qualifies me as a scientist, I flatter myself by saying I have a fairly reasonable grasp of modern science as it filters out to the interested layman.

Certainly, you know that some Christian religious traditions and modern science have been at war with each other for over a century. However, please keep two things in mind about this.

One: "modern" science today is a very different thing from what "modern" science was a century ago.

Two: the Bible and religious tradition, no matter how sincere, are often two very different things. You may have heard some (certainly not all) traditionalists confidently proclaim that the Bible says the earth is only six thousand years old, or that the dinosaurs were the dragons of the Middle Ages. And I can well understand why you might then take that traditionalist's word on the matter and consider dumping the Bible in the garbage can, unread.

Please don't. I assure you that would be a huge mistake. The Bible has much to say of vital interest to you today. I simply ask that you take the time to read this series of lessons and judge for yourself whether or not you should take the Bible seriously.

2

SECOND—TO THE TRADITIONALIST: I am an evangeli-
cal Christian. This means I view the Bible as the infallible Word of
God, and, all other things being equal, I tend to side with traditional
understandings of what any particular passage of the Bible means.
However, like most evangelicals, given a reasonable argument, I am
willing to amend my understanding of that biblical passage and
dump any minor tradition with relatively little fuss or bother.

Ask yourself why you honor the Bible. Is it because it has shown
itself to be the infallible Word of God, or is it because it's your
church's or family's tradition? Is the Bible true because your pastor
says so, or because all of creation declares it so?

This book grew out of my frustration with the well-meaning sil-
liness that often passes itself off as creation science in most of the
available texts. Watching a church equip their Christian students with
such nonsense and then send them off for slaughter at college simply
makes me cringe—especially since the carnage is so unnecessary.

Please—given that the stakes are so high—don't let your assumptions about what you think the Bible *means* keep you from taking
the time to look a bit more closely at what the Bible actually *says*.

THIRD—TO THE OLD-EARTH CREATIONIST: The science
in the first section of this book dovetails with the standard day-age
approach to the creation story that views the word *day* as a synonym
for *age* or *era*. You may already be familiar with most, though maybe
not all, of the parallels between the creation story and modern science presented in section one. However, while I certainly wish Dr.
Hugh Ross and his organization "Reasons to Believe" well, this book
presents a different approach. (By the way, I sat down with Hugh
once about twenty years ago, and we determined that we were in no
way cousins, despite the similarity of our names and the tracks our
lives had taken to that point.)

While you may think you understand the "Revelation Days"
approach to the creation story that this book takes, the odds are

against it. The last three sections of this book place that approach firmly in the context of the Exodus and explore implications you may not have considered before. I think you will be pleased with this book.

THE BOOK'S METHODOLOGY: First, to paraphrase Isaac Newton: When several ways exist to interpret a passage from the Book of God's *Word* (the Bible), evidence from the book of God's *works* (science) can rightly settle the issue.[1] Some find this the rankest heresy. They consider the objective world so intrinsically evil that any attempt to use it to interpret the Word of God is blasphemous. However, in spite of their praiseworthy respect for the Bible, it seems to me that they ignore at least three important Biblical truths.

- Truth # 1: In the Old Testament, a prophet's words were not validated by a committee of orthodox theologians; they were validated by observed events:

  "When a prophet speaketh in the name of the Lord, if the thing follow not . . . the Lord hath not spoken, but the prophet hath spoken it presumptuously." (Deuteronomy 18:22)

  None of this business of "religious truth"—either the thing was demonstrably and observably true, or it was simply false.

- Truth # 2: Jesus said to Nicodemus:

  "If I have told you earthly things, and ye believe not, how shall ye believe, if I tell you of heavenly things?" (John 3:12)

---

1. Schaeffer, 1976, p.142, cites Newton's *New Organon.*

This implies that earthly knowledge is more basic than heavenly knowledge, and that ignorance of the first often blocks knowledge of the second. It bemuses me to see someone take pride in their ignorance of "worldly science," thinking this somehow makes them more competent to handle the Word of God.

- Truth # 3: This universe is God's creation. According to Paul:

"For the invisible things of him [God] from the creation of the world are clearly seen, being understood by the things that are made." (Romans 1:20)

In other words, the Bible itself says that the natural world tells us many true things about the nature and works of God. In orthodox theology, going back centuries, the natural world is called "God's primary revelation," while the Word of God is called "God's secondary revelation." As impious as this may sound at first, if you haven't first learned to speak and read from human society around you, and you didn't have access to actual symbols, you would have no objective Word of God. This means that for us the natural, physical world is primary (occurs first).

Second, we are only going to skim the surface of a whole library's worth of material. We will not have time to do more than mention a few other viewpoints. This book offers only a simple introduction to what it considers the best information available today. If, as is likely, future evidence makes some of that information obsolete, then neither the author nor you should be particularly shocked.

Third, many evangelicals have a problem with the huge numbers casually batted around by cosmologists and paleontologists. However, we will not deal with dates until chapter four, "Trouble with Tradition." So, if this is a problem for you, I ask that you be patient and wait until then to raise objections. Just pretend you're reading a novel and suspend your disbelief for now. I think you will find as we go along that the old dates are the Bible's friends.

THE SCIENCE TEACHER'S VERSION: Unless otherwise noted, all biblical quotes come from the King James Version of the Bible (the KJV), since, as a literary standard, the KJV has had the largest impact on how the general public visualizes the creation, Garden of Eden, and flood stories. However, in the first three chapters and in chapter seven, I refer to my own translation of the creation story, called the "Science Teacher's Version of the Creation Story," (the STV or the STeVe—Oh, stop groaning!) I have appended a table in the back of each of those chapters showing how the STV was derived. Once you have had a chance to see the logic of the translation, I offer the complete STV at the end of chapter seven.

Please don't take the STV to imply that I, the author, am a towering Hebrew scholar. Yes, I have trained to pastor a church, and yes, I have researched this material for the past forty years. And, yes, I have attempted a translation of the creation story. However, like most pastors, I have only the sketchiest grasp of the Hebrew language, and have had to rely on the many excellent reference books now available to the linguistically challenged. Hopefully, you will not give the STV more weight than it deserves, but will merely use it as a springboard for your own research.

THE ISSUE: For nearly 1,700 years the Bible stood at the foundation of the thinking and values of Western civilization. As late as the mid-twentieth century, the American legal system viewed the Bible as "organic to the constitution" and admitted it in court as legal precedent. The practice of requiring witnesses to take an oath with one hand on the Bible was more than a quaint tradition. Those who publicly rejected the Bible could be and on occasion were banned from giving testimony in court.[2]

---

2. Barton, pp. 47–82.

However, in the second half of the nineteenth century, the Western world's academic elite had begun to view the Bible with increasing suspicion and doubt. The rise of scientific rationalism and especially the speculations of paleontology and archaeology resulted in the casting of increasing doubt on the Bible's reliability and even its authenticity. It was then that "higher criticism" laid out complex and scholarly analyses to insist that the Old Testament Bible had "evolved" from primitive verbal traditions and did not become something similar to our modern Bible until as late as 200 BC.

By the early twentieth century, among the American intellectual elite, the matter was settled. While the Bible had retained its status as a cultural and literary standard, in their view only religious zealots or uneducated bumpkins could possibly take the Bible seriously as history or science.

Finally, in the mid-twentieth century, the Federal Supreme Court felt confident enough to issue its famous "no prayer in the public schools" decision without referencing a single line of any legal document, ignoring all precedent, and scorning the wishes of well over 95 percent of the voting public.[3] The opinion of the elite carried more weight. The Bible was no longer considered appropriate material for serious academic study, and America was no longer considered an officially Christian nation.

This brings us to the beginning of the twenty-first century. Given the mainstream academic confidence of the last 150 years, we would expect that by now cosmology, paleontology, and archeology would have driven the last nail in that particular coffin, ratifying the end of the Judeo-Christian era of Western civilization. However, most inconveniently for that elite group, it just hasn't worked out that way.

In fact, scientific orthodoxy now routinely refers to the greatest catastrophe known in the history of human civilization as Noah's flood. Furthermore, recent excavations in the Mediterranean and the Nile Delta have confirmed many of the background details of

---

3. Ibid., pp. 147–149.

the Exodus story. Worse yet for that elite group, in spite of the Scopes Monkey Trial and the huge creationism vs. Darwinism debate in the public schools, virtually every detail of the events of the Bible's creation story have been confirmed, in order, by the traitorous fields of cosmology and paleontology.

Now, this is not to say that so-called "Scientific Creationism" or the old Sunday school teacher's flannel board have come through all that well themselves. Modern science has pretty much savaged both sides of that particular feud. So, while religious tradition hasn't fared so well, a more literal reading of the Bible's Hebrew language has done very well indeed.

DAY ONE

Since the Bible's creation story remains the focus of the controversy that makes the seven o'clock news, we will begin with a word-by-word study of the creation story. Remember, you can turn to the back of each chapter to find the STV word study tools to see how and why the STV differs from the KJV passage.

(Genesis 1:1a STV) In the beginning, and most importantly . . . For most of the twentieth century, non-Christian cosmologists argued with Christians about the birth of our universe. Until recently, most taught that the universe is stable with some parts collapsing into black holes while other parts spew out from quasars. This "steady-state" view taught that the physical universe stretched into infinity past in an endless cycle and had no beginning.

When in 1927 a Belgian Roman Catholic priest (and professor of physics and astronomer) named Georges Lemaiter published evidence to suggest that our universe had a definite beginning, he grossly offended their secular tastes. In derision, they dubbed that nonsense the "Big Bang Theory," refusing to take it seriously.[4]

---

4. http://www.catholiceducation.org/articles/science/sc0022.html#, accessed October 19, 2009.

However, astronomical observations over the past thirty years have rudely supported that view.[5] Using the Hubble telescope that orbits the earth, astronomers have confirmed that our universe is expanding at an increasing rate. By looking far into the universe, given the limited speed of light, they can thus peer thirteen billion years into the past and see actual shock waves of an original "Big Bang." All matter originated from one tiny spot; it exploded into existence all at once, and it came from no detectable source. In other words, the universe had a definite beginning, just as Genesis says.

Note also that the word translated as "In the beginning" implies more than just a start; it implies the greatest importance.

(Genesis 1:1b STV) Almighty God created . . . According to the creation story, the most important thing to remember is that our universe begins in a deliberate, willful, creative act. Mathematicians currently working with cosmology have emphasized the arbitrary randomness of the laws or "universal constants" that were set during the process of the Big Bang and that govern our universe— things like the limiting speed of light and the intensity of gravity. On its face, it appears that some intelligent will set the laws in motion that made our universe possible. However, most secular cosmologists absolutely refuse to accept this for all the same reasons they refused to accept the Big Bang theory until observed facts rubbed their noses in it.

So, they've moved their arguments back a step, and proposed that the fundamental fabric of reality somehow constantly generates billions of universes, and that the unique constants that make our universe possible were simply a result of a random, non-thinking process. They find it easy to accept that the fabric of existence is both eternal and infinitely complex. But, for some reason they find it impossible to accept the possibility that that same infinitely complex fabric could have a conscious will at least as complex as that generated by our three-pound brains.

5. McGraw Hill, vol. 4 p. 471.

Dr. Hugh Ross, in 1989, outlined the main points of this issue in his book, *The Fingerprint of God*. He used his background in astronomy and physics to present a history of the debate over the Big Bang and outline the developments that have undermined the opposing theories. Currently, Dr. Ross heads the organization "Reasons to Believe"[6] based in Glendora, California, which spearheads the current day-age approach to the creation story.

(Genesis 1:1c STV) whirling flows . . . Take a close look at the KJV word *heaven*. In the English language the word heaven is simply the past participle of the word to heave, which means to throw with great force, or to vomit (for example: "Give him the old heave ho!" or, "He suffered from the dry heaves"). This may seem like a strange or even rude source for the word for heaven. But, this compares closely with the Hebrew word for heaven: *shaamayim*. This is itself a combination for two words: *shaa* (rushing, dizzy) and *mayim* (water, wine, urine, or liquid.)

The first word, *shaa*, implies rushing, headlong speed. According to the current inflationary model, the early universe expanded at many times the speed of light, since the universal constant of the limiting speed of light had not yet kicked in; certainly, it expanded at "dizzying" speed.

Was the original material of the universe a liquid? For centuries, most school children learned that matter comes in one of three states: solid, liquid, or gas. However, modern physics has added a fourth state of matter to the list: plasmas—magnetically supercharged gasses—that under extreme heat and pressure collapse on themselves and flow like liquids. Since plasmas make up the bodies of most stars, including our own sun, they comprise the most common state of matter. Until recently, most of us had never seen plasma on the surface of the earth. It only existed in such rare natural phenomenon as ball lightning, or was artificially produced in the scientist's laboratory. However, today many of us have seen the very weak plasma in a plasma lamp.

6. http://www.reasons.org

The original material of our universe consisted only of whirling plasmas. Certainly, the ancient Hebrew language could only have described it as *shaamayim*. So, while modern cosmology has only just discovered that our universe began as an explosion of dizzily rushing liquids, the Bible knew it 3,500 years ago.

(Genesis 1:1d STV) and then solid matter . . . Notice, the earth comes second, a minor point, but a point nonetheless.

When we say "the earth," we usually think of the planet earth. However, to the ancients, any solid ground was "earth." Nothing hinders us from taking the Hebrew *aarets* from referring to all solid matter, not just our own planet. Modern cosmology tells us that the creation of solid matter represents the second major step in the development of our universe. Soon after the Big Bang, the expanding shock waves of whirling plasmas began to clump up in "gravity wells." Cosmologists use this term to describe what happens on a stellar scale, as gravity causes the matter in any given region to contract inward on itself.

With all that compact plasma in the infant universe, huge stars formed quickly. As more and more plasma rushed inward, the crush of gravity at each star's core forced protons and neutrons to fuse together, creating heavier elements, and releasing even more heat as a by-product. On a much smaller scale, this process of nuclear fusion heats our own sun.

However, these huge protostars in the infant universe sucked in so much matter so quickly that they simply could not absorb it all. So, they exploded in supernovas. In those explosions most of the cores' solid matter blew away. Some solid chunks became the "seeds" to begin more gravity wells and create more stars. Other pieces simply shot-gunned their way between the stars. So, in a literal sense, solid matter started with its own big bang.

During the processes of star seeding, the fusion of smaller sub-atomic particles into heavier elements, along with supernova explosions, the infant universe expanded and cooled. Eventually, it entered its childhood.

(Genesis 1:2a STV) And the solid matter was empty desolation. . . . Earlier, the condensation and explosion process had been much too intense and violent for anything like what we now call a planetary system to exist. However, as the universe continued to expand and cool, and as enough of the original plasma condensed, vast voids began to spread between the stars.

(Genesis 1:2b STV) And, darkness . . . After the first generation of protostars, a stellar formation of a different nature began. Today, astronomers can watch this process through their telescopes. Instead of collapsing plasmas, they see interstellar clouds called nebulas, primarily made of light elements like hydrogen. While the infant universe roared with incredible light and radiation, nebulas look like huge black clouds.

(Genesis 1:2c STV) wrapped a turning sphere deep in a surging mass . . . These nebulas wrap the smaller gravity wells of swirling chunks of solid matter. As some of those chunks begin to cluster and clump, they create relatively dense whirl pooling disks within the body of the nebula. Increasingly, these pull in more and more matter, thinning the nebula between the various gravity wells. Eventually, the nebula thins to the point that the starlight from outside it begins to blow the nebula back on itself, exposing the dark whirlpools of debris and denser gases.[7] As the edge of the nebula withdraws, it gives the illusion that it has left oblong seeds or eggs in its wake. Astronomers call these star pods.

Within each star pod, gases and solid debris whirl and collide in utter darkness. Only dim red sparkling impacts on the forming planets and center masses (that will eventually combine to make the center star) give any light. Astronomers call this the Hadean stage of planetary formation, after the Greek word for hell: *Hades*. What better description of the interior of a nebular star pod could we hope for than what Genesis gives us: "shapeless desolation, and emptiness, and darkness?"

---

7. Whipple, p. 214.

Far away from the wildly spinning center masses, other chunks have established almost circular orbits in the plane of the spinning star pod. The further-out planets usually represent larger pieces that never joined the central whirlpool. The nearer and smaller planets represent tiny droplets that have splashed off collisions within the center masses. The center star has not yet ignited. Although it glows from the heat of contraction and its many collisions, the surrounding nebular gases shield it from view.

The same gases that pour into the center masses flow into and around those planets. Indeed, since the planets lie in the heart of a nebular star pod, each one's atmosphere extends many thousands of miles. Today, earth has a bare skin of an atmosphere, a mere fifty miles deep. But even that thin skin exerts a pressure at sea level of fourteen pounds on every square inch. Think of the pressure exerted by thousands of miles of atmosphere. It would literally reduce the planet's surface into a pressure cooker. Cosmologists call that primitive pressure cooker a stage-one atmosphere.[8]

The word the KJV translates as *face* here in "upon the *face* of the deep" actually relates to any object that is round or spherical and turns. It closely relates to the word for pearl. Here you have a great description of the stage-one planet earth before the ignition of the sun. Imagine what a stage-one planet would look like. Against the velvety dark background of the swirling nebular star pod, the planet has a faint, shimmering pearl-like glow. The friction of the inward whirling dust storm of debris creates vast ionic charges, which in turn release lightning storms and auroras much larger that the beautiful northern lights that we see today.

Let's take a short detour to something you may have learned in your math classes. "The sum of the squares of the two legs of a right triangle equals the square of its hypotenuse." Remember that? It's called the Pythagorean Theorem, named after a Greek philosopher and mathematician who lived between 500 and 600 BC. Well,

---

8. McGraw Hill, Vol. 2, p. 166.

Pythagoras has another claim to fame: "Credit for the idea that the Earth is spherical is usually given to Pythagoras . . . and his school, who reasoned that, because the Moon and Sun are spherical, the Earth is too."[9]

This was really revolutionary stuff in the early Iron Age. But, wait a minute! We just saw that Genesis casually uses the word for sphere to refer to the earth, long before the birth of any of the Greek philosophers. So, next time you sit in a science class that gives Pythagoras the credit for first saying the earth is a sphere, raise your hand, and let them know that Genesis said it first. Not only that, note that the Hebrew word for sphere also implies turning. This is why this word is also translated as face. People have round heads that turn laterally. Even Pythagoras didn't know that the earth turned.

(Genesis 1:2d STV) And, the breath of Almighty God . . . Currently many cosmologists looking at nebulas believe that they see mists of organic compounds. According to this view, many of the basic building blocks of life literally blew onto the infant earth from the nebular cloud, like the breath of God.

(Genesis 1:2e STV) fluttered like a nesting hen . . . The Hebrew word for move in the KJV refers to the action of a hen on her nest. Since you may not have grown up on a farm, you might not know that when a hen sits on her nest, and it gets cold outside, she gently flutters and shakes her feathers over that egg, so friction and her activity can keep it warm.

That stage-one earth was like a giant egg, complete with a shell, liquids, and living seed. Geologists call the few patches of earth's crust that remain from this era the Archeozoic layer of the Precambrian. (Geological names like these can refer either to the rock layers themselves or the periods of geological history during which those layers formed.)

Without stretching the metaphor too far, note that hens sit on their nests for several weeks. In using this metaphor, Genesis im-

---

9. Encyclopedia Britannica Vol. 17, p. 534.

plies the passage of time. Even most traditionalists who believe that each of the creative days lasts only twenty-four hours are willing to concede that this passage takes place before the first day and may therefore cover any length of time, even billions of years.

When scientists examine rocks from this earliest period under their microscopes, they see traces of the amino acids that form the building blocks of life. Even at that early date, chemical processes created amino acids much like those found in the white of an egg. "Molecules of formaldehyde and hydrogen cyanide were chemically synthesized in the early atmosphere . . . [and precipitated] into the oceans . . . which eventually led to the chemical synthesis of amino acids."[10] Another source states: "Experiments by S. L. Miller in 1953 . . . showed that a mixture of methane, ammonia, water, and hydrogen, when subjected to an electric discharge gave significant yields of simple amino acids, hydroxyl acids, aliphatic acids, urea, and possibly sugars. Ultra violet light gives similar results. [Therefore] it is thought that [these] compounds . . . were present in the oceans of primitive Earth."[11]

God brooded over the fertile planetary egg, protecting it, letting the seed of life grow, and making sure that the next event didn't destroy its fragile balance.

(Genesis 1:2f STV) on the turning sphere of waters . . . During this period, the earth's crust is much too unstable and volcanic, and the atmosphere much too thick to have a permanent layer of water. However, the inward flowing nebular cloud constantly adds water to the atmosphere until water bathes the whole surface by way of pouring hot rains that gush over millions of shifting pools, each stained with its own colored minerals and amino acids. Think of a soggy Yellowstone National Park magnified a million times.

(Genesis 1:3 STV) And Almighty God said, "Be light," and it was light . . . A few years back astronomers saw something amazing hap-

---

10. McGraw Hill, Vol. 10, p. 46.
11. Magill, p. 115

pen. They saw that a star pod had turned on like a neon light—an apt analogy, since the thin gases that fill the nebula are quite similar to the gases that fill the glass tube of a neon light.[12]

The center masses at the star pod's core, in spinning and grinding against each other, had overcome the centrifugal force of their spinning dance and merged into a much larger single mass. This increased the crunch of gravity in the star's core, which in its turn triggered a regularly recurring fusion reaction, like the heartbeat of millions of hydrogen bomb explosions in its core.

The outpouring of electromagnetic radiation not only lit up the star, it lit up the entire star pod with a bright, though relatively cool glow of excited ions. In addition, the intense visible light given off by the infant star itself reflected through the entire star pod. If you have ever ridden in a car in a thick fog at night, you many have noticed this. If the driver turns the headlights on high, then the light bounces around off the fog's water droplets and lights up even the back of the car. When the sun lamp switched on, light poured into the watery planet from all directions, with no dark spot or night forming shadow anywhere.

(Gen. 1:4a STV) And Almighty God saw the light, "That's good" . . . Many modern people have a lot of trouble with thinking of God as evaluative or judgmental. And certainly, they are right that the thought of an evaluative God leads to lots of uncomfortable conclusions. However, we will leave those implications to a later chapter. Here we see God call the light "good, pleasant, fitting."

This raises the question, "Could the light have been bad?" Scientists estimate that life has reached this same stage on many millions of planets, only to be blasted away by the wrong light—too cold, too hot, too unstable, too radioactive. According to modern science, the light could have been bad in a thousand ways. Yet, like Goldilocks tasting Baby Bear's porridge, this light was just right. Surviving the ignition of the Sun was the first huge milestone in the development

---

12. McGraw, Vol. 16 pp. 592–593.

of life on earth. Paleontology points to several milestones, crises in the history of earth's life. We will find that one of those milestones correlates to each usage of the word *good* in the creation story.

(Genesis 1:4b STV) And then Almighty God separated the light from the darkness . . . Scientists have continued to watch as that newly ignited star pod blows brightly colored feathers of gases straight out from below and above the star pod's center. You see, light pushes. It doesn't push much, but it does push. Some have called this light pressure, "the wind from the Sun." Some have even gone as far as to suggest that NASA could build spaceships with huge sails to catch the Sun's light and "sail" from planet to planet.

So, like a huge feather duster, that star has begun the process of sweeping the remaining nebular gases out the system's back door. This is why scientists work so hard to have space probes take samples from the tails of comets. Those comets are the leftover sweepings from when our Sun first ignited.

Let's return to our point of view just above the stage-one planet. In the process of the solar wind blowing the nebular gases from between the planets, it begins blowing away the thick outer layer of the earth's atmosphere, relieving the surface pressure, speeding the cooling process.

As the haze clears, the planet casts a distinct shadow for the first time, and the darkness pulls away from the light; until finally, a clear-cut line divides light from darkness. For the first time, earth has day and night.

(Genesis 1:5a STV) And Almighty God called the light day and the darkness He called the twist away. . . Notice that the word for night here is simply a twist or turning away. Furthermore, the night does the turning, not the light. Also remember that the Hebrew word used earlier for the face of the earth implies the act of turning. These two words combined strongly suggest that it is the earth itself that does the turning. This may seem an obvious point, but think about it. Before Copernicus, virtually everyone believed that the earth stood still

and the Sun did the turning. Yet here, three thousand years before Galileo's infamous trial, we have Genesis say that the spherical-turning earth turns away from the Sun to produce night.

(Genesis 1:5b STV) And was evening and was morning, Day One. This simple phrase has much more import that you may think at first glance.

Of course, the traditional view takes this to refer to the newly made day and night just mentioned. And then, when the similar phrase comes up a few verses later, "And this was evening, and this was morning, Day Two," tradition takes that to say that God created all those other things in just one day. Tradition then reasonably goes on to say that Genesis claims that God created at least our whole solar system—Sun, Moon, Earth, and all its life forms—in just six days (or five if you exclude the first day.)

However, archaeology has shown us that this innocent-looking phrase may have much more to say to us. Sixty-something years ago, a retired British Officer named P. J. Wiseman spent quite a bit of time in the Middle East studying up on the writing conventions of the cuneiform tablets left over from the early Bronze Age. In 1949 he published his findings in "Creation Revealed in Six Days."

One of those conventions consisted of closing a clay tablet with a note about the time and occasion on which the tablet was written. The closing note was called a colophon.

This is a simpler form of our convention of closing a letter:

Sincerely yours,	Polite nothing
	Space for a signature authenticating the letter
John Doe	Printed, readable version of the signature
8/13/2009	Date of the letter
slr	lowercase initials of the secretary typing the letter

Wiseman concluded that the periodic "This was evening and this was morning, Day #" had all the earmarks of the standard Middle-Eastern colophon for legal documents.

If so, this would mean that the "Day #" formulas in the creation story referred not to how long it took God to do the things recording in the passage, but rather was a note about exactly when the scribe recorded God's message. Wiseman concluded that the creation story represented a record of successive days of revelation to Moses during the first seven-day feast of unleavened bread, the actual Exodus itself.[13]

When Wiseman published his theory, any connection between early written Hebrew and cuneiform was problematic at best. And so, while many scholars agreed that this approach potentially fit the passage, it garnered little popular support at the time.

However, recent findings have demonstrated the connection between cuneiform and written Hebrew (which we will outline in the next chapter). So, given the current findings, Wiseman's work has been building in popularity with Evangelical Bible scholars.

So, what's the point? As interesting as it may be to us to see these parallels between the creation story and modern science, we have to ask that question.

For us here and now in this context, the point may be that in these last days, when the Bible itself has been under such concentrated attacks, God gives us proof of his hand in the writing of the story. Neither Moses nor any number of clever committees could have written this story just a few centuries ago.

During the last century and a half, many attempts were made to push the writing of the creation story forward into the late Babylonian Empire of 500 BC. In a later chapter we will look at the findings of the last few decades that have completely squashed that idea. However, even if we stipulate that nonsense, we would still have a

---

13. Wiseman, 1948.

modern document that paradoxically dates to 2,500 years ago. It's like we peeled back the page and found a giant eye winking at us.

That's very nice for us; however, we're only the latest generation. Did everyone else waste their time when they read the creation story? Hardly.

First, the story gives context to the Bible itself. When God dramatically shows up at the dawn of literacy, he starts his conversation with us by telling us who he is and how he relates to who we are. He lets us know that he's been here all along, and what he is doing now is not an accident but part of a very well-thought-out plan.

Second, he assures us that not only does he have a plan, he has the longevity and power to make sure everything continues to go according to that plan.

In this chapter we have gone over detailed word-by-word parallels between modern science and the creation story's "day one." We could easily show a condensed Science Channel–style history of cosmology with every word of day one of the creation story in order as a voice-over. As we proceed through the remaining "days," we will find the same thing, only in greater detail. No other religious tradition has any passage that even remotely fits modern science the way the Bible's creation story does.

Recommended Reading: I don't know about you, but when I take any course, the first thing I look for is a list of important books to read. Here's my pick of the five best that relate directly or indirectly to this book:

1.) Dr. Francis A. Schaeffer, *How Should We Then Live: the Rise and Decline of Western Thought and Culture*, 1976, Crossway Books.

This highly influential book has nothing to do with creationism. However, it has much to say about the eighteenth–twentieth century mind shifts that have produced our modern culture.

2.) Dr. Hugh Ross, *The Fingerprint of God*, 1989, Promise Publishing Company.

This book provides a good background in the issues and debate that led to the acceptance of the Big Bang by mainstream science. Dr. Ross heads the organization "Reasons to Believe" at www.reasons.org.

3.) William Ryan & Walter Pitman, *Noah's Flood*, 1998, Simon & Schuster Paperbacks.

This is not a Christian tract. Mainstream geologists, Ryan and Pitman, outline the research in the 1990s that led to the discovery of the Upper Neolithic Black Sea flood that they believe lies at the base of the many flood myths we find all over the world.

4.) K. A. Kitchen, *On the Reliability of the Old Testament*, 2003, Wm. B. Eerdmans Publishing Co.

If you actually already have some college background in Middle Eastern history, I highly recommend you go out and buy a copy of this excellent book and read it at least twice. While Kitchen's work has little or nothing to do with the topic of creationism, in section four I will refer to it quite a bit and even disagree with it once, with much fear and trembling. Certainly, this hefty book is much more scholarly and heavier reading than the one you are now reading, but well worth wading through if you have the background.

5.) David A. Dorsey, *The Literary Structure of the Old Testament*, 1999, Baker Books.

Chapter nine leans heavily on this unexpectedly wonderful book—NOT light reading.

The STV: Day One Table

King James Version of the Bible	Transliterated Pronounceable Bible	Literal Bible with Vertical Strong's #s Bolded Quotes are from Strong's Hebrew Lexicon {Alternate information in braces}	The Science Teacher's Version
1:1 In the beginning	Bree'shiyt	|7225| In the beginning **"the first, in place, time, order or rank"**	In the beginning, and most importantly,
God created	baaraa'	|1254| created **"choose, create (creator), cut down, dispatch, do, make"**	Almighty God created
	Elohiym	|0430| God **"plural of (a deity); gods in the ordinary sense--from [strong]"**	
	'eet	|0853| **"used to point out more definitely the object of a verb or preposition . . . untranslated"**	
the heaven	'hashaamayim	|8064| the heavens **"from an unused root meaning to be lofty; the sky"** {homograph: shaa (rushing or dizzy)+ mayim (waters)}	whirling flows,
and	w'eet	|0853| and	and *then*
the earth.	haa'aarets	|0776| the earth **"probably meaning to be firm"**	solid matter.
1:2 And the earth	Whaa'aarets	|0776| and the earth	And, the solid matter
was	haaytaah	|1961| was	was
without form,	tohuw	|8414| without form **"to lie waste; a desolation (of surface) . . . confusion, empty place, without form,"**	empty desolation.
and void;	waabohuw	|0922| and empty, **"undistinguishable ruin: --emptiness, void."**	
and darkness was	Wchoshek	|2822| and darkness **"the dark; . . . figuratively, misery, destruction, death, ignorance, sorrow, wickedness"**	And, darkness
upon	`al-	|5921| on	wrapped
the face of	pneey	|6440| the surface of **"from to turn; the face (as the part that turns)"** {by implication a sphere or ball}	a turning sphere
the deep	thowm	|8415| the deep **"an abyss (as a surging mass of water), especially the deep (the main sea)"**	deep in a surging mass.
And the Spirit of	Wruwach	|7307| and the Spirit of **"wind; by resemblance breath, i.e. a sensible (or even violent) exhalation"**	And, the breath of
God	Elohiym	|0430| God	Almighty God
moved	mrachepet	|7363| moving gently **"to brood; by implication, to be relaxed: --flutter, move, shake"** {Refers to a hen sitting on her eggs.}	fluttered like a nesting hen
upon	`al-	|5921| on	on
the face	pneey	|6440| the surface of	the turning sphere

22

of the waters	hamaayim	|4325| the waters **"water; … juice; by euphemism, urine, semen"**.	of waters.
1:3 And God said	Wayo'mer 'Elohiym,	|0559| Then said |0430| God,	And, Almighty God said
Let there be	Yhiy	|1961| Let be	"Be
light:	'owr	|0216| light	**light,"**
and there was	wayhiy-	|1961| and was	and it was
light.	'owr.	|0216| light.	light.
1:4 And God saw	Wayar' 'Elohiym	|7200| And saw |0430| God	And, Almighty God saw
	'et-	|0853| -	
the light,	haa'owr	|0216| the light	the light,
that	kiy-	|3588| that	"That's
it was good.	Towb.	|2896| good	good."
and God	Wayabdeel	|0914| and separated	And *then*,
divided	'Elohiym	|0430| God	Almighty
	beeyn	|0996| between	God separated
the light	haa'owr	|0216| the light	the light
from the	uwbeeyn	|0996| and	from
darkness.	hachoshek	|2822| the darkness.	the darkness.
1:5 And God	Wayiqraa'	|7121| And called	And,
called	'Elohiym	|0430| God	Almighty God called
the light	laa'owr	|0216| the light	the light
Day,	yowm	|3117| "day,"	day
and the darkness	wlachoshek	|2822| and the darkness	and the darkness
he called	qaaraa'	|7121| He called	He called
Night.	laaylaah	|3915| night **"from (to fold back; a spiral step-winding stair) properly, a twist"**	*the* twist away."
And	wayhiy-	|1961| and was	[And was
the evening	`ereb	|6153| evening,	evening
and the	Wayhiy	|1961| and {it} was	and was
morning	boqer	|1242| morning,	morning,
were the first	yowm	|3117| day	Day
day.	'echaad.	|0259| one.	One.]

Spelling Out Days
Two, Three, and Four

Bible Passage: Genesis 1:6-19

The ABCs of Literacy

As we open, consider a simple, common thing you probably learned by kindergarten—a simple thing full of wonder and awesome importance that has come to us through the toil and blood of two hundred generations—the alphabet.

In first grade you may have engaged in contests to see who could rattle it off the fastest. You may even have been one of those six-year-old show-offs who could rattle it off backwards in one breath. By the time you were eight years old, through applying some basic phonics rules to this alphabet, most of your classmates could puzzle their way through reading most of the words they used in everyday conversation.

Despite how hard it may have seemed at the time to learn to read, today we tend to view attaining reading and writing skills as, literally, child's play. We view the common use of reading and writing as an integral part of everyday life. We take it for granted that we belong to a large group of people who share a common written code system, and who have pooled a common treasury of shared knowledge that any of us can easily access. We call this literacy.

But, do not confuse literacy with the simple act of writing and reading. Reading and writing are individual skills, while literacy is a group skill. For instance, I could create my own special code system, and could then learn to read and write it quite well. However, no matter how good I got at reading and writing that special code, I could not be *literate* in it until a sizable group of people also learned to use my code, and then we created a stored treasury of coded works that we could all access. When I accessed and became familiar with that code treasury, then and only then could I say I was literate in that code.

Now, while I was inventing such a code, it could go through any number of variations. If one day I got a bright idea on how to improve it, I could make the change with little trouble. However, the more that people got involved with using my code, the harder it would get to make changes. Worse yet, once my code system became a vehicle for a shared literacy, those improvements would become very difficult, if not impossible, to make.

Think of all the many millions of school children and adults who have complained about the seemingly irrational spellings in our English language. Always, someone is on a crusade to clean up the spelling of the English language, yet the improvements never seem to happen, for obvious reasons. First, everyone who went to all the trouble to learn the old system would have to now learn the new and improved system. Second, even if we could magically teach everyone the new system, we would still have to go back to all our millions of libraries and rewrite all the old books using the new system.

This means that, as a side effect of a culture crossing the threshold into literacy, the alphabet for that language suddenly freezes in time. And, while changes in font, the appearance of the letters, may develop over time, the alphabet itself solidifies. This means when archaeologists and linguists examine the alphabets from the various world cultures, they can examine the form it solidified in to tell the date when that culture became literate.

However, for most of human history literacy didn't even exist— at least not in the way we think of it today. Archaeologists talk about something called the "dawn of literacy," which started in the fifteenth century BC and that changed forever the whole course of human history.

For Western civilization, writing and reading had already been around for several thousand years by the fifteenth century, in, for instance, both Middle Eastern cuneiform and Egyptian hieroglyphics.

CUNEIFORM: You probably have seen pictures of ancient Middle Eastern clay biscuits covered with these densely packed scratches. However, cuneiform writing and reading had remained almost exclusively the domain of government bureaucrats, lawyers, and religious officials.

Today, archaeologists routinely dig up small mountains of palm-sized clay tablets, neatly stacked in their own little adobe houses and then forgotten and covered over by more mud and sand. The task of translating and transcribing these thousands of tablets is a tedious and generally unrewarding task, since they comprise almost exclusively shopkeeper kinds of receipts and legal documents. These were not really ever meant to be read, any more than you sit around reading your grocery receipts. They existed only to keep everyone honest and were only pulled out of storage by a lawyer if a legal dispute arose.

Occasionally, someone will strike upon the library of some palace or temple. These generally larger tablets each weigh several cumbersome, fragile pounds, and usually contain government treaties, or propaganda or religious stories. However, even these were not meant to be read in the way we think of reading.

Instead, they were lined up side by side on a ledge, so a professional of some sort could memorize the text of each one before moving on to the next for future recitation to an audience of some sort. None of this business of curling up with a good book—for instance, this book you have in your hands would have weighed a couple of hundred pounds and probably would have crumbled under its own weight if you attempted to hoist the whole thing onto your lap.

Even the most famous of the cuneiform documents, the "Code of Hammurabi," which stood in a public place, was not meant to be read by the general public. Instead, this ominous monolith of black granite covered with mysterious scratches stood like a threatening judge. The general public could only watch in awe as lawyers and judges tiptoed up to it and spiraled their way around and around it, muttering its words out loud as if in prayer, bowing before its weighty import, and bending ever lower as the text spiraled around and down the rock.

EGYPTIAN HIEROGLYPHICS: The next writing tradition comes to us from the other great river civilization—Egypt. Egyptian hieroglyphics tended to serve a different purpose. While cuneiform looks like the stark, clerkish thing it was, Egyptian hieroglyphics were quite literally enchanting works of art. An Egyptian scribe combined the office of clerk with those of artist and magician.

To the Egyptian, the painted symbols themselves were magic incantations. The symbol was the spirit of the reality. To write someone's name was to encapsulate their very soul. And, as art, Egyptian hieroglyphics were actually designed to make reading relatively easy. So, while only a trained scribe-artist-magician actually wrote, most nobles and skilled artisans knew how to read its pictures. However, it paid for its ease of reading by taking up lots of space on very expensive sheets of papyrus or on the walls of palaces and tombs, leaving most texts out of the reach of the general public.

THE MIDDLE BRONZE AGE ALPHABETS: Our modern alphabet descends from something called the Middle Bronze Age Alphabets that first appear in Egypt about the time of Abraham at about 2,000 BC.

Egypt had always been deeply suspicious of foreigners. Yet, as the old kingdom went into decline, fragmenting due to various civil wars, economic pressure prompted them to begin buying foreign slaves, especially Middle Easterners—Canaanites, whom they called "Asiatics." It is this thriving Egyptian market for Canaanite slaves that gets Joseph swept into slavery in Egypt.

Now, these Canaanite Egyptian slaves had the very businesslike Middle Eastern attitude toward writing and didn't have the patience or religious imperative to render every written word as a magical work of art. Instead, over the course of several centuries, they abbreviated twenty to thirty-five common Egyptian hieroglyphics into a few simple strokes of a paint brush or chisel, and used these alphabets to write, not in Egyptian, but in some Canaanite dialect, which was often Hebrew. (Yes, Hebrew is considered a Canaanite language. Remember, the patriarchs spent a couple of centuries there before Joseph's adventure. As simply one family in Canaan, they of course spoke Canaanite.)

Hints of this development were first discovered in "proto-Sinaitic script" found carved in the walls of the Egyptian

> . . . turquoise mines of Serabit el-Khadem in the western Sinai. . . . Apparently it was the Semitic workmen [slaves] there who were responsible for developing the first alphabetic script. Using modified forms of Egyptian signs, but interpreting and applying them to a western Semitic dialect.[14]

Over the last century, more and more examples of alphabetic Canaanite writing have been found in Egypt and Palestine, with the oldest examples turning up deep in Egypt.

---

14. Cornfield, p. 90.

PHOENICIAN/PHONICS: When you learned to read, likely you learned something called *phonics*, the skill of sounding out words. The word *phonics* is simply a variation on the word *Phoenician*. Our modern English alphabet came to us from the Romans, who got theirs from the Greeks, who learned theirs from sailor/merchants of Tyre, a city on the coast of Canaan, whom they called Phoenicians and who did business in Greek ports.

When I was in school many, many years ago, I was taught that the Phoenicians invented the alphabet. However, we now know this isn't true. Phoenician itself was simply a descendant of the Middle Bronze Age alphabets by way of something scholars call the Proto-Canaanite alphabet.

> The Proto-Canaanite alphabet "is a consonantal alphabet of twenty-two acrophonic glyphs, found in Levantine texts of the Late Bronze Age (from ca. the 15th century BC), by convention taken to last until a cut-off date of 1050 BC, after which it is called Phoenician. About a dozen inscriptions written in Proto-Canaanite have been discovered in modern-day Israel and Lebanon." [15]

Now as it happens, 1050 BC, the date Phoenicians crossed the threshold into literacy, is a significant date in biblical history. It is the beginning of what is referred to as the Golden Age of Israel, the reign of King David. Even more significant is the fact that the Phoenicians first appear here in the Bible: "And Hiram king of Tyre sent messengers to David, and cedar trees, and carpenters, and masons: and they built David an house" (2 Samuel 5:11).

For better or worse, this begins a long trade alliance between Israel and the Phoenicians (Jezebel was Phoenician.)

For many years some used this to claim that the Phoenicians obviously taught Israel the alphabet, and then the Hebrews used

---

15. http://en.wikipedia.org/wiki/Proto-Canaanite_alphabet, 2009-07-06, cites Ouaknin, Marc-Alain: Bacon, Josephine (1999), *Mysteries of the Alphabet: The Origins of Writing.* Abbeville Press.

that alphabet to write down stories that their priests and poets had recited for centuries around the firelight at night. However, as more evidence came to light, we learned that it was the other way around. Israel probably gave literacy to the Phoenicians. "While a descendant script from the Egyptian hieroglyphs, it is also the parent script of Phoenician. . . . The Hebrew alphabet remains the closest to its predecessor, as only the form of the letters has been modified."[16]

In Southern Egypt at Wadi el-Hol, archaeologists found a much more ancient style of Canaanite script. Since early Hebrew script resembles this script much more than Phoenician does, this strongly implies that written Hebrew solidified in the fifteenth century BC, about four hundred years before written Phoenician solidified.

This means that the Hebrews crossed the line into becoming a literate society at about 1,450 BC. This in turn means they had then just developed a common pool of written information large enough to freeze their alphabet. Coincidentally, this just happens to be the traditional date for the Exodus and the writing of the Creation Story.

Now you don't need to remember all the complicated names for these forms of alphabet; just remember that currently the physical evidence indicates that, by the time of the Exodus, Moses and whoever helped him write the Law, had a fully working Hebrew alphabet already at hand. Prior to the Exodus, this first alphabet was simply a method to ease some of the drudgery of slavery. However, in the hands of a free people, and with the writing of the Law, it became the vehicle for what is now one of the world's first known literate societies.

(A note from the Author: One of the aggravating problems I've had writing this text has been the fact that archaeology keeps popping up with new finds faster than I can keep up. For instance, on January 7, 2010, *Fox News* published the following article:

---

16. http://en.wikipedia.org/wiki/Proto-Canaanite_alphabet, accessed July 6, 2009

By decoding the inscription on a 3,000-year-old piece of pottery, an Israeli professor has concluded that parts of the bible were written hundreds of years earlier than suspected.

The pottery shard was discovered at excavations at Khirbet Qeiyafa near the Elah valley in Israel -- about 18 miles west of Jerusalem. Carbon-dating places it in the 10th century BC, making the shard about 1,000 years older than the Dead Sea scrolls.

The proto-canaanite text of this inscription resembles several Bible passages, and was found in what would have been a very marginal town in ancient Israel. Frustratingly, while this would provide concrete confirmation that written Hebrew itself, and not just its alphabet, had already been long established by the time of King David, it will take a couple of years to see if the professor's translation holds up to debate, or if the professor was a little over confident.)

BACK TO THE CREATION STORY: In the last chapter we looked at day one of the creation story, pointing out parallels between the passages' Hebrew and the detailed observations of modern cosmology.

In telling a story or making a description, the writer in effect asks you to look through the lens of a camera set in a particular place and see things from a particular angle, at a particular time, though a particular set of eyes. We call this setting of the imaginary camera "point of view," or POV.

In this study of the creation story, we have gone through some shifts in POV. In the last chapter, we began outside the universe and stood back to watch the Big Bang. Then we "zoomed in" to see inside a star pod and to hover above the infant planet earth. Finally, we descended into the earth's atmosphere to tell the remainder of the story from the POV of the planet's surface. We will now continue from that POV.

DAY TWO

(Genesis 1:6 STV) And, Almighty God said, "Let an open space split the flows. And let it divide flows from the flows" . . . The ignition of the Sun's fusion reaction begins a new phase in the development of its inner planets.[17] While those infant planets swept along with the orbiting currents of the nebular star pod's gasses, they had atmospheres several times thicker than the planets themselves, atmospheres primarily composed of hydrogen. Now, the same light pressure that swept away the star pod's dust also swept away nearly all that original atmosphere, reducing the atmospheric pressure on the inner planets' surfaces.

If you have ever watched someone cooking with a pressure cooker, you know that a time comes when they remove the cooker from the stove and carry it to the sink. Then, possibly with a wooden spoon, they depress the pressure release button, venting volumes of hissing steam. If you could see into that pressure cooker, you would see the seemingly calm water inside begin to wildly boil, producing yet more steam. The water continues to boil until the pressure equalizes.

The same thing happened to the infant earth. Volcanoes erupted, spewing out much of the liquids and gases trapped under the surface in a process called out-gassing. Whole seas of water steamed out of lava vents, creating a new, oxygen-less atmosphere composed of water vapor, caustic volcanic gases, formaldehyde, and one hundred times the modern weight of carbon dioxide. Torrents of muddy acid rain fell hissing through smoky orange and yellow fog onto the steaming surface of a forming sea. During this process, an eyewitness would have had difficulty identifying the boundary between the mineral-streaked waters of that ancient boiling sea and the dense rivers of gases roiling over its surface.

Eventually, a shallow ocean, which paleontologists call Panthalassa, covered the entire earth. As it cooled and ceased its sim-

---

17. McGraw Hill, Vol. 2, p. 166.

mering, the earth's interior pressures fell to reach equilibrium with the reduced weight of the new atmosphere. Like the oil, water, and spices in a shaken bottle of Italian salad dressing, the storm ceased, the skies calmed, and then settled into layers.

This stabilization provided an important boost for the sea's microscopic life forms. During this period, these life forms absorbed vast quantities of carbon dioxide into their micro skeletons, depositing it on the shallow ocean floor as mountains of calcium carbonate. You touch a remnant of this period of earth's childhood every time you walk to a blackboard and pick up a piece of chalk.

At the same time, these microorganisms release equally vast quantities of formaldehyde, ammonia, and methane into the atmosphere.[18] Normally, methane is transparent. However, "solar UV radiation would have caused the formation of an organic haze layer similar to that observed today on Saturn's largest moon, Titan."[19]

So, an organic orange sea in the upper atmosphere formed a translucent ceiling above the orange waves of the oily lower sea.

(Genesis 1:7, 8a STV) And, Almighty God showed the open vault separating the flows under the space, and the flows above the space. And it was so. And Almighty God called the open space, whirling flows . . . Remember that God has already created the heavens in verse one. Does this mean that God created the heavens twice? By descriptively naming the stage-two atmosphere a whirling flow (in the STV transliteration column, note the lack of the definite article *ha-*), this simply means that both the original plasmas of the Big Bang and the stage-two sky share the characteristics of rushing, dizzy flows.

"Now, wait a minute!" some may say. "The Bible says waters above—not colored gases above." Before we can answer why the author would describe the stage-two atmosphere as "waters above," we need to consider where the writer of the creation account got

---

18. McGraw Hill, Vol. 2, p. 166; Budyko, p. 26; Walker p. 217.
19. Kasting, J. F.; Pavlov, A. A. Methane Greenhouses and Anti-Greenhouses During the Achaean Era American Geophysical Union, Fall Meeting 2002, abstract #B52C-03, http://adsabs.harvard.edu/abs/2002AGUFM.B52C..03K, accessed August 24, 2009.

his information. Later we will look at evidence that suggests that God gave the creation story itself as an objectively visible revelation. For now, note that the strong visual descriptions given in the story support the impression that we have here an eyewitness account.

When Moses describes a vast open space with flows below and flows above, he gives a good eyewitness description of the late stage-two atmosphere. If, via some science-fiction-style time machine we could get a glimpse of that scene, we would find it difficult to know which side of the picture was up. High in the sky, a bright orange and yellow canopy of organic gases would mirror the oily orange and yellow currents of the Panthalassa Sea.[20] Sandwiched between those two seas, a dense atmosphere of transparent nitrogen and carbon dioxide would blow vast whirling orange and yellow clouds of water, formaldehyde, and ammonia around the earth.[21]

Moses, as an eyewitness, naturally does not mention the myriad of microscopic life forms that filled the sea during this stage of the earth's life. In the cooling sea, we enter that period called the Proterozoic. Using microscopes, paleontologists can see traces of the microscopic life forms that began to fill the sea. Genesis only hints at this major microscopic activity below the ocean's surface when it mentions the nesting aspect of God's Holy Spirit in day one, and only indirectly mentions them in day two by recording the hugely significant changes they made in the atmosphere.

(Genesis 1:8b STV) And was evening and was morning, Day Two.

DAY THREE

(Genesis 1:9, 10a STV) And, Almighty God said, "Gather the flows under the Whirling Flows into one place and expose bare land." And, it was so. And, Almighty God called the bare land earth . . . Two forces combined to produce the earth's first permanent continent. First,

---

20. Walker, p. 217.
21. Budyko, p. 128.

with the cooling of the ocean, the earth itself cooled enough to thicken its crust and reduce its volcanic activity. Second, under the earth's seemingly stable crust, molten magma still flowed in convection currents, just like oatmeal boiling in a pot or warm air circulating in a room. Warmer magma from the earth's interior flowed upward in one current, while cooler magma flowed downward to replace the warm in another current. These currents of molten magma dragged the crust along with them as they flowed, cracking that crust into plates, creating new crust in the cracks, and forcing some plates to collide and pile up in what we call mountains. This process raised a single massive low-laying continent above sea level. Geologists call that initial continent "Pangea."

(Gen 1:10b STV) and the gathered flows He called roaring seas . . . In waiting until now to name the sea, the creation story makes an interesting reference to the factor that made the next step possible. This Hebrew name for the sea refers to the sound of surf pounding on the land's shore. This band of frothy surf provided a key factor in breaking the equilibrium in the battle between two key forms of life that had long since fought to a standstill during the previous age. Notice also that the word for *gathered* used here can also refer to a meeting place, as in where the sea meets the shore.

The emphasis here is not on the whole sea, which had existed long before the first continent appeared. Instead, this passage emphasizes the roaring surf, the brand new shallow seas surrounding the new continent. This arena plays a key role in the historic triumph of aerobic life.

Today, most people think of life in terms of the aerobic (air-breathing) organisms that we call plants and animals. Plants consume carbon dioxide and release free oxygen as a waste by-product, while animals consume that oxygen and release the carbon dioxide as their waste by-product.

However, in contrast, most of the microbes in the early Panthalassa Sea were what we call anaerobic organisms. This means they did not depend on the exchange of oxygen and carbon dioxide.

These anaerobes consumed sulfur, nitrate, and carbon compounds, and represented an entirely different form of life from what most of us know. Today, we can still find these organisms underground or around volcanic vents at the bottom of the ocean. Probably, most of us have heard of *clostridium botulinus*, the organism responsible for botulism food poisoning. Yet, as deadly as it is, the organism itself is fragile and quickly dies when exposed to oxygen.

This is typical for the two life forms. Many anaerobes tend to release by-products that kill most animals. On the other hand, plants release free oxygen, which kills most anaerobes on contact. This is why most kitchen faucets have aerators on their openings to mix air bubbles with the water you drink.

As long as the anaerobes filled the Panthalassa Sea, the microscopic plant and animals limited themselves only to the top thin layer of the water. The green plankton oxygenated only the top layer of the water, while what oxygen that escaped into the atmosphere stayed in the lower levels, since the formaldehyde and ammonia produced by the dominant anaerobes filled most of the sky and quickly burnt the oxygen away.

However, the churning surf on the shallow shores created an entirely new oxygen-rich haven for both plankton and protozoans, holding the anaerobes at bay.

Here we enter that major group of fossil layers called the Paleozoic (ancient life) era. The aerobic protozoans form the base in a food chain for things like sponges, trilobites, and mollusks. Their remains formed the first layer of plentiful fossils in what is called the Cambrian period of the Paleozoic era.

Since, this all happened out of view of the Exodus eyewitness, we only see it referenced in the names God gives to the surf and the shore.

(Genesis 1:10c STV) And, Almighty God saw, "That's good" . . . Here we have the second major milestone in the progress of life on earth. In this vast universe, almost certainly untold millions of

planets have reached this point in their development yet lack the conditions to foster advanced aerobic organisms. God considers the whole condition of the shore and the atmosphere and concludes that things are coming along very well indeed.

(Genesis 1:11a STV) And, Almighty God said, "Earth, sprout tender sprouts" . . . We start with tender plants, plankton, algae, and lichen. Pangea provided an entire new air-exposed environment that favored the aerobic organisms. The fossil record shows that after having been held in check by the anaerobes for so long, the sea's plankton quickly overran the infant continent's low marshes and valleys, piling up in huge mats and blanketing waves of green. Paleontologists refer to this period as the Early Silurian.

(Genesis 1:11b STV) "glistening greens seeding seeds" . . . Next, the Late Silurian records shiny green plants that scatter seeds or spores, things like mosses and ferns. Note the conspicuous absence of flowers from the entire account. With this passage's attention to visual imagery, this may disappoint some. However, the fossil record shows that flowers did not appear until much later.

(Genesis 1:11c STV) "fruit trees showing fruit" . . . . Third, Genesis refers to the earth's first forests that paleontologists see in the Devonian fossil layer. God put plants with solid stalks in swamps, allowing them to raise high to take full advantage of the air and sun.

Note that paleontology gives the same order for the progression of plant life that Genesis does: first, simple shiny green plants like mosses, then plants that scatter seed or spores like ferns, then third, plants with solid stalks and seed bearing fruit or cones.

In the Carboniferous level we find the remains of the full-blown reign of the plants. Note the distinction between plants scattering seed and fruit trees producing fruit. While the Carboniferous forests didn't have modern-style flowering fruit trees, they did abound with the cones and fleshy seeds of conifers and other plants, which Hebrews would classify as fruit.

Such fruit implies the presence of something to take advantage of fruit, and by that, help spread the seeds for the trees. And, sure enough, the fossil record clearly shows insects, millipedes, centipedes, and thousands of different kinds of bugs, along with the green plants.

You may think this poses a problem, since the creation story does not directly mention animals until the fifth day. Furthermore, the newly elevated oxygen levels allowed some bugs to grow to three feet across—certainly large enough that an eyewitness like Moses would surely have noticed them.

So, how do bugs fit in the creation story? The answer is simple. Many, if not most, ancient cultures classified bugs not as animals but as simply the moving variety of plants. And, this would place bugs firmly in the third day with the other plants and not with the animals.

Actually, the Bible has very little to say about bugs. While the Bible mentions a few specific bugs, like locusts, the bald locust, the fly, the beetle, and lice, none of those particular bugs turn up in the fossil record for the Carboniferous.

Part of the problem is that biblical Hebrew lacked any word to refer to insects or bugs in general. In the whole Old Testament we only find one phrase used twice in the dietary code: "flying-creeping-thing." (Leviticus 11:21–23). Reasonably, the threefold combination of flying-creeping-thing has persuaded many that since the fifth day of creation has both flying and creeping things, the fifth day must therefore include flying-creeping-things. However, the creation story does not use that specific three-part phrase.

(Genesis 1:11c-12a STV) reproducing its sort in itself on the earth." *And, it was so. And the earth brought out tender sprouts, glistening greens seeding seed of its sort, solid plants showing fruit reproducing its sort in itself . . .* Notice the key phrase: "of its sort." In the KJV this is translated as "after his kind." Many have pointed to this to resist the idea that one species of plant or animal could arise from another species of animal.

However, the word is an inflection of the word for "out." A literal translation here simply tells us that certain kinds of fruit come out of their certain kinds of tree. Nothing here suggests that God would or would not make a new species out of an old one.

The traditional view has God mold full-grown adult plants and animals directly out of the mud, with God creating each of the organisms' billions of duplicate cells and genetic structures all at once. To them the suggestion that God may have only slightly altered one seed from one organism and then let that seed grow naturally into a slightly different organism seems to diminish the story.

This is the backdrop for the old controversy: "Which came first, the chicken or the egg?" The traditionalist says, "The chicken, since God fashioned each creature fully grown out of the clay." The scientist and the old-earth creationist both answer, "The egg, since the first chicken's mother may not quite have been a chicken." However you answer that question, remember—what's at stake here is the reliability of a tradition, not the Bible.

(Genesis 1:12b STV) And Almighty God saw, "That's good." . . . Here we have a third great milestone in life's history. According to the geological record, a huge disaster of some kind called the Permian Catastrophe struck the earth soon after this, killing off almost all of its life. If the Carboniferous had not been robust enough or good enough, life may not have survived at all.

(Genesis 1:13 STV) And was evening, and was morning, Day Three.

DAY FOUR

(Genesis 1:14a STV) And, Almighty God said, "Be lamps in an opening of the whirling flows, to distinguish between the day and the twist away" . . . For many years, critics of the Bible pointed to this placing of the sun and moon after the creation of the light and the plants as a major error in the Bible. But, think about it. Any primitive could tell you that until you had the sun, you would not have had either light or plants. Indeed, at the time of Moses, many cults actually worshipped the sun. Every natural pressure would

have kept Moses from making such a "mistake" if he had made up the creation story on his own.

Interestingly enough, modern science has come to verify Moses' eyewitness account. Modern science now affirms that while the early earth did have day and night, the sun, moon, and stars were not visible from the earth's surface until after the dominance of the green plants.

At first, constantly billowing ash and volcanic gases kept the sky opaque. Then, through the age of the anaerobes, like translucent stained glass, a thick cloud canopy laced with ionized methane blocked any view of the sun and the moon, even while letting much of the light pass through.

With the appearance of the green plants on dry land, the balance of power between the aerobic and anaerobic organisms shifted. Outward from the frothy waves on the continent's seashore, volumes of free oxygen poured into the air and water. On one hand, with the rising oxygen levels, the anaerobes began a steady retreat into the depths, producing smaller and smaller quantities of ammonia and formaldehyde. On the other hand, as the sea's plankton and the land's plants began to thrive, they produced ever larger quantities of free oxygen.

This completely and suddenly changed the atmosphere. A geologist can show you the one-inch-thick fossil layer of nitrate compounds in every elevated formation surviving from that time, from when the sky burned away. The free oxygen combined with the whirling flows of methane and ammonia to create a rain of solid nitrate fertilizer, identical to what many factories produce to fertilize fields today. Not only that, the fading of the stage-two canopy allowed much brighter light to reach the earth's surface and the plants growing there, further accelerating the process.

(Genesis 1:14b STV) "and let them be for beacons, and for formal assemblies, and for days, and annual cycles" . . . Of all the creative days, this one is most plainly about something more than the presentation of the objects themselves. Later we will examine a symbolic layer of the creation story. This, in short, will make a case that this fourth day is as much about the creation of the Bible itself, in both its Old and New Testaments, as it is about the sun and moon.

Be that as it may, historically, man's awareness of the steady rhythms of the celestial realm has always been an early step in the development of any kind of formal science.

(Genesis 1:15 STV) "And, be for lamps in an opening of the whirling flow to shine on the earth." And, it was so . . . With increasing light and the bonus rain of fertilizer, the plants really took off. Like the parting curtains on a stage, the orange and yellow stage-two atmosphere folded back, revealing the lamps of the sun and the moon for the first time in "an opening" of the sky.

Again, look closely at the transliteration of this passage. While the second day has *the* open space, here on day three the sun and moon are presented in *an* open space. Furthermore, this verse emphasizes seeing the lamps themselves, as opposed to the light they have long shed. The sun and moon are part of the heaved-up-things created on the first day. What happens here is that now we see the lamps themselves, not just the light cast by them.

(Genesis 1:16 STV) And Almighty God showed two great lamps: the greater lamp to rule the day and the lesser lamp to rule the twist away and the stars . . . In passing, note that the KJV implies that God creates the stars here for the first time. In actuality, all that the verse says is that the moon rules the stars. The witnesses to the creation story would have seen plenty of stars displayed on the first day of creation before their POV descended into the nebular star pod.

(Genesis 1:17–18 STV) And, Almighty God presented them in an opening of the whirling flow, to shine on the earth, and to rule over the day and over the twist away, and to distinguish between the light and the darkness. And, Almighty God saw, "That's good." . . . This is a fourth "good"—a fourth milestone. Scientists still have not agreed on what caused the Permian Extinction event. However, most theories involve a major disruption of the earth's atmosphere.

With the regular appearance of the sun and moon, the crisis has apparently passed and life is ready to make a full recovery—definitely good.

(Genesis 1:19 STV) And was evening and was morning, Day Four.

The STV: Days Two, Three, & Four Table

King James Version of the Bible	Transliterated Pronounceable Bible	Literal Bible with Vertical Strong's #s "Bolded Quotes are from Strong's Hebrew Lexicon" {Alternate information in braces}	The Science Teacher's Version
1:6 And God said,	Wayo'mer 'Elohiym,	|0559| And said |0430| God,	And, Almighty God said,
Let there be a firmament	Yhiy raaqiya`	|1961| Let be |7549| a space **"from [to expand (by hammering)]; properly, an expanse"**	"Let an open space
in the midst of	btowk	|8432| in the middle of **"a bisection, i.e. (by implication) the center"**	split
the waters, and let it divide	hamaayim wiyhiym abdiyl beeyn	|4325| the waters, |1961| and let it |0914| dividing |0996| between	the flows. And, let it divide flows from
the waters from the waters.	mayim laamaayim.	|4325| waters |4325| the waters.	the flows."
1:7 And God made	Waya`as	|6213| And made **"to do or make, in the broadest sense and widest application . . . serve, set, shew"**	And, Almighty God showed
	'Elohiym 'et-	|0430| God |0853|	
the firmament,	haaraaqiya`	|7549| the space,	an open space
and divided	wayabdeel beeyn	|0914| and He separated |0996| between	separating
the waters which	hamayim 'sher	|4325| the waters |0834| which	the flows under
were under	mitachat	|8478| under	
the firmament from	laaraaqiya `uwbeeyn	|7549| the space |0996| and	the space, and
the waters which	hamayim 'sher mee	|4325| the waters |0834| which	the flows
were above	`al	|5921| above	above
the firmament:	laaraaqiya`	|7549| the space	the space.
and it was so.	wayhiy-keen.	|1961| and it was |3651| so. **"from [to be erect]; properly, set upright; hence (figuratively as adjective) just"**	And, it was so.

1:8 And God called	Wayiqraa' 'Elohiym	|7121| And called |0430| God	**And, Almighty God called**
the firmament	laaraaqiya`	|7549| the space	**the open space**
Heaven.	shaamaayim	|8064| "heavens."	**whirling flows.**
And the evening and the morning *were the* second day	wayhiy- `ereb wayhiy- boqer Yowm sheeniy.	|1961| And {it} was |6153| evening, |1961| and {it} was |1242| morning, |3117| day |8145| second.	**[And was evening and was morning, Day Two.]**
1:9 And God said,	Wayo'mer ' Elohiym,	|0559| And said |0430| God,	**And, Almighty God said,**
Let the waters under the Heaven	Yiqaawuw hamayim mitachat hashaamayim'	|6960| Let be collected |4325| the waters |8478| under |8064| the heavens	**"Gather the flows under the whirling flows**
be gathered together unto	el-	|0413| to	**into**
one place	maaqowm echaad	|4725| place |0259| one,	**one place**
and let the dry land appear.	wteeraa'eh hayabaashaah	|7200| and let appear |3004| the dry land. **"from (to be ashamed, confused or disappointed) dry ground"**	**and expose bare land."**
and it was so.	wayhiy- keen.	|1961| And it was |3651| so	**And, it was so.**
1:10 And God called	Wayiqraa' 'Elohiym	|7121| And called |0430| God	**And, Almighty God called**
the dry land	layabaashaah	|3004| the dry land	**the bare land,**
Earth;	'erets	|0776| "earth,"	**earth,**
and the gathering together of	uwlmiqweeh	|4723| and the gathering of **"collection, caravan, drove"**, *convention*	**and the gathered**
the waters called he Seas:	hamayim qaaraa' yamiym.	|4325| the waters |7121| He called |3220| "oceans." **"from an unused root meaning to roar; a sea (as breaking in noisy surf)"**	**flows He called roaring seas.**
and God saw	Wayar' 'Elohiym	|7200| And saw |0430| God	**And, Almighty God saw,**
that *it was* good.	kiy- Towb.	|3588| that |2896| good	**"That's good."**
1:11 And God said,	Wayo'mer 'Elohiym,	|0559| And said |0430| God,	**And, Almighty God said,**

44

Let the earth	Tadshee'	|1876| Let sprout	"Earth,
bring forth	haa'aarets	|0776| the earth	sprout
grass,	deshe'	|1877| tender sprouts,	tender sprouts,
the herb	`eese	|6212| plant **"from an unused root meaning to glisten (or be green); grass (or any tender shoot)"**	glistening greens
yielding seed,	bmazriya` zera`	|2233| seeding |2233| seed	seeding seeds,
and the fruit tree	`eets	|6086| of tree **"from [a primitive root; properly, to fasten (or make firm)]; a tree (from its firmness); hence, wood"**	fruit trees
	priy	|6529| fruit	
yielding	`oseh	|6213| producing	showing
fruit	priy	|6529| fruit	fruit,
after his kind,	lmiynow	|4327| after its species, **"from an unused root meaning to portion out; a sort, i.e. species: --kind."**	reproducing its sort
whose seed is in itself,	'sher zar`ow-bow	|0834| which |1931| it	in itself
upon	`al-	|5921| on	on
the earth	haa'aarets	|0776| the earth.	the earth."
and it was	wayhiy-	|1961| And it was	And, it was
so.	keen.	|3651| so.	so.
1:12 And the earth brought	Watowtsee'	|3318| And gave birth to **"a primitive root; to go (causatively, bring) out,"**	And, the earth
forth	haa'aarets	|0776| the earth	brought out
grass,	deshe'	|1877| tender sprouts	tender sprouts,
and herb	`eeseb	|6212| plant	glistening greens
yielding seed	mazriya` zera`	|2233| seeding |2233| seed	seeding seeds
after his kind,	lmiyneehuw	|4327| after its species,	of its sort,
and the tree	w`eets `	|6086| and tree	solid plants
yielding	oseh-	|6213| producing	showing
fruit,	priy	|6529| fruit	fruit
whose	'sher	|0834| which	reproducing its sort in
seed was in itself	zar`ow-bow	|2233| its	itself.
after his kind:	lmiyneehuw	|4327| after its species.	
and God saw	Wayar' 'Elohiym	|7200| And saw |0430| God	And, Almighty
that it was good.	kiy- Towb.	|2896| that good.	God saw, "That's good."
1:13 And the evening	Wayhiy- `ereb	|1961| And it was |6153| evening	[And was evening
and the morning	wayhiy- boqer	|1961| and |1242| morning,	and was morning,
were the third day.	yowm shliyshiy.	|3117| day |7992| third.	Day Three.]

45

1:14 And God said,	Wayo'mer 'Elohiym,	|0559| And said |0430| God,	And, Almighty God said,
Let there be Lights	Yhiy m'orot	|1961| Let be |3974| lights "from [to be . . . luminous]; properly, a luminous body or luminary, i.e. (abstractly) light (as an element): figuratively, brightness, i.e. cheerfulness; specifically, a chandelier: bright, light"	"Be lamps
in the firmament of	birqiya	|7549|in the firmament of	in an opening of
the heaven	hashaamayiml	|8064| the heavens	the whirling flows,
to divide	habdiyl	|0914| to divide	to distinguish
	beeyn	|0996| between	between
the day	hayowm	|3117| the day	the day
from	uwbeeyn	|0996| and	and
the night;	halaaylaah	|3915| the night	the twist away,
and let them be	whaayuw	|1961| and let them be	and let them be
for signs,	l'otot	|0226| for signs "from [to come] (in the sense of appearing); a signal (literally or figuratively), as a flag, beacon, monument"	for beacons,
and for seasons,	uwlmow`diym	|4150| and for seasons "from [to fix upon (by agreement or appointment]; properly, an appointment, i.e. a fixed time or season; specifically, a festival; conventionally a year; by implication, an assembly"	and for formal assemblies,
and for days, and years:	uwlyaamiym wshaaniym	|3117| and for days |8141| and years. "from [to fold, i.e. duplicate]; a year (as a revolution of time)"	and for days, and annual cycles.
1:15 And let them be	Whaayuw	|1961| And let them be	And, be
for lights	lim'owrot	|3974| for lights	for lamps
in the firmament of	birqiya`	|7549| in the space of	in an opening of
the heaven	hashaamayim	|8064| the heavens,	the whirling flows,
to give light	lhaa'iyr	|0215| to give off light	to shine
upon	`al-	|5921| on	on
the earth:	haa'aarets	|0776| the earth.	the earth."
1:16 And God made	Waya`as 'Elohiym	|6213| And made |0430| God	And, Almighty God showed
	'et-	|0853| -	
two	Shneey	|8147| two	two
great lights,	ham'orot	|3974| the lights	great lamps:
	hagdoliym	|1419| great.	
	'et-	|0853| -	

the greater	hamaa'owr	|3974| The light	the greater
light	hagaadol	|1419| great	lamp
to rule	lmemshelet .	|4475| for the rule of **"feminine of [a ruler or (abstractly) rule: dominion, that ruled]; rule; also . . . dominion, government, power, to rule"**	to rule
the day,	hayowm	|3117| the day,	the day
and	w'et-	|0853| and	and
the lesser	hamaa'owr	|3974| the light	the lesser
light	haqaa	|6996| small	lamp
to rule	Ton lmemshelet	|4475| for the rule of	to rule
the night:	halaylaah	|3915| the night,	the twist away
he made	w'eet	|0853| and	and
the stars *also*	hakowkaabiym	|3556| the stars.	the stars.
1:17 And Almighty God set them	Wayiteen	|5414| And set **"to give, used with greatest latitude of application (put, make, etc.) . . . bestow, bring (forth, hither)"**	And, Almighty God
	'otaam'	|0853| them	presented
	Elohiym	|0430| God	them
in the firmament of	birqiya`	|7549| in the space of	in an opening of
the heaven	hashaamaayim	|8064| the heavens	the whirling flows,
to give light	lhaa'iyr	|0216| to give off light	to shine
upon	`al-	|5921| on	on
the earth,	haa'aarets.	|0776| the earth,	the earth,
1:18 And to rule	Wlimshol	|4910| and to rule	and to rule
over the day	bayowm	|3117| over the day	over the day
and over the night,	uwbalaylaah	|3915| and over the night,	and over the twist away,
and to divide	uwlhabdiyl	|0914| and to separate	and to distinguish
	beeyn	|0996| between	between
the light	haa'owr	|0216| the light	the light
from	uwbeeyn	|0996| and	and
the darkness:	hachoshek	|2822| the darkness	the darkness.
and God saw	Wayar' 'Elohiym	|7200| And saw |0430| God	And, Almighty God saw,
that	kiy	|3588| that	"That's
it was good.	Towb.	|2896| good.	good."
1:19 And the evening	Wayhiy-`ereb	|1961| And was |6153| evening	[And was evening
and	wayhiy-	|1961| and	and was
the morning	boqer	|1242| morning	morning
were the	yowm	|3117| day,	Day
fourth day.	rbiy`iy.	|7243| the fourth.	Four]

3

The Fifth, Sixth & Seventh Days
Bible Passage: Genesis 1:20-2:3

DAY FIVE

Many of us have sat in a traditional Sunday school class as small children and watched our teacher present the fifth day of creation. Here, she would stick pictures of fish, birds, and a whale onto her flannel board. If we use only a surface reading of the KJV, this makes sense. However, if we look closer at what the fifth day actually says, we find something drastically different.

For instance, nowhere does the fifth day use the word *fish*. The creation story does not mention fish until verse 28 in God's blessing of man. So, while the creation story uses the word *fish*, it does so in the sixth day, not the fifth day. Let's look more closely at the words used instead of fish.

(Genesis 1:20a STV) And, Almighty God said, "Let the waters swarm with swarming . . . Note that the Hebrew word the STV translates as "swarm" has the connotation of swarming in large groups and breeding.

(Genesis 1:20b STV) breathing . . . The word the KJV translates as "living" literally means breathing. While we understand today that fish breath water, no ancient Hebrew would have applied the word for breathing to fish, since breathing referred to making wind. Instead, we have here a good description of air-breathing amphibians, swarming into shallow water to sing and breed.

(Genesis 1:20b STV) frisky beasts . . . This word isn't just to be alive, but rather to be lively, again with sexual overtones.

While small amphibians had been around for quite a while already, until now they had been too small for the Exodus eyewitness to notice. Only in the Early Triassic, after the plants had produced the stage-three atmosphere and raised the concentration of oxygen up above modern levels, did the giant amphibians appear.

(Genesis 1:20c STV) and shrouds . . . The Hebrew word for bird refers to the cloaks of feathers they wear. Most of Eurasia to this day refers to many birds as "shrouds," similar to a cloth shroud draped over a dead body. Birds not only wear shrouds, scavenger birds enshroud any dead body left unattended.

(Genesis 1:20d STV) flapping on the earth . . . For most of the last century, paleontologists classified the dinosaur with the reptile. However, current studies of dinosaur bone structure and metabolism have convinced most that the dinosaurs were closely related to birds. In fact, China has fossil beds made from compressed very fine sand (volcanic ash) that show that many, if not most, small or young therapod dinosaurs had feathers. This is why some children's picture books have even shifted to portraying therapod dinosaurs as colorfully plumed birds.

These feathered dinosaurs appear quite early in the Triassic, the first period of the Mesozoic. Furthermore, the Triassic marks the appearance of another birdlike characteristic. Dinosaurs laid hard-shelled eggs like birds. This allowed them to roam far away from the wetlands that the amphibians needed to breed in. In this fossil layer we suddenly find dinosaur nests scattered all over the continents.

(Genesis 1:20e STV) and on the turning sphere of the open whirling flow . . . Only in the Late Triassic, after the dinosaurs had covered the land, do we find flying dinosaurs. Paleontologists mark their arrival by the sudden extinction of the giant flying insects they had preyed on.

(Genesis 1:21a STV) and every shroud with flaps to its sort." And, Almighty God saw, "That's good." . . . Here we have the fifth "good," the fifth milestone. Every major biome on the planet now has bloomed into fully mature life systems. It's as if a sculptor has roughed out the structure and overall shape of his work—seas here, wetlands, jungles, plains and mountains there, all with their own fully functioning systems of life. "Ah, this is good! This is ready, time for detail work."

(Genesis 1:21b STV) And Almighty God created . . . Despite the fact that we are on day five of the creation story, we have here only the second thing God is said to create. The first verse says "God created the heaven and the earth." However, after that, the KJV says "make." The STV says "shine" or "show" until now. God now creates something spectacular enough to rate comparison with the entire heaven and earth.

(Genesis 1:21c STV) huge long monsters . . . This word literally means a long, stretched-out monster of some kind. In the middle ages, some took this to mean that the Bible taught that monsters haunted the oceans, so they occasionally translated this word as sea serpent. But, notice how the word is used in the following verses:

> "And Aaron cast down his rod before Pharaoh . . . and it became a *serpent*" (Exodus 7:10, emphasis added).

> "Thou shalt tread upon the lion and the adder: the young lion and the *dragon* shalt thou trample under feet" (Psalm 91:13, emphasis added)

Even in the KJV the word translated as whale in day five rarely, if ever, applies to a water animal. Remember that a translator depends heavily on context to rightly translate a word. The traditional pre-conception that the fifth day referred to life *in* the sea, as opposed to life coming *out* of the sea, predisposed the translators into looking for a word pertaining to a water animal like a whale or sea serpent, instead of a word that usually referred to any kind of long, drawn-out land monster.

Here we see a good description of the monsters lumbering in the shallow waters and swamps of the Upper Jurassic on through the huge, long sauropods and finally on to the titanosaurs of the Cretaceous. We would be hard pressed to think of a better description in ancient Hebrew than what the Bible gives us here.

While the sheer grandeur of these giants may seem to merit the word *create*, I have to admit that I keep expecting science to come up with something more amazing about them than just their size. Then, despite my best intentions, my mind wanders, I hope not irreverently, to the famous Gary Larson "The Far Side" cartoon, titled "God as an Adolescent." It shows a T. Rex in battle with a triceratops. From the clouds above comes a voice balloon exclaiming, "Cool!"

*(Genesis 1:21d STV) and all sorts of breathing, frisky scampering-*beasts *breeding in the water to their sorts* . . . Notice the word that the KJV translates as "that moveth" here. Everywhere else in the Bible this word refers to small things that scamper on all four legs, definitely not to fish. We call breathing things that scamper on all four legs and breed in the water "amphibians."

(Genesis 1:22a STV) And Almighty God blessed them, saying "Be fruitful and multiply, and fill the waters of the roaring sea . . . By the titanosaurs of the Cretaceous—the last of the three periods of the Mesozoic era—the dinosaurs had become more associated with dry land. However many of the dinosaurs had returned to dominate the sea, like the plesiosaur and the giant crocodilians.

(Genesis 1:22b STV) and shrouds multiply on the earth"... By the end of the Cretaceous, a vast diversity of dinosaurs and other life forms roamed forests and flowering grassy plains very similar to our modern ones.

(Genesis 1:21c-23 STV) And was evening and was morning, Day Five.

DAY SIX

(Genesis 1:24a STV) And Almighty God said, "Earth, bring out breathing friskies of their sorts... Paleontologists call that era from the disappearance of the dinosaurs until today the Cenozoic. Notice that we already had "friskies" created on day five. However, the frisky amphibians and reptiles of the fifth day differ entirely from the frisky mammals of the sixth day. The Hebrew language lumped mammals and other kinds of animals together with this word, explaining why we see friskies twice in the creation story. Nearly all of our modern mammals, including man himself, date from the most recent epoch of the Cenozoic, which we call the Pleistocene. The words used in the Creation Story's sixth day all seem to relate to mammals from the Pleistocene.

(Genesis 1:24b STV) large mammals... We get the English word *behemoth* from this Hebrew word. The Hebrews themselves borrowed *bheemaah* from the Egyptian word for the water ox. However, they used it for any large unspeaking mammal, like the hippopotamus or even the elephant. For instance, in Job 40:15, the behemoth has a "tail like a cedar," a reference to the elephant's trunk. However, behemoth often plainly referred to other more familiar animals. We can take the word to refer to any large mammal. Interestingly, most children's picture books that deal with the Pleistocene usually start with a page or two of the giant mammals for which the age is famous.

(Genesis 1:24c STV) and scampering-beasts... This next word used is another word also used in day five. This Hebrew word in practice referred to all the smaller non-domesticated animals. This

leads us to wonder why God would show us scampering-beasts twice. However, again this makes good biological sense. You see, the Hebrew language did not distinguish small amphibians and reptiles from small mammals; it called both scampering-beasts. So, while the language lumped those two categories together, Genesis rightly distinguishes between the two groups by using the same word on two different days to refer to two entirely different kinds of animals.

(Genesis 1:24d STV) and the frisky-herds of the earth of their sorts, and it was so . . . Again, the word the STV translates as "frisky-herds" is used in day five, but not in conjunction with the word *earth*. Note that the KJV occasionally translated this word for herd as troop or company:

> And the Philistines were gathered together into a **troop**. (2 Sam 23:11)

> Rebuke the **company** of spearmen, the multitude of bulls. (Psalm 68:30)

(Genesis 1:25a STV) And Almighty God showed frisky-herds of the earth to their sorts, and large mammals of their sorts . . . Picture a vast Pleistocene savanna covered with thousands of animals each clustered in their distinct herds—a multicolored patchwork quilt spread to the horizon.

(Genesis 1:25b STV) and all mannish scampering-beasts of their sorts . . . The KJV translates this as "beast of the earth," as if it were the same phrase used in the previous verse. But it's not. The word used here is an inflection of the word translated as Adam or man in the rest of Genesis. We could translate it as "mannish." This word relates to the word for red or reddish, probably a reference to man's pink flesh. This is why the KJV decided that it must refer to red clay.

The translators for the KJV didn't think it would make any sense to translate the phrase as "beast men," so they stayed with the "beast of the earth" from the previous verse. However, today, the term *beast-men* makes lots of sense, given all the "missing links" posted in museums all over the world.

For the last 160 years paleontologists have grappled with human or near-human fossils. They blundered through false starts—and some outright hoaxes. They misassembled some skeletons and lost others to invading armies. They have made wild guesses and fought and argued constantly with each other. In short, they have handled the evidence and applied the scientific method about the way Homo sapiens usually has.

Rather than go into a detailed history here, let's look at the basic conclusions that paleontologists generally agree on. The Stone Age, or Paleolithic (*paleo* = ancient + *lith* = stone) refers to a layer of stone tools that lies at the top of the fossil record. With minor variations, these stone tools fall into three distinct types or layers that they call the Lower, the Middle, and the Upper Paleolithic (lower and upper as in lower and higher rock layers. Lower levels would therefore be older and upper levels younger.)

THE LOWER PALEOLITHIC contains only the simplest kinds of chipped scraper and hand axes, and covers all of Europe, Asia, and Africa. It lasted two to three million years. Evidence also indicates the use of fire during this period. Skeletons from this lower Paleolithic show that a variety of manlike hominids, now grouped together as Homo erectus, used these simple tools and fire. During those millions of years, none of those hominids showed signs of what the Bible calls the image of God. So, despite their simple tools and use of fire, we see little cumulative culture or innovation over the course of millions of years. While Homo erectus had a slightly larger brain than the modern chimpanzee, we have no evidence that Homo erectus had any significant culture or abstract language skills.

THE MIDDLE PALEOLITHIC contains more complex chipped stone tools, which gradually appear. But after they appear, they also show very little improvement over the course of hundreds of thousands of years. This is the age of the Neanderthal and the Early Moderns.

For a while some pointed to the Neanderthal as a kind of missing link. Today, most consider them simply as the most sophisticated of the Homo erectus species. Granted, they had brains slightly larger than even ours today. However, the Neanderthal never showed a significant surge in culture or artifacts.

For a while some believed that the Neanderthal seemed to begin a surge of their own, and that they began to show many of the same advancements as modern man of the same period. However, increasingly, opinion shifted to considering those improved tools as simple borrowings from modern men. When a Neanderthal saw modern men make an improved tool, suddenly the Neanderthal could make an inferior version of that tool also. However, no evidence indicates that they originated much on their own.

The Neanderthal hung on for another fifteen thousand years after the appearance of modern man, but all trace disappears by 35,000 BC. For a while, genetic studies tried to determine whether Neanderthals interbred with modern man, and thus perhaps didn't disappear at all. But, those genetic studies came back negative. Current opinion has it that the Neanderthal was never fully human, and that they definitely were not a missing link in our family tree.

(Genesis 1:25c) And Almighty God saw, "That's good" . . . Here we have a sixth "good," a sixth milestone. With the appearance of pre-human beast men, the stage is fully set. Everything is good and ready for the final step.

THE UPPER PALEOLITHIC: Paleontologists' studies of the top fossil layer show that about forty thousand-plus years ago a sudden explosion of constantly improving flint work, arts, and crafts hailed the dawn of modern humanity.

(Genesis 1:26a STV) And Almighty God said, "Let Us make man in our image, to be like us . . . This all happens during the rise of the last glacial period, when the advancing ice sheets have reached about two-thirds of what will be their maximum. This is the great age of the mammoth hunters and the cave painters. Note that humanness appears with no transition; it's not that things got slowly more sophisticated. With no discernable transition, suddenly modern man appears. God has impressed his image on the earth's clay.

This, of course brings us to the question, "Just exactly what is the 'image of God'?" We would expect a good communicator like God to not casually use undefined terms. When God uses the term, "in our image" in verse 26, then our first impulse should prompt us to look in the first 25 verses to see if God describes himself there. And, as you would expect since I've brought it up, I think I do find a description of God in the first 25 verses of Genesis. This description attributes four main characteristics to God.

God the Creator: God truly creates, shapes, makes, and originates. That means our imaginations reflect God's creativity. However, our image differs from God's reality. God does not just think stars and new things; he does stars and new things. In contrast, no matter how hard we squint our eyes or twitch our nose, we cannot think matter into existence.

Regardless, as much as we differ from God's kind of creating, we can say some things for certain. The image of God in us imagines. Then it prompts us to actively give shape to the things we imagine. While we do not expect a high degree of creativity from any of the animals, a man with little imagination, or stifled creativity, or no artistry in his soul is a poor man, a spiritual cripple, an object of pity.

Now, this does not mean that everything produced by our creativity is automatically good. However, it does mean that even the people who "imagine a vain thing" (Psalm 2:1), and the evil and violent men "which imagine mischiefs in their heart" (Psalm 140:2) have to use their Godlike imaginations to do it.

God the Communicator: Note that the first "God said" is preceded by an image of intimacy. "And the breath of Almighty God fluttered like a nesting hen on the watery sphere. And Almighty God said 'Be light,' and it was light" (Genesis 1:2c–1:3a STV).

God does not merely mouth words at an unresponsive world; he truly communicates. He communes.

God communicates within his own diverse nature. Both Jewish and Christian theologians have long recognized that the communicative aspect of God implies multiple persons within the Godhead. Jews talk of the seven spirits of God, while Christians talk about the Father, Son, and Holy Spirit. Yet, these are not the separate, potentially hostile gods of the Greek mode. These personalities in the Godhead commune and cooperate and create on a level that can only be called loving intimacy.

Traditionally, many have said that God created man to have an object for his love. But, this may miss a key point. God has never been lonely (or, maybe only once on the cross). Like children well loved by our parents, we were the products of love before we became the objects of love. God engaged in intimate communion long before he created us.

God the Evaluator: We have already seen God call some things "good" in the creation story. In the garden story we also see the phrase, "It is *not good* for man to be alone." This may seem trivial, but it makes an important point. If God was simply some kind of impersonal cosmic force, then everything would be equally good or not good to him. Yet, the creation story clearly says that God evaluated his creations. Some things were better and some things were worse than others.

Of all the aspects of God, our world today finds this one the hardest to accept. They find it hard to believe that God would pick sides—that he could disapprove or even approve of anything. For instance, notice the public revulsion when someone calls any disaster the judgment of God. They do not usually say, "There is no God, and so this cannot be the judgment of God." Neither do they say, "What we do pleases God, and therefore he would not judge us." Instead, they firmly assert, "God is impartial; he does not judge anything. He only observes."

Tragically, in recent years, the word spiritual has often come to suggest a detached yogi sitting on a mountaintop, utterly unresponsive to the real world. Yet, any human being that has seared away his capacity to form judgments is spiritually deficient, less than fully human. The ability to form judgments, to appreciate and depreciate, to enjoy and to revile, to accept and reject, to love and to hate—these are not the failings of the human heart; they are the marks of our creator and spring from the image of God in us.

God the Instructor: In the very act of giving the creation story, God shows himself to be a teacher.

Recently, much has been made, especially on the various science channels, of the tool and language skills of both chimpanzees and mountain gorillas. Some have even claimed that their learning capacity can match or occasionally out-do that of a human three-year-old child. However, these advanced primate skills generally come only after intensive instruction from human trainers.

Recent studies have discovered a very basic difference between how human children and other primates learn. The advanced primates can observe and mimic and thus acquire fairly impressive sets of skills. However, humans teach, and human children expect to be taught. Chimpanzees will closely watch the trainer and thereby learn a skill. However, the human child expects the teacher to actively help them learn, and will trust and follow a teacher's instructions even when those instructions make no apparent sense, or yield no immediate reward.[22]

Humans deliberately and meticulously build bodies of knowledge, something we call culture. It is even built into our life cycles. Humans have prolonged childhoods and prolonged old ages, some-

---

22. http://www.ncbi.nmi.nih.gov/pubmed/15549502.accessed July 7, 2009.

thing the other primates don't. Microscopic studies of the tooth enamel of all forms of Homo erectus show that they had reached full adulthood by the age of nine at the latest, and died of sudden-onset old age by at most the age of forty.[23] In contrast, we humans have whole stages of life dedicated to learning and instruction.

Have you ever noticed how small children love to hear favorite stories told over and over again? They want to hear these stories repeated even when they know them so well that they will stop you if you leave something out or try to change something.

Well, this has a flip side. Since I've developed gray hair and now stand on the threshold of geezer-hood myself, I have become increasingly aware of the urge to tell the same stories over and over again. It's built into my genes. And, worse yet, it's built into your genes to sit there and politely nod as I tell the same story for the two-hundredth time, no matter how deadly bored you are. It's part of what makes you distinctively human, and why you're not sitting naked on a jungle floor right now picking at lice and munching on bananas and beetles.

(Genesis 1:26b STV) and to rule over the fish of the roaring seas, and over shrouds of the whirling flow, and over the large mammals, and over all the earth, and over all scampering-beasts *scampering on the earth."*. . . In passing, notice that this list doesn't include the large amphibians and dinosaurs that figure so prominently in day five. They didn't exist anymore; the day of the dinosaurs had long past.

(Genesis 1:27 STV) And Almighty God created the man in His image. In the image of Almighty God He created him. Male and Female He created them . . . The Upper Paleolithic appears so suddenly that it is called the Paleolithic Revolution. The shift from beast-man to fully modern man happens suddenly with no known transition period. While we can speculate about natural processes in the evolution of life on earth, clearly the Bible teaches that modern man himself is the result of direct divine intervention.

---

23. Lewin.

The creation story itself uses the word for create only five times. First, God creates the heavens and the earth. Second, God creates the giant dinosaurs. Finally, the story uses the word *create* three times when God creates the image of God in man.

To understand that you need to understand a quirk of the Hebrew language. Hebrew lacks the good-better-best comparison as an inflection. Instead it says good, good-good, or good-good-good. By using the word *create* three times in this passage, the creation story establishes the creation of man as the focus of the entire creation story.

That the third *create* occurs on the stress of man as male and female may tell us something as well. This may imply that human sexuality is at the peak of our nature and importance. This has a whole set of its own implications. For instance, modern anthropology identifies human sexuality as the fuel that drives the engine of culture and civilization. This in turn suggests that the peak of our importance to God rests in our aggregate interactions. And this, of course, leads us to the concept of the church, a rabbit trail you can follow on your own.

Does this prove that man is the most important thing God ever created? Probably not—it's a big and ancient universe we live in. But, we can say with confidence that the creation of modern man is the point of the creation story. The creation story is not about the whole universe; it's about us. God is telling us who we are, where we came from, and how we relate to him.

And, Almighty God knelt to bless them. And, Almighty God said to them, "Be fruitful and multiply, and fill the earth, and tread on it. Rule over the fish of the roaring seas, and over the frisky-beasts scampering on the earth."

And, Almighty God said, "Look! I have presented to you every glistening green seeding seed, which is on the turning sphere of all the earth, and every solid plant

which has in it fruit, solid plants seeding seed, to you it will be for food. And, to all the friskies of the earth, and to all the shrouds in the whirling flows, and to all the scampering-beasts on the earth which are frisky breathers—all the green glistening greens for food."
And, it was so.

And Almighty God saw all that He had showed, and, "Look! Very good!"

Here we have the seventh and final "good." The "very" and the seven count would indicate that this is the completion milestone for life on earth. The stage has been fully set; the curtain is about to rise. Let the real show begin!

And was evening and was morning, Day Six.

And so, we finish the six creative days. I hope you noticed that every word, every phrase, falls in step in proper order with the findings of modern science.

On one hand, in the next three sections we will demonstrate that the creation story talks about much more than modern science. On the other hand, while science is the lesser theme of the story, the story still has detailed and accurate science far beyond anything humanly possible even two hundred years ago, let alone 3,500 years ago.

In review, go over the seven milestones and thirty-five parallels listed in the following chart:

Cosmology/Paleontology Parallels List

DAY ONE

1.	In the beginning	The universe has a definite beginning
2.	Dizzy-rushing	and initially expands at many multiples of the speed of light.
3.	Flow	The universe begins as a liquid/plasma and
4.	Solids	solids come second
5.	Empty desolation	As matter condenses, empty desolate space appears,
6.	Darkness	along with cold, light-blocking nebulas.
7.	Face/turning sphere	Planetoids aggregate
8.	Deep in a surging mass	deep in nebular cocoons.
9.	Breath	Inward blowing organic compounds enrich the planet.
10.	Brooded	allowing the earliest forms of life to incubate.
11.	Face of the waters	Earth acquires most of its water suspended in a turbulent atmosphere.
12.	Be light	The sun ignites with just the right kind of light.

"That's Good" #1	**Life's First Milestone: the Proterozoic**
13. Light and dark separated	Light pressure blows away the remaining gases and excess atmosphere so the first night appears.
14. Night named Twist Away	A reference to the laterally turning earth producing the day and night cycle.

DAY TWO

15. Waters divided	Thinning of the atmosphere and cooling of the crust permit the first universal sea, Panthalassa, matched by an ionized methane haze canopy above.

16. Second whirling flows | Rushing clouds of steam, formaldehyde and ammonia stream across the lower atmosphere.

DAY THREE

17. Bare ground | Further cooling of the crust allows the first permanent raised land mass, Pangea.
18. Roaring sea | With the first continent comes the coastal surf, an important new biome. Oxygenated water becomes a haven for aerobic organisms.

"That's Good" #2 | **Life's Second Milestone: the Phanerozoic**

19. Soft sprouts | Early Silurian: glistening green mosses and algae blanket the earth.
20. Plants seeding seeds | Late Silurran: ferns and taller plants produce spores and bare seeds.
21. Fruit trees showing fruit | Carboniferous: palms and conifers attract bugs, "moving plants," for pollination and dissemination.

"That's Good" #3 | **Life's Third Milestone: a robust biome, preparation for the Permian Extinction event**

DAY FOUR/Atmospheric Interlude

22. Moon/Sun in an opening | Atmospheric changes allow first view of moon and sun.

23. (Not stars) | Moon said to rule stars, but stars already created "in the beginning."

"That's Good" #4 | **Life's Fourth Milestone: the Permian Extinction event survived, signaled by the clearing of the sky**

DAY FIVE

24. Breathing, frisky beasts	Early Triassic: the amphibians rise.
25. Shrouds	Late Triassic: the theropods rise.

"That's Good #5   **Life's Fifth Milestone: a robust biome reestablished**

26. Long monsters created	Cretaceous: the giant dinosaurs rise (possible mysterious significance).
27. "Fill the waters"	Dinosaurs move back into the sea,
28. Shrouds multiply	and a vast diversity fills the terrestrial biome.

DAY SIX

29. "Frisky mammals"	The Cenozoic: the mammals rise.
30. "Large mammals"	The Pleistocene: filled with giant mammals
31. "Scampering-beasts"	wild mammals
32. "Frisky herds"	mammal herds, and
33. "mannish beasts"	Homo erectus and then the Early Moderns.

"That's Good" #6   **Life's Sixth Milestone: Preparation for the dawn of modern man**

34. The image of God created	Modern man appears
35. Male/female emphasis	Human sexuality forms the foundation for cumulative culture.

"Look! Very Good" #7   **Life's Seventh Milestone: The stage is complete (7 = completion); all is ready**

DAY SEVEN

(Genesis 2:1–2a STV) And finished were the whirling flow and the earth and all their troops . . . The creation story doesn't limit itself to the six creative days. Instead, it ends with the establishment of the Sabbath celebration.

(Genesis 2:2b STV) And on the seventh day Almighty God finished His angelic message which He had showed . . . Notice that here the entire creation story is called an angelic message.

Strong's says we could translate *mla'ktow* as "a deputation, a delegated task," or even an "angelic revelation." We see it used in that sense in Haggai 1:13: "Then spake Haggai the Lord's *messenger* in the Lord's *message* unto the people" (emphasis added).

(Genesis 2:2c STV) On the seventh day he stopped all his angelic message which he had showed . . . Notice here that the word for stop doesn't actually mean to rest, as the KJV has it. He simply stops. To those who hold the Six-day Revelation view, this is a reference to the action of the cloud that leads the Hebrews out of Egypt. The book of Exodus records that on every seventh day the cloud stopped. Traditionally, most have said that the cloud stopped *because* God rested on the seventh day, not that the cloud stopping was itself the "rest."

(Genesis 2:3a STV) And Almighty God knelt to bless the seventh day, and made it special . . . Here we see that God stops, not to rest from his creation, as if he were tired from all that work, but rather to commune with and bless what he has made. God is not a drone, drudging away with no purpose. Instead, his creation is a work of art, and he pauses to take joy in it.

(Genesis 2:3b STV) because He stopped on it from the entire angelic message which Almighty God created to show . . . Remember how I said that the creation story only claims God created three things: the universe, the dinosaurs, and man? Actually, here we see that God created a fourth thing: the angelic revelation that is the creation story itself.

Notice also that here we have the triple emphasis on the combination of the words *angelic message* and *to show*. This gives us a clear indication that God gave the creation story as a definite, visible, and probably public event, and not just a prophet's mystic dream or inspiration. The use of the triple superlative structure indicates that the scribe felt this showing was the peak of all showings.

When we couple this with the fact that the creation story calls itself an "angelic message," we don't get the impression that the creation story was given as the simple musings of some prophet. Even a dramatic revelation with a prophet face down on the ground (like John receiving the book of Revelation) would barely qualify. Visions don't seem concrete enough to qualify as creations, in this context.

This is one more reason why those who hold the Revelation Days view of the creation story suspect that this story was visually shown to all of the hosts of Israel by the cloud of fire during the first six evenings and mornings of the Exodus from Egypt.

The STV: Days Five, Six, & Seven Table

King James Version of the Bible	Transliterated Pronounceable Bible	Literal Bible with Vertical Strong's #s "Bolded Quotes are from Strong's Hebrew Lexicon" {Alternate information in braces}	The Science Teacher's Version
1:20 And God said,	Wayo'mer 'Elohiym,	|0559| And said |0430| God,	And, Almighty God said,
Let the waters bring forth abundantly	Yishrtsuw	|8317| Let swarm **"to wriggle, i.e. (by implication) swarm or abound: breed (bring forth, increase) abundantly"**	"Let the waters swarm
	hamayim	|4325| the waters	
the moving	sherets	|8318| swarmers **"from [to wriggle]; a swarm, i.e. active mass of minute animals: creep(-ing thing), move(-ing creature)"**	with swarming,
creature	nepesh	|5315| a life **"from [to breathe]; properly, a breathing creature"**	breathing,
that hath life,	chayaah	|2416| living. **"alive; raw (flesh); (wild) beast, company, congregation, living (creature, thing), running, springing, troop."**	frisky *beasts,*
and fowl	w`owp	|5775| And birds **"from [to cover]; a bird (as covered with feathers),"**	and shrouds

that may fly	y`owpeep	|5774| let fly around **"to cover"**	flapping
above	`al-	|5921| over	on
the earth	haa'aarets	|0776| the earth,	the earth
in the	`al-	|5921| on	and on
open	pneey	|6440| the surface of	the turning sphere
firmament of	rqiya	|7549| the space of	of the open
heaven.	`hashaamaayim.	|8064| heavens.	whirling flows,
1:21 and every	kaal-	|3605| every	every
winged fowl	`owp	|5775| bird	shroud
	kaanaap	|3671| wing **"from [to project laterally]; an edge or extremity; specifically (of a bird or army) a wing, (of a garment or bed-clothing) a flap"**	with flaps
after his kind:	lmiyneehuw.	|4327| after its species.	of its sort."
and God saw	Wayar' 'Elohiym	|7200| And saw |0430| God	And, Almighty God saw,
that	kiy-	|3588| that	"That's
it was good.	Tow	|2896| good	good."
And God	Wayibraa'	|1254| And created	And,
created	'Elohiym	|0430| God	Almighty God created
	'et-	|0853| -	
great whales,	hataniynim	|8577| the sea monsters **"intensive from [to elongate; a monster]; a marine or land monster"**	huge long monsters
	hagdoliym	|1419| great	
and	w'eet	|0853| and	and all sorts of
every	kaal-	|3605| all	
living	nepesh	|5315| life	breathing,
creature	hachayaah	|2416| living	frisky
that moveth,	haaromeset	|7430| that crawls **"properly, to glide swiftly, i.e. to crawl or move with short steps"** {This word includes amphibians, small reptiles, and small mammals, and refers to crawling on all four legs}	scampering-*beasts*
which	'sher	|0834| which	
the waters	Shaartsuw	|8317| swarmed	breeding in
brought forth abundantly,	hamayim	|4325| the waters	the water
after their kind . . .	lmiyneehem	|4327| after their species,	to their sorts.
1:22 And God blessed them,	w'eet Waybaarek 'otaam 'Elohiym	|0853| - |1288| And blessed |0853| them |0430| God	And, Almighty God blessed them,
saying,	lee'mor	|0559| saying,	saying,
Be fruitful,	pruw	|6509| Be fruitful	"Be fruitful
and multiply,	uwrbuwuw	|7235| and be many,	and

			multiply, and fill
and fill	mil'uw 'et-	|4390| and fill |0853| -	and fill
the waters	Hamayim	|4325| the waters	the waters
in the seas,	bayamiym	|3220| in the oceans.	of the roaring sea,
and let fowl	whaa`owp	|5775| And the birds	and shrouds
multiply	yirebba	|7235| let multiply	multiply
in the earth.	a'aarets.	|0776| on the earth.	on the earth."
1:23 And	Wayhiy-	|1961| And was	[And was
the evening	`ereb	|6153| evening	evening
and	wayhiy-	|1961| and {it} was	and was
the morning	boqer	|1242| morning,	morning,
were the fifth	yowm	|3117| day	Day
day.	chmiyshiy.	|2549| fifth.	Five]
1:24 And	Wayo'mer	|0559| And said	And,
God said,	'Elohiym,	|0430| God,	Almighty God said,
Let the earth	Towtsee'	|3318| Let bring forth	"Earth,
bring forth	haa'aarets	|0776| the earth	bring out
the living	nepesh	|5315| life	breathing
creature	chayaa	|2416| living	friskies
after his kind,	hlmiynaah	|4327| after its species,	of their sorts,
cattle,	bheemaah	|0929| cattle **"properly, a dumb beast; especially any large quadruped or animal (often collective)"**	large mammals,
and creeping thing,	waaremes	|7431| and crawlers, **"from [to glide swiftly, i.e. to crawl or move with short steps]; a reptile or any other rapidly moving animal."**	and scampering-*beasts,*
and beast	wchaytow-	|2416| and its animals	and frisky-
of the earth	'erets	|0776| of the earth	*herds* of the earth
after his kind:	lmiynaah	|4327| after its species.	of their sorts."
and it was so.	wayhiy-keen.	|1961| And so it was.	And, it was so.
1:25 And God made	Waya`as 'Elohiym	|6213| And made |0430| God	And, Almighty God showed
the beast of	'et- chayat	|0853| - |2416| the animals of	frisky-*herds*
the earth	haa'aarets	|0776| the earth	of the earth
after his kind,	lmiynaah	|4327| after its species	of their sorts,
and	w'et-	|0853| and	and large
cattle	habheemaah	|0929| the cattle	mammals
after their kind,	lmiynaah	|4327| after its species,	of their sorts
and	w'eet	|0853| and	and
every	kaal-	|3605| all	all
thing that	remes	|7431| crawlers	mannish scampering-
creepeth upon the earth	haa'daamaa.	|0127| of the ground **"from [to show**	*beasts*

		blood (in the face), i.e. flush or turn rosy]; soil (from its general redness): country, earth, ground, husband[man]” {an inflection of the word man, mannish}	
after his kind:	hlmiyneehuw.	|4327| after their species	of their sorts.
and God saw	Wayar'	|7200| and saw	And,
	'Elohiym	|0430| God	Almighty God saw,
that	kiy-	|3588| that	“That's
it was good.	Towb.	|2896| good	good.”
1:26 And	Wayo'mer	|0559| And said	And,
God said,	'Elohiym,	|0430| God,	Almighty God said,
Let us make	Na`seh	|6213| Let us make	“Let Us make
man	'aadaam	|0120| mankind “from [to show blood (in the face), i.e. flush or turn rosy]ruddy i.e. a human being (an individual or the species, mankind”	a man
in our image,	Btsalmeen	|6754| in Our image, “from an unused root meaning to shade; a phantom, i.e. (figuratively) illusion, resemblance; hence, a representative figure”	in Our image,
after our likeness:	uwkidmuwteenuw	|1823| according to Our likeness; “from [to compare]; resemblance; concretely, model, shape; adverbially, like”	to be like us,
and let them have dominion	wyirduw	|7287| and let them rule	and to rule
over the fish of	bidgat	|1710| over fish of	over the fish of
the sea,	hayaam	|3220| the ocean	the roaring sea,
and over the fowl of	uwb`owp	|5775| and over birds of	and over shrouds of
the air,	hashaamayim	|8064| the heavens,	the whirling flows,
and over the cattle,	uwbabheemaah	|0929| and over the cattle	and over the large mammals,
and over all the earth,	uwbkaal- haa'aarets {*}	|3605| and over all |0776| the earth	and over all the earth,
and over every creeping thing	uwbkaal- haaremes	|3605| and over all |7431| crawlers	and over all the scampering-beasts
that creepeth	haaromees	|7430| crawling	scampering
upon	`al-	|5921| on	on
the earth.	haa'aarets.	|0776| the earth.	the earth.”
1:27 So God	wayibraa'	|1254| And created {1-declarative}	And,
created	'Elohiym	|0430| God	Almighty God created
	'et-	|0853| -	

70

man	haa'aadaam	|0120| the mankind	the man
in his own image,	btsalmow	|6754| in His image,	in His image.
in the image of	btselem	|6754| In the image of	In the image of
God	'Elohiym	|0430| God	Almighty God
created he him;	**baaraa'** 'otow	|1254| He created {2-comparative} |0853| him;	**He created** **him.**
male	zaakaar	|2145| male	**Male and**
and female	uwnqeebaah	|5347| and female	**Female**
created he them.	**baaraa'** 'otaam.	|1254| He created (3-superlative} |0853| them.	**He created** **them.**
1:28 And God blessed them	Waybaarek	|1288| And blessed **"to kneel; by implication to bless God (as an act of adoration), and (vice versa) man (as a benefit)"**	**And,** **Almighty** **God knelt to** **bless them.**
	'otaam ' Elohiym.	|0853| them |0430| God,	
and God said unto them,	Wayo'mer laahem	|0559| and said |0000| to them	**And,** **Almighty** **God said to** **them,**
	'Elohiym,	|0430| God,	
Be fruitful,	Pruw	|6509| Be fruitful	**"Be fruitful**
and multiply,	uwrbuw	|7235| and multiply,	**and** **multiply,**
and replenish	uwmil'uw 'et-	|4390| and fill |0853| -	**and fill the** **earth,**
the earth,	haa'aarets	|0776| the earth,	
and subdue it:	wkibshuhaa	|3533| and it subdue **"to tread down; hence, negatively, to disregard; positively, to conquer, subjugate"**	**and tread on** **it.**
and have dominion	uwrduw	|7287| And rule	**Rule**
over the fish	bidgat	|1710| over fish of	**over the fish** **of**
of the sea,	hayaam	|3220| the ocean,	**the roaring** **seas,**
and over the fowl	uwb`owp	|5775| and over of birds	**and over the** **shrouds of**
of the air,	hashaamayim	|8064| the heavens	**the whirling** **flows,**
and over every	uwbkaal-	|3605| and over all	**and over all**
iving thing	chayaah	|2416| animals	*the* **frisky** ***beasts***
that moveth	haaromeset	|7430| crawling	**scampering**
upon	`al-	|5921| on	**on**
the earth.	haa'aarets.	|0776| the earth.	**the earth."**
1:29 And God said,	Wayo'mer 'Elohiym,	|0559| And said |0430| God,	**And,** **Almighty** **God said,**
Behold,	Hineeh	|2009| Behold,	**"Look!**

I have given	naatatiy	|5414| I have given	**I have presented**
you	laakem	|0000| to you	**to you**
	'et-	|0853| -	
every	kaal-	|3605| every	**every**
herb	`eeseb	|6212| plant	**glistening green**
bearing	zoreea`	|2232| seeding	**seeding**
seed,	zera`	|2233| seed	**seed,**
which	'sher	|0834| which	**which** *is*
is upon	`al-	|5921| on	**on** *the*
the face of	pneey	|6440| the surface of	**turning sphere of**
all	kaal-	|3605| all	**all**
the earth,	haa'aarets	|0776| the earth,	**the earth,**
and	w'et-	|0853| and	**and**
every	kaal-	|3605| every	**every**
tree,	haa`eets	|6086| tree	**solid plant**
in the which is the	sher-bow	|0834| which in it	**which has in it**
fruit of	priy-	|6529| fruit of	**fruit,**
a tree	`eets	|6086| tree	**solid plants**
yielding	zoreea`	|2232| seeding	**seeding**
seed;	zaara`	|2233| seed.	**seed,**
to you	laakem	|0000| to you	**to you**
it shall be	yihyeh	|1961| will it be	**it will be**
for meat.	l'aaklaah.	|0402| for food,	**for food.**
1:30 And to every	Uwlkaal-	|3605| and to every	**And, to all**
beast	chayat	|2416| animal of	**the friskies of**
of the earth,	haa'aarets	|0776| the earth	**the earth,**
and to every	uwlkaal-	|3605| and to every	**and to all**
fowl	`owp	|5775| bird of	*the* **shrouds in**
of the air,	hashaamayim	|8064| the heavens,	**the whirling flows,**
and to every thing that creepeth	uwlkol rowmees	|3605| and to every |7430| crawler	**and to all** *the* **scampering-** *beasts*
upon	`al-	|5921| on	**on**
the earth,	haa'aarets	|0776| the earth	**the earth**
wherein there is	sher-bow	|0834| which in it	**which are**
	nepesh	|5315| a life	**frisky**
life,	chayaah	|2416| living	**breathers**
I have given	'et-	|0853| -	
every	kaal-	|3605| every	**—all the**
green	yereq	|3418| green	**green**
herb	`eeseb	|6212| plant	**glistening greens**
for meat:	l'aaklaah	|0402| for food.	**for food."**
and it was	wayhiy-	|1961| And it was	**And, it was**

72

so.	keen.	|3651| so.	so.
1:31 And	Wayar'	|7200| And saw	And,
God saw	'Elohiym	|0430| God	Almighty God saw
	'et-	|0853| -	
every thing	kaal-	|3605| all	all
that	'sher	|0834| which	that
he had made	`aasaah -	|6213| He had made	He had showed,
and, behold,	whineeh	|2009| and, look,	and, "Look!
it was very	Towb	|2896| good	Very Good!"
good.	m'od	|3966| very!	
And	wayhiy-	|1961| And was	[And was
the evening	`ereb	|6153| evening,	evening
and	wayhiy-	|1961| and was	and was
the morning	boqer	|1242| morning,	morning
were the sixth	yowm	|3117| day	Day
day.	hashishiy.	|8345| sixth.	Six.]
2:1 Thus the	Waykuluw	|3615| And were finished	And so,
heavens and	hashaamayim	|8064| the heavens	the whirling flows
the earth were finished,	whaa'aarets	|0776| and the earth	and the earth
and all	wkaal-	|3605| and all	and all
the host of	tsbaa'aam.	|6635| their army. **"from [to mass (an army or servants)]; a mass of persons (or figuratively, things), especially reg. organized for war (an army)"**	their troops were finished.
them.			
2:2 And on	Waykal	|3615| And finished	And, on the
the seventh	'Elohiym	|0430| God	seventh day
day God	bayowm	|3117| on day	Almighty
ended	hashbiy`iy	|7637| the seventh	God finished
his work	mla'ktow	|4399| His work **"from [to despatch as a deputy; a messenger; specifically, of God, i.e. an angel (also a prophet, priest or teacher): ambassador, angel, king, messenger.]; properly, deputyship, i.e. ministry; generally, employment (never servile) or work (abstractly or concretely)"** *{1-declarative}*	His angelic message
which	'sher	|0834| which	which
he had made;	`aasaah	|6213| He had made. *{1-declarative}*	He had showed.
and he rested	wayishbot	|7673| And He ceased **"to repose, i.e. desist from exertion; ... cease, celebrate, cause (make) to fail, keep (sabbath)"**	On the seventh day He stopped
on the	bayowm	|3117| on day	
seventh day	hashbiy`iy	|7637| the seventh	
from all	mikaal-	|3605| from all	all
his work	mla'ktow	|4399| His work *{2-comparative}*	His angelic message

which	'sher	|0834| which	**which**
he had made.	`aasaah.	|6213| He had made. *{2-comparative}*	**He had showed.**
2:3 And God	ybaarek	|1288| And blessed	**And,**
blessed	'Elohiym	|0430| God	**Almighty God knelt to bless**
	'et-	|0853|	
the seventh	yowm	|3117| day	**the seventh**
day,	hashbiy`iy	|7637| the seventh	**day,**
and sanctified	wayqadeesh	|6942| and sanctified	**and made it**
it:	'otow	|0853| it,	**special,**
because	kiy	|3588| because	**because**
that in it	bow	|0000| in it	**He stopped**
he had rested	shaabat	|7673| He ceased	**on it**
from all	mikaal-	|3605| from all	**from the entire**
his work	mla'ktow	|4399| His work *{3-superlative}*	**angelic message**
which	'sher-	|0834| which	**which**
God **created**	**baaraa'**	|1254| had created	**Almighty**
	'Elohiym	|0430| God	**God created**
and made.	la`sowt.	|6213| to make. *{3-superlative}*	**to show.**

Section Two:

Disputes over the Creation Story

Double-Trouble with Tradition

FAIR WARNING: this particular chapter is somewhat downbeat, since it deals with two essentially negative events in the last few centuries of church history. If you absolutely insist on stories with happy endings, or can't abide or chronically misunderstand sarcasm, then you should probably just skip this chapter.

We live in an era that takes a conflict between religion and science for granted and even accepts it as a necessary part of life. This began as a conflict between some Christian traditions and the declarations of popular science a century ago, and has moved on to a popular modern acceptance of irrationality as the price of humanity. Nice, caring people are assumed to embrace irrationality. In popular culture, *Star Trek*'s contrast and pairing of Spock and McCoy has become the norm.

For instance, those of you who watch *NCIS* on TV can see this in the characters of Abby and Ducky. Both are highly competent forensic scientists who escape the inherent ghoulishness of their jobs by engaging in irrational behavior. Abby, the younger woman, embraces a Goth-new-age look and the over-sentimental affect of a ten-year-old girl. Ducky embraces the affect of a pre-WWII English gentleman, politely conversing with corpses while he performs graphic autopsies on-screen.

Today, this makes the characters more sympathetic to the viewing audience. Things have changed. Sixty years ago it would have landed them in mental hospitals, and we would have carefully kept them away from sharp objects or children.

If the above statement leaves your eyebrows pushing your hairline, then I highly recommend that you read the works of the late Dr. Francis Schaeffer, especially *How Should We Then Live.* He called this disconnect between reason and humanity "fragmentation." We will not have time to explain that in more detail here. Suffice it to say, most of this "fragmentation" can be traced back to the loss of a Christian consensus in the Western world, which itself began with a major conflict between rising modern science and two popular Christian traditions.

THE FIRST LOST BATTLE

In the course of fighting a war, even the side that ultimately wins may lose some battles along the way. Sometimes circumstances just favor the enemy. But even when overwhelmed by superior forces, the loss can remain a source of pride; remember, for instance, the Alamo.

However, it's harder to take pride in losing a battle to a tactical blunder. The poem, "The Charge of the Light Brigade" may honor the courage of the fallen, but it forever mocks military bureaucracy.

It's interesting to note that an organization exists today called the Association for Biblical Astronomy. They apparently publish detailed and complex articles arguing that earth is the center of the universe, and all the mainstream astronomy of the past 450 years is a satanic plot to undermine the Bible. You can easily look them up on the Internet if you want.

Personally, I've only given them a quick look, and really can't tell if they are serious, or if it's all a put-on to make fun of fundamentalist Christianity. Assuming they are on the up and up, I did notice that the group views the KJV as the only true Bible. (I can't tell what they think the church used before the KJV was published, or what they think non-English speaking churches use for a Bible.) However, their insistence on the KJV makes sense, since all their biblical supports for rejecting Copernicus seem to depend on poetic idioms. For instance, they view Psalm 113:3, "From the rising of the Sun, to the going down of the same," as proof positive that the Bible teaches that the sun goes around the earth and not vice versa.

(By the way, after I wrote the above paragraph, I looked up Psalm 113:3 and was reminded to my amusement that the Hebrew here is literally "From the east of the sun to the west of the same" with no implication of moving up and down involved.)

COPERNICUS VS. ARISTOTLE: We probably have all heard of Copernicus and how he waited to publish his book claiming the earth went around the sun until he was on his deathbed in 1543. He knew that the church would view this proposition as rankest heresy, since it went against an important church tradition from the time of Saint Thomas Aquinas three hundred years earlier.

Following Thomas's lead, the Roman church had mixed the teachings of the pagan Greek philosopher Aristotle with church doctrine. Eventually, the teachings of Aristotle became equal to the Bible. And, since Aristotle had taught that the earth was the center of the universe, this became official church doctrine. By challenging Aristotle, Copernicus had challenged a beloved church tradition.

However, we should not just blame the Roman Catholics. The very elderly Martin Luther, who heard about Copernicus about a year after the book was published, railed against the idea before even the Catholics did. He reasoned that since man was the peak of God's creation, and Christ died for man, then the earth, man's home, must be the center of God's universe. To devalue the earth was to devalue man, and thus to devalue Christ's sacrifice. It seemed like perfectly sound logic at the time.[24] About fifty years later, Galileo faced his famous trial for heresy, and went under house arrest for the rest of his life for daring to publish what he saw though his telescope.

In fact, for a century after even that, pious Christians in virtually every denomination fought valiantly against what they saw as a demonic attack on the Bible. Then, Isaac Newton, a Reformation Christian himself, published his *Principia* in 1687, which, among other things, laid out the general theory of gravity and mathematically and finally demonstrated that Copernicus was right.

But even after that, any educated Christian who owned a telescope and had a reasonable background in mathematics had to duck his head and keep his mouth shut in church. The piously ignorant would only think he was some kind of heathen if he spoke up.

Today, hundreds of millions of dedicated Christians, who have faithfully studied and applied the Bible for most of their lives, can only scratch their heads and wonder what all the fuss was about. The Bible simply doesn't declare anywhere that either man or the earth is the center focus of God's universe. In fact, many verses plainly say precisely the opposite. So, where did all that theological thunder come from? The answer is simple. We should all grab our fiddles, climb on a roof, and start singing, "Tradition!"

So how did the church finally come around to exonerate poor Copernicus? The answer is, "they didn't." What happened was that, within each denomination, a generation of Christians would come along whose general knowledge of both the Bible and of science allowed them to see the folly of their elders' ranting. They just shut their mouths, kept the peace, and waited for the older generation to die. Then they went on as if there had never been any controversy.

Historically, this happened much sooner in the many smaller Reformation denominations. They had already broken with many

24. Drake, p. 468, note 9.

traditions, and one more didn't make that much difference. Since these denominations flourished primarily in the American colonies, we see that the concept of a conflict between science and religion was just not an issue for Americans. The American colleges were also the American seminaries. Any serious theologian was also expected to be a serious scientist, or lawyer, or academic. This is one reason why Christianity continued to be a major force in American life long after Christianity began its decline in Europe.

THE PEACE OF WESTPHALIA: However, in Europe, events took a much different course. You are probably aware that in the wake of the Reformation and Counter-Reformation, what is now Germany was ravaged by a long series of brutal wars, which was calmed, if not pacified, by a series of treaties in 1648 that came to be called the Peace of Westphalia.

One of the terms of this peace stipulated that the currently reigning prince or duke of each small principality/town would decide whether the town's official church was Lutheran or Roman Catholic. Eventually, after a bit more squabbling, the choices were expanded to include a third option: Calvinist.

Since none of the three options were particularly tolerant of the other two, this also meant that two options in any given area usually faced hard times. To avoid this initially, many people simply relocated to friendlier areas. But, as time went on and succeeding princes changed allegiances, this caused lots of emotional and economic stress.

This was so bad that most protestant Germans, when forced to pack up their homes and move to a friendlier region, chose to leave the German states entirely and emigrated to the American colonies. This is the primary reason America's largest 19th century traditional immigrant group was not English, Scottish, or Irish, but rather German. In fact, by the opening of the twentieth century, so many Protestant Germans had emigrated to America that Germany, the birthplace of the Protestant Reformation, had a Roman Catholic majority.

One force that tried to avoid the wrangling and establish some kind of stability was the university systems of Germany and France. This was not terribly effective, and academia soon developed an increasing disgust with all churches in general. This led to various attempts to develop a value system that bypassed Christianity. France produced the tacitly atheistic Enlightenment, and Germany spawned the infamous "German philosophers" who attempted to deduce some kind of grand idealism apart from religion of any kind.

In the context of the churches' continued ranting against Copernicus, both groups found it fairly easy to convince many college students that all religion was a breeding ground of bigoted ignorance. With, of course, the (wink-wink) obvious exception of whatever religion the university town's current prince held to.

If you have ever had to study these German philosophers, one thing in particular will stand out. They loved to invent vast and intricate systems of jargon. To some, this gave them an air of super-intellect and mystical learning. However, to most, it was simply incoherent and deadly boring. Carl Jung, the famous psychologist, even charged that the writings of Hegel, the worst offender, were simply schizophrenic gibberish completely out of touch with reality. So, while these atheist philosophers appealed to self-important college students, it took a couple more generations for their attitudes to filter out to the general Continental public.

Now, since the English churches had long ago dropped their anti-Copernican tradition, a strange tension developed. On one hand, many in the English colleges and the English upper class highly respected Continental education and philosophy. So, a significant minority of them shared the Continental contempt for religion and the Bible. On the other hand, the English general public considered the Continental mind-set blasphemous, immoral, and generally vile. It was during this period that people began saying "Pardon my French" to mean "Pardon my obscenity."

Many English atheists and academics were highly disgusted by the fact that the English-speaking world simply refused to follow along with the Continental progress. They recognized that the Continental churches' stubborn opposition to Copernicus had been the atheists' strongest weapon, and felt that English Christianity had somehow cheated when they didn't go along with the program.

What was needed, they generally agreed, was to find some other clear-cut scientific issue where they could publicly and loudly expose Christianity as bigoted, superstitious nonsense. They needed to find a major religious tradition they could attack with some clear and easily understood scientific fact.

Unfortunately, this wasn't working out very well for them at all. In fact, Reformation Christianity was using science to score big points by pointing out that modern science was historically the child of Christian theology. Furthermore, incomprehensibly to the atheists, Christian English-speaking science and technology were perversely leading the world.

THE SECOND LOST BATTLE

Things looked pretty bleak for the English atheists until finally, in the early nineteenth century they found their issue.

The crucial tradition was established in 1650 by an Anglican bishop by the name of James Ussher. Bishop Ussher drew on his vast knowledge of both the Bible and history to publish his *Annals of the Old Testament*. In this book he claimed to have precisely dated creation to "the evening of October 22, 4004 BC."[25] He dated biblical events by paying close attention to the genealogies of the Old Testament, the "so-and-so lived a jillion years and begat so-and-so" passages scattered though the Old Testament that go on for chapters at a time.

Clearly, Ussher's dating system had benefits. First, it helped date biblical events. Second, it produced some clear patterns. For instance, Old Testament history fell into four clearly defined blocks of one thousand years each. The fall of man to the birth of Noah equaled one thousand years. The birth of Noah to the call of Abra-

---

25. New Encyclopedia Britannica, 15th Ed. p.754.

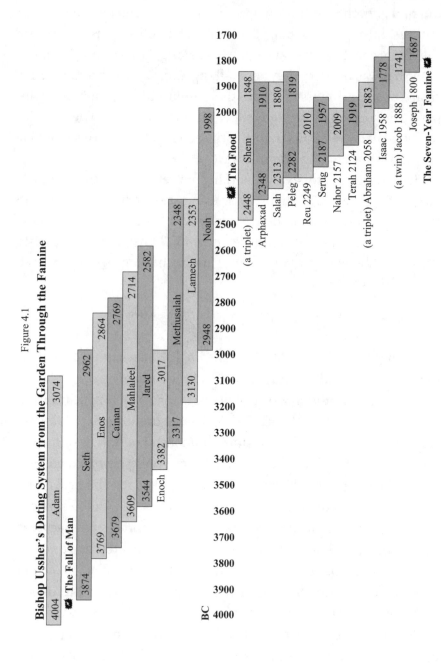

Figure 4.1

Bishop Ussher's Dating System from the Garden Through the Famine

ham equaled one thousand years. The call of Abraham to the dedication of Solomon's temple equaled one thousand years, and the dedication of Solomon's temple to the birth of Christ equaled another one thousand years. Furthermore, subdivisions of those four millennia easily yielded even more neat and tidy patterns.

This regular rhythm of the Old Testament stories was taken as another support for the truth that, while many different men over a long period of history wrote the individual books of the Bible, a single author, God himself, had welded the whole into a unified story.

Finally, Ussher's genealogical dating system reflected the current attitude that all of human history was a neat and orderly affair under the lordship of God, reflecting the English ideal of a proper and civil society under the lordship of the King of England. By the early 1800s, Ussher's dates had gained such traditional support that many equated them to the Word of God itself. Indeed, many Bibles as late as the early twentieth century went as far as to include Ussher's dates at the heading of each page.[26] However, from the very beginning, not everybody agreed that the genealogical dates could give us as firm a historical reference as Ussher had derived.

First, from the earliest church ages, the church fathers had taught that the days of creation represented long time periods far into the distant past. In other words, as strange as it may seem to some today, Ussher's view ran against some important church traditions. Dr. Hugh Ross has documented this:

> Many of the early church fathers and other biblical scholars interpreted the creation days of Genesis 1 as long periods of time. This list includes the Jewish historian Josephus (1st century); Irenaeus, Bishop of Lyons, apologist, and martyr (2nd century); Origen, who rebutted heathen attacks on Christian doctrine (3rd century); Basil (4th century); Augustine (5th century); and later Aquinas (13th century), to name a few.

---

26. Scofield.

The significance of this list lies . . . in that their scriptural views cannot be said to have been shaped to accommodate [modern evolutionary] secular opinion.[27]

Next, concerning the genealogical lists themselves, conflict arose over the usage of the Hebrew word translated as "begat"—*yaw-lad'*. Many contended that *yaw-lad'*, to howl, closely related to the word for birth pangs, and in usage it simply meant "became the male ancestor of a like male." After all, it is the woman, and not the man who howled with birth pangs. A woman giving birth to a man's great-great-grandson was still thought to bear that man's seed. Remember, the Jews called themselves "the seed of Abraham."

Furthermore, Bible scholars pointed out that when you compare similar genealogical lists in the Bible, you often find that one or the other would routinely skip minor ancestors.

Worse yet, some of the generations in Ussher's list didn't actually contain the "lived so many years and begat so-and-so" formula. In other words, Ussher simply made guesses—lots and lots of guesses.

Thus, these people felt that genealogical dating could only give a "no later than" kind of date. This meant that, while the story of Adam could have happened no later than Ussher's 4,000 BC, it could have happened much earlier than that date.

All these factors warn us that we cannot absolutely rely on Ussher's genealogical dating system. In fact, few evangelical Bible scholars still place the Garden of Eden at Ussher's 4,000 BC. Even many young–earth creationists now place the Garden of Eden at 10,900 BC, while some young-earthers even go back as far as 60-40,000 BC.

THE NEEDED SCIENCE: About the time of the American Revolution, a boy named William Smith developed the passionate hobby of collecting fossils as he wandered the hills on his uncle's farm in southern England. In school he learned the basic principles

---

27. Hugh Ross, p. 141.

of surveying, and at eighteen years old he got a job helping a surveyor. Eventually, he became a surveyor himself, working on building canals for a coal company. All this time he continued to keep up his hobby of collecting fossils. Eventually, he became quite good at identifying the different sorts. His job and his hobby soon came together.

William Smith noticed that all over England the rocks made layers like slices of bread. Not only that, but the different kinds of fossils were sorted into distinct layers, and these fossil layers kept the same order no matter where you went in England. Furthermore, the coal beds generally kept their place in one particular layer. Knowing how the different kinds of fossils related to the position of the coal-bed, "carboniferous," layer made the hunt for coal much easier. In 1799, Smith began telling other surveyors what he had found. And, since this discovery meant saving the coal companies lots of money, word traveled quickly through the coal-producing community.

Future generations would remember William Smith by the title, "The Father of Geology." However, as a side effect, Smith's discovery clearly implied that the lower rock layers were significantly older than the upper rock layers. This dovetailed with the published observations of other "natural philosophers," as they called themselves, who were beginning to suspect that the earth may be much older than the "Bible's" six thousand years.

Up until Smith's discovery, most people had been willing to accept that all those animal bones had simply been laid down by Noah's flood. However, when William Smith pointed out the distinctiveness of each layer of rock, this completely junked the idea that Noah's flood could have created the fossils. If these animals were simply truants from the ark, what possible action of the flood sorted them into such neatly organized layers? Obviously, each layer represented many generations, sometimes thousands of generations, of one sort of animal living and dying before the next slightly different sort of animal even came into existence.

Word of this discovery made its way to an elderly "natural philosopher" by the name of Erasmus Darwin who speculated in writing that Smith's discovery may indicate that life on earth may have gradually developed from a "single living filament."[28]

In 1815, William Smith published what came to be known as "The Map That Changed the World." Suddenly, with the popularity of this map, not just a few coal companies and natural philosophers but most academics saw proof positive that the earth was vastly older than the "Bible's" six thousand years, and that life had gone though a long series of gradual changes over the course of many eons, a process they eventually came to call "evolution."

Erasmus Darwin's grandson, Charles, was just six years old at the time.

Now please wrap your mind around the scope of this disaster. The Protestant Reformation had had relatively little trouble discarding the Roman Catholic tradition that had overlapped the teachings of Aristotle over the Bible. But now, things were different. It wasn't some popish superstition at stake; it was their very own tradition. So, even with the example of Copernicus fresh in front of them, many church leaders plunged blithely into the fray. "We are God's people; we couldn't possibly be glaringly and embarrassingly wrong! Could we?"

Every few years, another scientist would make another discovery indicating that the earth was very old. And, in response, church leaders would thunder against the evil scientist, rallying the faithful with often specious and silly arguments. While such arguments inspired the faithful, they only served to push more and more academics and college students into the antichurch camp. Eventually, on most college campuses the mere fact that the church opposed something became in itself an argument in the topic's favor. It was Copernicus all over again.

---

28. Zoonomia from http://www.gutenberg.org/files/15707/15707-h/15707-h.htm, accessed October 19, 2009.

Up until 1859, this debate had fought to a draw, and the English public had remained unmoved. The primary problem was that nobody could demonstrate any such principle of evolutionary change.

Some, like LeMarc, thought that environmental forces on the parents directly affect the characteristics of the offspring. If a child's parents spent their lives lifting heavy loads, then that meant their children would be a little bit stronger and able to lift even heavier loads. But that was pure mysticism, and no laboratory had demonstrated any such thing.

THE CRISIS: However, in 1859, Erasmus Darwin's grandson, Charles, published his famous *On the Origin of Species*. Now, Darwin's research and conclusions had little or nothing to do with any battle between the church and Continental systems of philosophy. He had simply been raised in a family famous for its natural philosophers, and had long pondered his grandfather's question about whether some natural principle existed that could change species. Darwin was a quiet man, and not in the least spoiling for a fight. Nevertheless, today virtually everybody thinks they understand Darwin's theory and how it "conflicts with the Bible."

Thus, for a century and a half, many evangelicals have felt as if someone picked up Darwin by the heels and proceeded to beat them over the head with him, like a dog being beat with a rolled-up newspaper. Reasonably, they have developed hostility to the very name Darwin. However, just as it's not really the newspaper beating on the dog, but rather someone's hand holding that newspaper, we evangelicals should instead look at the hand that has been holding the science.

Immediately before Darwin's work was published, England's leading "agnostic," (a word he himself coined)—a man by the name of Thomas Huxley—read a preliminary copy from the publisher of Darwin's book and immediately picked it up and ran with it. The interesting thing was that, in private, he didn't fully agree with Darwin. Privately, he still tended to favor LaMarc's semi-pagan mystical evolutionary principal at work. His enthusiasm stemmed from his ability to recognize the elegant simplicity of Darwin's theory. The common man could easily wrap his mind around it. It was the kind of thing that could spark the imagination of even nine-year-old school children.

Huxley set out on a systematic campaign. First, he publicly and vocally rose to Darwin's defense, earning himself the nickname "Darwin's Bulldog." Second, he politely couched his arguments in the most inflammatory anti-Christian terms he could find. He wanted to draw the church into the fight. He did not want the English-speaking church to dodge the bullet as they had done with Copernicus.

Within a year, he had wrangled a public debate on the subject between himself and Anglican Bishop Samuel Wilberforce, nicknamed Soapy Sam by the newspapers for his unctuous and pompous style of public speaking. He was the son of William Wilberforce, the Christian philanthropist who had been the leader in the fight to abolish slavery in the British Empire. The debate was sponsored by the British Association, a leading scientific organization, and took place at the Oxford University Museum. While the debate was purportedly amiable enough, and both sides felt they had done well, by most accounts Huxley had carried the day.

Certainly, once the debate had ended, he had persuaded most of England's intellectual elite to his point of view, and virtually everyone knew that regardless of whether Darwin was right or wrong, his theory was sound science, and it was not going away.

One last note: Huxley went on to hold many very prominent positions in English academic life. Among them, he sat on the London School Board during the earliest development of what we call public schools. Prior to this, the church had offered the only available free education system for the poor. Many thought that the new developing state schools should work closely with the existing denominational schools. However, Huxley was absolutely adamant in opposing this. Almost single-handedly he made sure that the free, church denominational schools were not allowed to be part of the London school system. Huxley believed that he could use the public school system as a tool to help destroy his great enemy, the Christian church.

With their nation's children firmly in hand, the English secularists knew they had finally joined England with the Continental mystic philosophers.

At the beginning of this chapter, I warned you that this material would be negative. By clinging to two traditions—the first from Aristotle and the second from Bishop Ussher—first the Continental European and then the English-speaking church lost major battles. But the war is not over; no armistice has been declared. It is time to learn from our mistakes and regroup and then reengage the enemy. And, our enemy is not Copernicus or Darwin. It is the hopeless, meaningless, and ultimately irrational secular mind-set that currently cripples our culture.

5

Mystical Darwinian Disasters

In its original meaning, Darwinism referred to a very specific method used to explain the origin of species, taken from the title of Darwin's book. In itself, it is actually quite innocuous. If the church had been more concerned about the truth of the Word of God and less concerned about upholding a silly tradition, it would have had no negative impact whatsoever.

THE LIMITS OF ACTUAL DARWINISM

Of course, in that era before the science of genetics, Darwin's theory begged the question of where all those random mutations had come from. At the time this seemed like an extremely minor issue. After all, plainly they did occur. Darwin himself tended to believe the Victorian idea that the circumstances of a mother directly affected the unborn child. People who had buck teeth tended to believe that their mother had been startled by a rabbit.

Figure 5.1

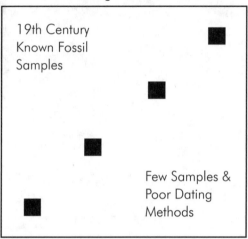

In the nineteenth century, it looked like the fossil record supported the idea that life had gone through slow, steady changes over a long time. However, this was based on the nineteenth century's limited sampling of the fossil record. Darwin confidently believed that paleontologists would fill in the missing links between the then currently known fossil forms, and that would show that life had smoothly and steadily advanced as if up an inclined plane or ramp.

Figure 5.2

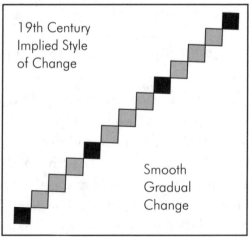

PUNCTUATED EQUILIBRIUM: However, this traditional form of Darwinian Evolution has fallen on hard times in recent years. This began in 1972, when Niles Eldredge of the American Museum of Natural History and Stephen Gould of Harvard University proposed a theory they called "Punctuated Equilibrium." They insisted that the fossil record did not show the kind of slow, steady change that Darwin predicted.

Figure 5.3

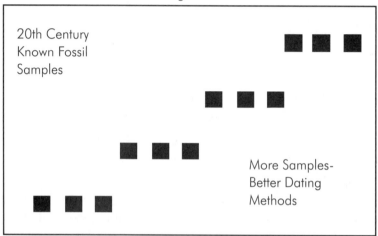

Paleontologists over the last century have collected many thousands of different fossils using vastly better dating methods. While they have filled in many of the gaps in the fossil record, contrary to expectations, the fossil record doesn't look like a ramp at all. Instead, the record shows long periods of relative stability, punctuated by short bursts of revolutionary change. This creates a stair-stepping of the fossil record. After much debate, punctuated equilibrium has taken the field.

Figure 5.4

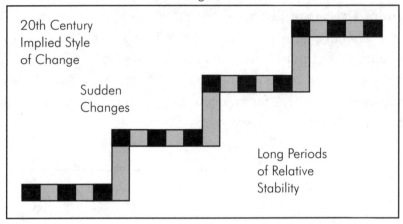

20th Century
Implied Style
of Change

Sudden
Changes

Long Periods
of Relative
Stability

Now, you have to understand how awkward this is for traditional Darwinists. Forty years ago they could confidently claim to understand speciation. By conceding fossil stair-stepping, however reluctantly, they must admit they no longer have as confident an answer for exactly how speciation takes place, since they no longer have those millions of years to play with.

Remember that minor question about exactly how species produce those random mutations? One day they may actually have an answer they like. And, just because they don't have as confident and as clear an answer now as they did before doesn't mean they are completely confounded.

However, while real scientists research and debate this, I have been amused by the increasingly convoluted and often poetical blathering that mystical Darwinists hide behind in their desperate attempt to avoid publicly admitting that they no longer have as confident an answer to the question.

You hear a lot about "niches" today. What they say is that when one species goes extinct and leaves its place in the ecological network vacant, then another species rapidly changes to fill that slot or niche. But, all this really says is, "*this* happens and then marvelously *that* happens, and we have proved it happens!" What they have yet to establish is "*how* that happens."

Currently, we have seen a modified revival of the old Lamarckian system that proposed that long-term stress on an organism causes genetic modification of their descendants—that the genetic code is not as passive as once believed. Some long-term intergenerational studies have shown some possible results; however, the debate on this has only begun.

Others have suggested that the events leading to mass extinctions also deplete the earth's ozone layer, leading to a vastly increased rate of mutation.

Still others have proposed that an ecological group of distressed organisms begins to shed strands of DNA as quasi-viruses that can infect and modify the genetic makeup of other species in the system, leading to a vastly accelerated process of positive genetic mutation.

All of this bears on the current intelligent design debate that is getting so much attention in the public schools. Intelligent design, which we will look at in the next chapter, tends to view God as a genetic engineer. However, ultimately, for our purposes, it really doesn't matter what the mechanism actually turns out to be. As we have seen in the last three chapters, what the Bible says happened has been confirmed to have happened. For our purposes, the how is not relevant.

BE CAREFUL WHAT YOU WISH FOR

Remember those French Enlightenment and German mystic philosophers from the last lesson? They believed that if they could only have their way and remove the backward influence of the church, mankind would be freed from its chains of superstition and ignorance and a new golden age would dawn. They had been searching frantically for some mystical universal principle that would allow them to leap forward to that goal.

Once they saw the apparent success of Darwin's theory as a tool to combat the church, they almost universally became convinced that here they had the universal mystical principle they had sought for so long. In their minds, evolution became a mystical kind of life force, sort of like Mesmer's animal magnetism. They spoke of it as if it were a god. These mystical Darwinists believed the evil church would melt backward from the bright light of Darwin, and evolution itself would carry humanity ever forward to greater and greater heights. Well, the majority may not have said it in such a corny way, but in essence, this is what they thought.

However, these inhuman philosophies had been around for generations before Darwin, and they actually had nothing to do with Darwin or his theory. To them, science was just a tool to be used or misused as they desired. Ultimately, Darwinism and mystical Darwinism have nothing to do with each other. However, the public mind often confuses the two things. This is sort of like the current popular belief that the phrase *separation of church and state* has something to do with the American Constitution—completely false, but an entrenched belief nonetheless.

In the hands of these antichurch philosophers, the word *Darwinism* began to shift from its scientific meaning toward meaning that mystical principle. It became the fashion for these philosophers to use Darwin's essentially simple biological principle to justify their crackpot theories, to make them more palatable to the general public. In a surge of manic optimism, mystical Darwinism became the magic answer to all questions, the cure-all for every problem.

Understandably, things did not work as well as the mystic philosophers had wished. On one hand, they got their wish of discrediting the Christian church on virtually all college campuses. On the other hand, this didn't yield all those wonderful benefits they had envisioned. In fact, a very good case can be made to assert that the vast majority of preventable human suffering over the last century and a half can be directly laid at the feet of mystical Darwinism.

UTILITARIANISM: Just before Darwin, during the early industrial revolution, a political philosophy called utilitarianism, spearheaded by John Stuart Mill, had taught that the government should not pass laws to ease the harsh conditions in the factories.

It agreed that it was tragic that thousands of malnourished women and children slaved such long, hard hours as simple cogs in factories, sleeping on mats next to where they worked, freezing in thin rags. However, utilitarians insisted that by working for such long hours for such low wages, those factory workers produced lots of products at a low price, thereby raising the standard of living for many thousands of others.

They believed the government should reduce all moral issues to the question of what provides "the greatest good for the greatest number." They taught that society should judge laws by their utility, or usefulness, and not by emotion.

However, as leading Christians continued to relentlessly pound on the public mind, the scope of the suffering sank in. Utilitarianism began to be branded as so obviously cold-hearted and cruel that few politicians would publicly admit to supporting such a shameful position.

However, with the diminishment of the churches' influence and the rise of mystical Darwinism, utilitarianism surged back into respectability. Society became "our species" and utilitarians began to appear as stern but benign benefactors of humanity. Thus, mystical Darwinism combined with utilitarianism to help prolong the worst abuses of the middle industrial revolution.

SOCIAL DARWINISM: Over the next fifty years, various attempts were made to apply the "survival of the fittest" mentality to solve social problems. For instance, Charles Darwin's cousin, Francis Galton, began the eugenics movement, which embraced the belief that the government should pass laws forbidding the unfit to have children. Later historians called these schemes "Social Darwinism."

Social Darwinism differed from utilitarianism in one key way. On one hand, a certain egalitarianism underlined John Stuart Mill's utilitarian thought. The good that happens to individuals A and B overbalances the bad that happens to individual C. On the other hand, social Darwinism labeled the majority of humanity as bad in and of themselves, while the good resided in only the few strong individuals. The suffering of the poor went from being considered a necessary evil to being seen as an active good.

This political philosophy urged the government to not only do nothing to help the poor or the weak, but to actively go out of its way to make conditions for the weak even harsher. Our species would only suffer if we allowed the weak to even survive. Instead, we should allow evolution to take its course and purify our species by killing off the poor and ending their misery.

CUTTHROAT CAPITALISM: This is not the same thing as free enterprise, or even regular capitalism—the practice of businessmen pooling their capital and financial resources to build and operate factories.

Free enterprise teaches that if we want businesses to do well, we should let them freely compete, much like a race in the Olympics. To get runners to run their fastest times, we line them up at the starting block, and, at the sound of the starting pistol, have them compete against each other fairly for a prize. Here, competition for a reward insures that the audience gets to see the runners put forth their best effort.

In contrast, men began to approach capitalism from the "survival of the fittest" worldview. These "cutthroat capitalists" felt justified in lying, stealing, and actively destroying rival businesses. The ideal was to achieve a monopoly in which only your business provided vital products to the consumer.

Once you had a monopoly, you could raise your prices and make huge profits. Then, having made your money, you should spend it in huge and lavish ways so that everyone could see and envy your success. This would motivate them to work hard and ruthlessly too, thereby making more businesses strong.

Cutthroat capitalism held only to the values of greed, envy, and conspicuous consumption. Occasionally, you will hear someone point out the vast philanthropic works some of these barons of industry sponsored. However, this was simply a variation on the conspicuous consumption theme. "See how rich and wonderful I am! I gift your city with this museum!"

It would be as if the runners in the Olympics did everything they could to kill or maim the other runners in the locker room before they got to the track. At the call to start the race, one player wanders onto the field with a big grin. He nonchalantly strolls his way around the track, and then collects the big cash prize at the end. When he gets the prize, he waves it in the air, puts his thumb to his nose, and sounds a loud raspberry at the audience for being dumb enough to have paid money to watch the race. On the way out, the runner may deign to shower the nearby audience with a couple handfuls of coins, Roman fashion, to keep the peasants happy. The Parker Brothers game of Monopoly harkens back to the great railroad monopolies of the nineteenth century. One person wins; everyone else goes bankrupt.

COMMUNISM: A German philosopher by the name of Karl Marx began to view all of human history as an evolution of economic systems. Watching the abuses of cutthroat capitalism, he decided that the next logical evolutionary step was for the workers to rise, kill all the capitalists, take control of the factories themselves, and abolish private property. In his view, only the human species, which he called "the state," mattered. Furthermore, Marx believed the state should not hesitate to eliminate individuals who opposed this evolutionary process.

Now, Marx wrote *Das Capital* in 1838 and it languished as simply the ravings of a crank. However, when twenty years later Darwin published *On the Origin of Species*, others picked up Marx's theory and ran with it in the name of mystical Darwinism.

So, in the name of evolutionary progress, Communism slaughtered tens of millions of innocent people and enslaved hundreds of millions more to repressive states. Hence, the famous jibe, "I'm a communist. I love humanity, but hate people."

RACISM: Human beings have always tended to devalue anyone who was not part of their particular tribe. This is why the Bible strictly commands, "Thou shalt not oppress the stranger" (Exodus 23:9). However, in spite of its biblical heritage, slavery based on race developed in the American South for a combination of reasons.

First, with the growth of colonialism, Europeans developed an ethnocentric contempt for what they saw as the brutal backwardness of African cultures. Second, in the American South, a white slave who wandered off the plantation could easily blend into the countryside, never to be seen again. However, a black slave was easily spotted and returned. Third, the Southern educational system began to follow the Continental system, which emphasized the Greek and Roman classics much more than the Bible. While the Bible allowed slavery, it was strictly regulated and limited to only six years, which was the basis for the indentured servant model allowed in the North. However, the Greek and Roman classics viewed slaves as simply living machines to be exploited, tortured, raped, and even killed at will.

Finally, the Southern upper class was heavily influenced by the English East Indian Tea Company, which, in its later years, came under the heavy influence of Hinduism (all those Hindu nannies). Now, while the Hindu caste system was actually far more complicated than simple racism, to an outsider's first glance it seemed to say that the darker your skin, the lower down the reincarnation scale you stood. The South, in practice, eventually developed their own version of the Hindu caste system.

Prior to the American Civil war, the primary forces opposing slavery came from various Christian denominations. These included what we today would call Baptist, Presbyterian, and Methodist groups, joined by other groups we would not consider evangelical today, but who nonetheless stood loyal to the Bible.

In contrast, the Southern churches were almost exclusively Episcopalian and Roman Catholic, groups whose primary focus was on the church instead of the Bible. The antislavery denominations formed only a very small and despised minority in the South. In fact, the Southern Baptist (pro-slavery) denomination was founded as an attempt to get out from under the ongoing overt persecution Reformation Christians faced in the South for their strident opposition to slavery. (Some may be surprised to hear this, since they are so used to thinking of the South as the "Bible Belt." However, the South gained that reputation only after the Billy Sunday–style revivals that swept through the South early in the twentieth century. Prior to then, America's "Bible-Belt" was New England.)

After the bloodbath of the Civil War, you would think the issue had been settled. However, Charles Darwin published his *On the Origin of Species* in 1859, one year before the Civil War began. During the war, it quickly rose on the best seller list. So, as the Civil War proceeded, Darwin was misused to give that Southern caste system scientific respectability, since it fit so easily into the logic of their modified Hindu caste system.

If humanity had evolved as a species over millions of years, then the racial groupings from the earth's different continents represented competing variations on humanity. Some must be superior and some must be inferior, and it did not take these mystical Darwinists long to figure out which were which. We've all seen the evolutionary chart where an amphibian crawls out of the water on the left, while increasingly advanced animals progress their way though apes and ape-men into a modern European. Until recently, these evolutionary charts showed an African as the link to the missing link at the right, (something Darwin himself firmly and clearly opposed, despite allegations to the contrary.)

This poster once hung in the science lab of virtually every public high school and was very well known. However, today it is almost impossible to find. It has been scrubbed from most Web sites, and blocked as offensive material by most Web browsers. Given the on-going creation vs. evolution conflict, the "establishment" would like to pretend it had never existed.

NAZISM: Adolph Hitler took advantage of Germany's simmering hatreds over the oppression they had suffered following their defeat in WWI. He used mystical Darwinism to get great masses of people to view war as an evolutionary struggle. He created a state based on the ethic of strength over weakness.

Visitors to Germany before WWII often gushed over the universal employment of the German people and their wonderful health-care system. What they did not know was that the Nazis tossed the chronically unemployed, the seriously ill, and the mentally "defective" into the gas chamber. The German state did not have to worry about welfare for the poor, medical care for the chronically ill, or Social Security for the aged; it simply euthanized the weak.[29]

If the Nazis treated their own people so harshly, then no wonder they slaughtered millions of innocent civilians in an attempt to exterminate "inferior races." To their mystical Darwinist mentality, the mere fact that they *could* kill so many was in itself proof positive that those races were obviously weaker and deserved to die for the good of humanity.

BIBLICAL HIGHER CRITICISM: The leading Old Testament Bible professor in a German university, Julius Wellhausen, had made his distaste for much of the Old Testament plain years before Darwin's book came out. And, he had already published a book that purported

---

29. Schaeffer 1982, Vol. V: p. 340–342.

that none of the Law of Moses had been written until at least five hundred years after the reputed time of Moses. However, generally, this produced little excitement. But once Darwin's *On the Origin of Species* came out, Wellhausen pushed a fresh attack, this time couching his arguments in terms of mystical Darwinism. Bible passages that he deemed to have more "advanced" concepts obviously had to have been written later than passages with less "advanced" concepts.

The books of Moses were seen as a hodgepodge of material from four primary sources written centuries apart. Passages using the name *Elohim* came from one source; passages using the name *Jehovah* came from a second source. Passages referring to issues of interest to pre-Babylonian captivity Israel were called the *Deuteronomist*, while the most advanced religious concepts were evolved by Jewish priests during and after the Babylonian captivity. He divided the Bible into these four main sources, *Jehovist, Elohist, Deuteronomist, and Priestly*—abbreviated JED-P.

None of this was based on any actual archaeological evidence or comparison with other actual written documents from the purported time periods. It was all theory.

For example, one of Wellhausen's main opening arguments insists the account of a wilderness tabernacle and bronze altar was an obvious fiction from five hundred years later to support the claim of Solomon's temple to being the only legitimate location for national sacrifices.

Wellhausen confidently and logically proves that such a tabernacle and altar design was a complete anachronism and could not possibly have existed at such an early date, and furthermore, he doubted that such a structure as the Bible describes could actually be built. Unfortunately for his logic, archaeology later dug one up— in Egypt of all places.

An actual canopy frame belonging to Queen Hetepheres, the mother of Khufu, builder of the great pyramid at Giza, was discovered near the great pyramid.

This bedroom canopy, which is presently displayed in the Cairo museum, was covered with linen. The poles are elegantly decorated with gold foil and were set into sockets on a base and ceiling beams, thus constituting a frame. This discovery, along with the illustrations of purification tents from Meir and Giza, demonstrate the technical knowledge to construct booths or tent-like structures, like the Hebrew tabernacle, was known in Egypt over a thousand years before the exodus and the wilderness period.[30]

So, not only was such a structure possible, it was a typically royal Egyptian-style tent, something that would have been completely unknown at the time of Solomon's temple.

Despite the complete absence of any objective evidence to support Wellhausen's ivory tower, debate over this application of Mystical Darwinism to the Bible started a battle in the public arena that intellectually dominated an entire decade. In the public eye, this even eclipsed the debate on Darwin's scientific theory itself, which had absolutely nothing to do with literature.

Actually, it made perfect sense. The churches' enemies were bright enough to know that they had to discredit the Bible if they were going to move forward. Wellhausen's theory did this, so academia embraced it with enthusiasm, knowing full well that it was based on absolutely nothing. This "Biblical Darwinism" carried the day, and the intellectual elite, in effect, discarded the Bible. And, in doing so, they discarded the entire moral system built on the foundation of the Bible, which alone could have withstood the various Darwinian disasters that followed.

I'm sure I've scandalized some by classing what they see as these innocuous Bible scholars with the social Darwinists, the cutthroat capitalists, the communists, the racists, and the Nazis, but they well

30. Hoffmeier, 2005, p. 206.

deserve the honor. If the academic elite had dealt with the Bible with any degree of objective integrity, the abuses of the middle industrial revolution would have been greatly reduced, racism would have been radically curtailed, the communist slave labor death camps would have never been established, and Hitler's ovens would never have belched tons of human ash into the sky—if.

So, in a literal sense, the bloodiest and worst of all the Darwinian disasters was not Nazism or Communism. It was not an accident that both Lenin and Hitler had launched from post-Wellhausen Germany. The German university system's disastrous embracing of Wellhausen's higher criticism and rejection of the Bible had made all the other disasters possible.

"SCHOLARLY": People who advocated the Wellhausen form of biblical higher criticism put great store in the word *scholarly*. Often, the producers of the Science Channel, when wanting to present a debunking perspective when someone's archaeological find seemed to have confirmed a biblical passage, would interview someone who taught the Wellhausen form of higher criticism. Invariably, against a backdrop of well-stocked mahogany bookshelves, a bespectacled academic with a slight smile would explain his "scholarly" position, implying that obviously the opposition was just too uneducated to understand the facts of the matter.

However, you have to understand that the word *scholarly* had nothing to do with actual science, or studies of actual historical artifacts or written documents. The word *scholarly* just means they had carefully studied each other's books. As they toured and made additions to each other's ivory towers, those ivory towers became increasing elaborate and tall.

Imagine a first-grade classroom where both the teacher and the students came to the firm conclusion that two plus two could not possibly equal four. This of course would set off a quest to find out what two plus two actually did equal. Assuming that that class stayed together down through the years, by the time they reached the doc-torate level, the members of that class would find themselves forced to increasingly study and elaborate on each other's works and no others. Books by that unscholarly mob of four-damentalists would be too simplistic to even consider, since even as first-graders they had proved conclusively that two plus two plainly did not equal four. And there you have their version of "scholarly."

Biblical higher criticism made a good showing, and its adherents did succeed in dominating secular academic discussion of the Bible for a little over a century. However, as physical evidence mounted contravening Wellhausen's four divisions, these "scholars" began franticly re-dividing and embellishing the old system in an attempt to keep in standing, until it seemed that every verse had to have had a different author. But, by the 1990s, the winds of actual archaeolog-ical data and scientific evidence became too strong, and the whole ivory tower began to collapse.

Now, that tower lies in ruins. However, since many adults and teachers went to school before the 1990s, the word hasn't quite got-ten out yet. And, certainly, many will continue to cling to it as their own kind of religious tradition. So, for the next couple of decades, you inevitably will find yourself stumbling over someone spouting biblical higher critical nonsense. Try to be gentle with them.

6

Approaches to the Creation Story

Given the beating the church has taken at the hands of mystical Darwinism (not to be confused with actual Darwinism), the issue of just how we see the creation story makes a huge difference.

YOUNG-EARTH CREATIONISM

Some approaches to the creation story still attempt to keep Ussher's tradition and can be broadly grouped under the heading "Young-earth Creationism." Most of these you probably have already heard of. Very, *very* briefly, the three main ones follow:

SCIENTIFIC CREATIONISM: This approach is similar to that of the Association for Biblical Astronomy. They absolutely refuse to concede the facts of modern geology and publish detailed and very intricate books to prove that the earth is actually only about six thousand years old. (They have taken such a beating on this that many of their faction have moved their line back to 60-40,000 BC and continue to fight a rear-line action.)

To their credit, they argued in favor of catastrophism when it was out of fashion. Catastrophism is the theory that many of the earth's landforms and much of the geological record could only be explained by some kind of huge disaster. They used the neglected evidence in favor of catastrophes as an underpinning for their arguments in favor of a universal flood.

Unfortunately, when catastrophism came back into fashion, it came back on such a scale that it took the wind out of the scientific creationists' sails. When they then pointed to the Grand Canyon and huge deposits of coal beds and mountainous piles of dinosaur bones, they only provoked yawns. Such things are now fully integrated into mainstream science—dated, and mapped—and still provide no evidence for a universal flood.

Sadly, if you listen to their current lectures, they now depend more on sophist word games than actual logical argument. I don't voluntarily attend their lectures anymore since I don't enjoy cringing with embarrassment.

While I have met some Christians who have been encouraged by their work, I have yet to meet anyone who has accepted Christ because of it. I do know that if I had come across them before I became a Christian I probably would have taken their word for it that the Bible was utter nonsense and not bothered to read it carefully.

SATANIC CONSPIRACY BUFFS: They concede that the evidence clearly shows the earth is very old, but insist that demons (or sometimes God in a bad mood) run around magically faking that evidence. It's all a satanic plot. I have yet to meet anyone who held this viewpoint who had the slightest interest in logical discussion.

THE GAP THEORY: They concede all the vast ages of cosmology and the evolution of life on earth and posit that just before the garden story God had judged and completely wiped out all life on earth. They view the creation story as a re-creation event taking place between verses one and two of Genesis one.

Of all the young-earth creationist approaches, I think this one deserves the most respect, since it at least consciously *tries* to deal logically and honestly with both science and the Bible. The main drawback is that they throw away all the scientific supports for the creation story that we went through in the first three chapters.

OLD-EARTH CREATIONISM

Three main approaches to the creation story make no effort to maintain Ussher's tradition:

THEISTIC EVOLUTION: Usually, this approach views the creation story primarily as a work of inspirational literature and not as science at all. Those who hold to it tend to be members of old-line denominations who generally have a lower view of the Bible than most evangelical Christians.

Historically, we evangelicals have viewed ourselves much like the Moslem world describes us—we are the "People of the Book." For all our talk about getting "saved," or "accepting Christ," or being "born again," ultimately our understanding of salvation is shaped by our understanding of the Book. You take away the Book, and we have no Christ or salvation left. From our perspective, anyone who rejects the Book rejects Christ.

However, over the last few decades we have softened our stance somewhat, conceding that salvation rests in the hands of Christ himself, and not in our understanding. So, when someone from these old-line denominations acts and talks like a Christ follower, most of us swallow hard, suspend our disbelief, and let it ride.

Generally, theistic evolutionists tend to participate in the modern mind-set that divides basic humanity away from reason. They say lots of warm, fuzzy things, but rarely appeal to reason on any issue of values or humanness. In appealing to "religious truth," they ultimately have nothing objective left to say.

THE DAY-AGE THEORY: This is historically the most popular of the old-earth approaches. It looks at the word *day* in the creation story and takes it as a metaphor for a long age. It points out several verses where the Bible applies the singular word day to a much longer time. Also, they tend to lean heavily on 2 Peter 3:8: "But, beloved, be not ignorant of this one thing, that one day is with the Lord as a thousand years, and a thousand years as one day."

This approach has the advantage in that it is able to embrace all the comparisons between the creation story and the observations of cosmology, geology, and paleontology like those we pointed out in the first three chapters of this book. (Not that they should be blamed for any mistakes I've undoubtedly made.)

Currently, the strongest supporter for this position is the Reasons to Believe organization based in California and under the leadership of Dr. Hugh Ross, the author of *The Fingerprint of God* that I recommended in chapter one.

THE DAY/AGE APPROACHES AND INTELLIGENT DESIGN: Today, a theory called intelligent design has taken center stage in the ongoing battle about the teaching of evolution in the public schools, using two basic arguments.

First, with the mapping of the various genomes over the last forty years, we see a vast and intricate design on a molecular level. This essentially binary code in each of our bodies' cells makes our modern supercomputers look retarded. These codes in turn guide molecular machines in each living cell that make modern attempts at nanotechnology look pathetic. Intelligent design argues that it is ridiculous to imagine that these microcomputers and nanomachines just happened by accident.

Their opponents argue that, despite the complexity, they believe they have mapped out natural processes that could, given enough time, lead to just such a code.

Second, the intelligent design camp points out that the discovery of punctuated equilibrium in the fossil record has greatly reduced the time available for all that random mutation to happen. The fossil record doesn't show slow gradual change as Darwin expected; instead, it shows periods of extinction followed by rapid, revolutionary change.

Initially, their opponents took refuge from punctuated equilibrium in the niche-filling argument we mentioned in the last chapter. However, even they knew this was essentially a non-argument, since it does not actually address the issue of *how* organisms change to fit those vacant spaces in a stressed ecological system.

However, all the opponents complain that the intelligent design camp:

1. Grossly exaggerates the troubles of traditional Darwinism.
2. Unfairly portrays the position of their opponents.
3. Has an obvious religious agenda, which they dishonestly cover up.

While, ultimately, none of those three complaints is in itself germane to the issue, as Christians we should take those complaints seriously:

1. We should scrupulously avoid exaggeration. Admittedly, in the heat of argument this is difficult, but important nonetheless.
2. Under no circumstance should we distort our opponents' position. If we avoid arguing against their real position, then we tacitly concede that we ourselves have no real argument.
3. Of course we have a religious agenda. We should be open, even blatant, about it, and defiantly turn the other cheek to those who slap out at it. Too bad if the ACLU or the current judicial tyranny doesn't like it.

Personally, I like the idea of intelligent design. To say that God on occasion intervenes in a natural process in no way contravenes the rule of natural law—any more than my reaching out to catch Newton's falling apple would contravene the law of gravity.

Also, intelligent design gratuitously aggravates mystical Darwinists. Something less than redeemed in my soul just enjoys watching them squawk.

However, this raises the question of whether the Bible actually says God played genetic engineer. Remember, the creation story only says that God directly created two living things, the large dinosaurs and modern man. So, when it comes to those two items, I favor intelligent design, at least. On everything else, I just have fun watching the debate.

It will be interesting to see where that debate leads. However, barring someone coming across a written copyright stamp in the genetic code, I have no idea how the debate could be settled to everyone's satisfaction. I *am* confident that the "book of God's works" will have some surprises for us.

A final note: modern science and modern scientists are not our enemies—unless we make them so. If we don't get ahead of what the Bible actually says, and if we treat the modern scientist as a valuable source of truth, we should get along just fine.

THE REVELATION DAYS APPROACH

By now you have probably noticed that this book favors an approach to the creation story called the "Six-day Revelation of Creation" theory, or "Revelation Days" theory.

This approach is a variation of the classic day/age approach. Basically, it views the six creative days of Genesis one not as six days of creation, but rather as six successive days of revelation to Moses and the children of Israel about God's creation.

We already touched on this in chapter one, when we looked at Wiseman's view of the "day" formula at the end of each section of the creation story as a cuneiform scribal convention carried over into early written Hebrew.

Historically, given the Reformation's emphasis on the content of what the Bible means when it says something, the Hebrew literary devices used to actually pen the words themselves seemed relatively unimportant. However, in reaction against the JED-P crowd, evangelical scholars a few decades ago began to put much more effort themselves into studying the detailed literary structure of the Old Testament. This in turn required them to actually examine the literary structure of the "evening and the morning were the # day" phrase and conclude that it may have served a different function than the feel the KJV gave it.

This in turn has led many more Bible scholars to actually take the time to read up on the claims that had long been made by the proponents of the Revelation Days theory. Since then, support for this view among evangelicals has increased exponentially.

In passing, note that this approach takes the language of the creation story much more literally that the traditional day/age approach does, and relies much less on the use of poetic metaphor. In fact, the Revelation Days approach takes the Hebrew text of the creation story much more literally than even the traditional young-earth approaches do.

SIX MORE BIBLICAL SUPPORTS: In addition to viewing the "it was evening and it was morning, day #" phrases as colophon structures, the Revelation Days theory points to at least six other things in the Bible to support its view.

First, it focuses on the Hebrew word *mla'ktow*, translated as *work* in Genesis 2:2–3: "And on the seventh day God ended his *work* which he had made." Now, the Old Testament has several words translated as work. However, *mla'ktow* is an inflection of the word *mla'ak*, which the KJV Old Testament most often translated as angel.

We could translate *mla'ktow* as a deputation, a delegated task, or even an angelic revelation. We see it used in that sense in Haggai 1:13: "Then spake Haggai the Lord's messenger (*mla'ak*) in the Lord's message (*mla'ktow*) unto the people."

So, we could more literally translate Genesis 2:2b as, "And on the seventh day God finished His angelic message which He had showed."

Second, the creation story is tied to the Sabbath. A day-by-day correlation between a seven-day week and the creation story seems so obvious that Moses cited it as the main reason for keeping the Sabbath.

> But the seventh day is the Sabbath of the Lord thy
> God . . . For in six days the Lord made heaven and earth,
> the sea, and all that in them is, and rested the seventh
> day: wherefore the Lord blessed the Sabbath day, and
> hallowed it. (Exodus 20:10–11)

However, nothing in the Bible suggests that the children of Israel knew anything about a seven-day Sabbath rest before the Exodus. As slaves in Egypt, any conflict over a divinely mandated rest every seven days would almost certainly have made its way into the biblical account. Furthermore, only a few weeks after the crossing of the Red Sea, in the wilderness of Sin, in Exodus 16:22–30 we find Moses scolding the children of Israel for attempting to gather manna on the Sabbath.

Later, in Numbers 15:32–36, a man is caught breaking the seventh-day prohibition on work. Note verse 34: "And they put him in ward, because it was not declared what should be done to him." Clearly, this Sabbath thing was a new idea at the time.

By tying the creation story to the Sabbath, the Bible implies that the Hebrews were just as ignorant of the creation story before the

Exodus as they were of the Sabbath. Yet, within a few days after the Exodus, this entire hoard of harried and hurrying refugees had been clearly introduced to both concepts, even if they hadn't grown accustomed to them yet. In that era before the advent of mass media, we have to wonder how that possibly could have happened.

Third, Exodus 12 establishes a special seven-day ceremony, the first Feast of Unleavened Bread, which took place at the very beginning of the Exodus, just before Moses first instructed Israel about the Sabbath:

> This month shall be unto you the . . . first month of the year. . . . In the tenth day of this month . . . take to them every man a lamb. . . . And ye shall keep it up until the fourteenth day [the eve of the full moon] and the whole assembly of the congregation of Israel shall kill it in the evening. And they shall take of the blood, and strike it on the two side posts and on the upper door post of the houses. . . . and they shall eat the flesh in that night . . . with your loins girded, your shoes on your feet, and your staff in your hand: and ye shall eat it in haste: it is the Lord's Passover.
>
> And in the first day there shall be an holy convocation, and in the seventh day there shall be an holy convocation to you, no manner of work shall be done in them save that which every man must eat, that only may be done of you. In the first month, on the fourteenth day of the month at even [sunset—just as the new day begins], ye shall eat unleavened bread, until the one and twentieth day of the month at even. (Exodus 12:2–18)

Here we see that the Passover is established in effect as a New Year's celebration. The old year (old life) ends with the slaughter of the Passover lamb at the rising of the full moon in the last hour of the old year. The lamb is cooked as nightfall fully descends, and the feast itself is eaten in the first hour of the New Year. The fifteenth day of the moon (month) becomes day one of the seven-day Feast of Unleavened Bread.

While Passover full moons don't always fall on a regular Sabbath, in this first Passover, both the day the lamb is slaughtered (the last day of the old year) and the final day of the feast are by definition regular Sabbaths, since they began the seven-day cycle that we recognize to this day. Thus, we see that the actual Exodus begins with a formal day one, day two, and so on to day seven.

Fourth, if the revelation of the creation story was indeed given during the first week of Israel's trek out of Egypt, then the only two times available for such a revelation would be just after sunset after a long day's march and just after waking in the morning, before starting the next march. Or, (if they marched both day and night as many feel) during the evening and morning rests. Even though Israel didn't travel far that first day, they may have been busy all day long with the great fun of plundering their terrified Egyptian neighbors of all their easily carried valuables.

This perspective takes the phrase *and the evening and the morning were the # day* as much more than some kind of poetic device to emphasize the twenty-four-hour nature of the days of creation. Instead, it approaches the phrase more literally, as a statement of exactly when during the day the revelation was given—morning and evening—as opposed to night or daylight.

Furthermore, note that the evening-and-the-morning formula is conspicuously absent on the seventh day. This would make sense, since the congregation would have had no special limitation to either evening or morning, since they neither broke nor set up camp on the seventh day of that first Feast of Unleavened Bread.

Fifth, the appearance of the pillar of cloud by day and fire by night makes its first recorded appearance on the day the Hebrews leave Egypt, day one of the Feast of Unleavened Bread (Exodus 13:20-21).

The word translated as pillar here, Strong's |5982| *am-mood'* "a stand, i.e.platform" implies that the cloud functioned as a kind of speaking platform.

During the last few decades, some have tended to view the pillar of a cloud as simply a standard Egyptian-style banner/smoke pot. This is basically a smoke pot on poles that releases smoke during the day, and shows glowing flames at night to keep an army marching in the right direction. More recently, with the evidence indicating that the Sinai may have experienced volcanic eruptions during this period of history, some have identified the cloud as a volcanic plume, black during the day, and shot with hot ash and lightning bolts during the night.

However, the Bible describes that pillar of a cloud almost as if it were a living entity in its own right. It occasionally even descends to speak and settle disputes as in the dispute between Moses and Miriam, his sister: "And the Lord came down in the pillar of the cloud, and stood in the door of the Tabernacle, and called Aaron and Miriam. . . . And He said, 'Hear now my words!" (Numbers 12:5).

Then again, immediately after that first Feast of Unleavened Bread, and just before the crossing of the Red Sea, Exodus 14:19 ties the cloud to an angel: "And the angel of God, who went before the camp of Israel, removed and went behind them; and the pillar of the cloud went from before their face, and stood behind them."

Then in Exodus 16:10–11 we read,

> And it came to pass, as Aaron spoke unto the whole congregation of the children of Israel, that they looked toward the wilderness and, behold, the glory of the Lord appeared in the cloud, and the Lord spoke unto Moses, saying . . ."

This brings us to the heart of the Revelation Days tradition. It proposes that the six days recorded in Genesis are in fact a record of what God visually and audibly revealed to Moses and probably all the hosts of Israel from the "fiery speaking platform" during the "evenings and the mornings" on the six weekdays of the first Feast of Unleavened Bread as the Hebrews journeyed to the banks of the Red Sea.

Sixth, note the singular form of the word *day* in Genesis 2:4: "These are the generations of the heavens and of the earth when they were created, in the *day* [singular] that the Lord God made the earth and the heavens" (emphasis added).

Traditionally, scholars suppose that God simply uses the word *day* loosely here. However, look at the grammatical structure of the verse. Taken literally, it seems to say that the collected stories of Adam and Eve, the fall of man, Cain and Abel, and the several stories after that (the "generations of the heaven and the earth") all happened during the creation story's first day, before the creation of man on the sixth day. This seemingly absurd meaning is further emphasized by the phrase *when they were created* found in the middle of the verse. Naturally, since this literal, grammatical interpretation seemed to make no sense, traditional Bible scholars tended to pass it by and looked for a less literal sense for the verse.

However, if we view the days of creation as seven consecutive days of revelation to Moses, then Genesis 2:4 simply states that God revealed all these stories on the same day as the evening and morning revelations of day one. This would make sense, since Moses, Aaron, and Miriam may not have gone anywhere that day. Instead, at least one of them would have stayed with the angelic cloud while everyone else scurried around their neighborhoods like scary, happy children on Halloween, plundering Egypt and then gathering at Succoth. In contrast to how poorly other interpretations fit the verse, this more literal approach fits quite well.

Two Common Objections: First, look at Exodus 20:11. "For in six days the Lord made heaven and earth, the sea, and all that in them is, and rested the seventh day." This seems to declare fairly clearly that God actually made, not just revealed, his creation in those six days.

However, let's look at the following verses (emphasis added):

"Fear ye not, stand still, and see the salvation of the Lord, which he will *shew* to you today." (Exodus 14:13)

"*Shew* me a sign that thou talkest with me." (Judges 6:17)

Shew me a token for good. (Psalm 86:17)

Wilt thou *shew* wonders to the dead? (Psalm 88:10)

The word translated here as "shew, is the same word translated as "made" in Exodus 20:11 and, for that matter, in all of Genesis one. The Hebrew word *'asah* means to make or produce in the broadest sense, and closely resembles the word for to shine. If we substitute shew for the word made in Exodus 20:11, then we get "For in six days the Lord shewed [shined] heaven and earth." This would actively support the idea that God showed the creation story to all of Israel from the pillar of cloud and fire during the first Feast of Unleavened Bread.

Second, let's look at a passage that some say contradicts any form of old-earth creationism: "For since by man came death, by man came also the resurrection of the dead. For as in Adam all die, even so in Christ shall all be made alive" (1 Corinthians 15:21–22).

Traditionally, many teach that since death is an evil thing, death did not exist before the fall of man. They see 1 Cor. 15:21 as a clear statement that it was the fall of man that brought death into the world. Therefore, they cannot accept ages of animals living and dying long before the creation of man. They believe that God originally created the lion and the T. Rex as long-fanged vegetarians.

But, look at the whole passage. If we take verse 22 to say, "For as in Adam all animals die," then we have to take the rest of the verse to say, "even so in Christ shall all animals be made alive." Despite the popular fable about "doggie heaven," few adults seriously propose that every rat and cat will stand with us in line at the last judgment. Obviously, the topic in this passage is current human death, and not death as a simple biological process.

Furthermore, while current human death is a consequence of sin, biological death in general is not a sinful thing. Otherwise, God sinned in inflicting it, and Christ sinned in accepting it. In reality, the biological cycle of animal birth and death is a good thing. Otherwise, the world by now would be ten miles deep in just kittens alone.

Next, note that in Hebrew the word for garden literally means a fenced, defended area. What's the point of a fence if there is nothing outside the fence to defend against? Furthermore, the Garden of Eden contained something called "the Tree of Life." The very presence of a Tree of Life implied that, in contrast, death functioned on the rest of the planet. Think about it. If God had made everything inherently immortal, then what purpose did that tree serve?

Finally, note that God warned Adam that he would "surely die" if he ate of the Tree of the Knowledge of Good and Evil. If death did not exist before this time, then this statement may have been meaningless to Adam.

For example, the popular Christian philosopher, C. S. Lewis, unsuccessfully wrestles with this dilemma in his fantasy novel *Perelandra*, which replays the temptation of Eve on Venus. Lewis has the book's satanic figure attempt to convince Venus's Eve that her death would be a wonderful and noble thing. Meanwhile, Ransom, the protagonist, experiences great frustration trying to figure out a way to convince Eve that she really does not want to die. Eventually, Ransom gives up the effort at verbal persuasion as impossible, and wins the argument by physically assaulting the Satan figure.

So, while many teach that no biological death preceded the fall of man, we see that the idea has no real support in the Bible itself. It is just a tradition.

IMPLICATIONS: Embracing the Revelations Days approach to the creation story has a theological implication that many don't pick up on at first, and that others, when they do pick up on it, find objectionable.

Remember that we translated the KJV phrase *God made* as *God showed*. The creation story itself uses the word *create* on only three occasions:

1. The heavens and the earth (Genesis 1:1)
2. The long monsters (Genesis 1:21)
3. The image of God in man with the triple-use superlative (Genesis 1:27)

On one hand, we see that the story begins and ends with an emphatic emphasis on creation, which is obviously why we call it the creation story. In this, we agree with the traditionalists.

On the other hand, this means that the bulk of the story becomes about "showing" and not "creating." To the traditionalist it seems like we have gutted the story, removed the whole point.

We have to acknowledge that by tampering with the traditional point of the story we leave ourselves obligated to fill the void, to offer an alternative that is just as meaningful and just as satisfying. If we fail at that, then we have simply failed.

It is not enough to say, "But look! Isn't it neat that we no longer have to fight with modern science? That we no longer have to look like crackpots?" God could have done that quite easily by simply not giving it in the first place. God began his public conversation with humanity with this sweeping and compact story. Therefore, we have to acknowledge that every detail "showed" must have huge, possibly even vital importance in its own right

123

The next section's three chapters will all touch on the significance of the creation story as an outline of Genesis and perhaps the entire Bible—and some of its possible implications for world civilization and our time.

Section Three:

The Creation Story Expanded

The Garden of Eden & The Lower Neolithic Revolution

Bible Passage: Genesis 2:4-8

Like the first three chapters, this chapter also references the STV at its end.

(Gen 2:4 STV) The following are the family histories from *when the whirling flows and the solid earth* were *created,* given *on the day Yahweh-Almighty God showed the earth and the whirling flows . . .* Compare this translation with the KJV, "These are the generations of the heavens and of the earth when they were created, in the day that the Lord God made the earth and the heavens. . ."

Do you see the difference? The KJV's awkward wording stems from the fact that the translators assumed that the story of Adam and Eve was a retelling in more detail of Genesis 1:26, and so they ended up with a grammatical monstrosity trying to get it to say that. However, those with the seven-days-of-revelation POV have no such problem. The straightforward translation makes more sense. God gave the garden story on the same day he gave the day one story. This would tie the two stories closely together, and emphasize a symbolic layer of day one.

Notice also that this is the first usage of *Yahweh* in the Bible. Some scholars believe that this story may have been physically penned by a scribe other than the one who penned the creation story. They point to its much more fluid and elaborate style, especially compared to the rigid style of Genesis one. However, later we will make the case that Genesis One functions as a table of contents for the entire book of the Law, so of course it would have a "rigid" style, like any other table of contents.

Never-the less, even though Genesis is called one of the "books of Moses," many evangelical scholars have speculated that many sections of the Law may have been penned by Aaron, Miriam, or some unidentified prophet. In fact, the song in the chapter after the crossing of the Red Sea is specifically attributed to Miriam. Also, since Exodus specifically describes Aaron as the more eloquent brother, many have believed that he may have penned the garden story. Furthermore, if this story was given on the first day of the Exodus, then Moses may have been busy acting as general and organizer, leaving the recording of the garden story during the day to his brother or sister.

THE GARDEN STORY IN RELATION TO THE CREATION STORY: So, given our focus in this series, let's consider what modern science we can see here. Since this story deals with the dawn of modern man, let's summarize what paleontology has to say about the matter.

PALEONTOLOGY: MODERN MAN'S THREE BIG EARLY EVENTS

In the early history of modern man, paleontologists claim to see three big events that we are going to associate with three distinct

Bible narratives: the Upper Paleolithic, the Lower Neolithic Revolution, and the Upper Neolithic Revolution.

EVENT #1: THE UPPER PALEOLITHIC, 60–40,000 BC: We have already looked at the Upper Paleolithic in chapter three, when we looked at the sixth day. In short, the Upper Paleolithic refers to the sudden appearance of modern man, tools, art, and cumulative culture at about 40,000 BC. Hunter-gatherer bands of modern humans settle all the major continents with the exception of Antarctica. (Some evidence indicates that this may actually have begun much earlier in a region of Africa before spreading to the rest of the earth. But, while the debate still rages on this, it makes no difference to our study.)

EVENT #2: THE LOWER NEOLITHIC REVOLUTION, 10,900 BC: This primarily refers to the gradual dawn of agriculture in the Middle East, soon after the onset of the Younger Dryas glacial, (a reoccurring period of advancing glaciers during an ice age). Now, normally a glacial comes on slowly and ends suddenly for reasons still under debate. However, the Younger Dryas came on suddenly, possibly as a result of something called the Clovis Catastrophe.

Clovis refers to the human culture that occupied North America from the Upper Paleolithic through the end of the last major ice age, and the brief warming period that followed it. Then, according to some, literally out of the blue a comet struck North America; a fireball swept much of the north, and an ash cloud blanketed the planet, plunging the earth suddenly into a minor glacial period. However, the evidence for a comet impact is also still under debate.

Regardless, the onslaught of the Younger Dryas particularly impacted North America, wiping out virtually all species of large mammals, and most if not all of the Clovis culture. Although Eurasia on the other side of the earth escapes the blunt impact of the Clovis event, the sudden onslaught of the ice causes a dieback of most herd animals and the predators that depend on them, including man.

But, providentially, something positive happens. Instead of just hunting the wild herds, man begins tending the wild herds, driving away competing predators, protecting the herd's young, scouting for the best grazing lands and driving their herds in that direction, making up for the herds' disrupted migratory patterns, and even occasionally thinning the herds so more can survive times of famine.

Think of the Laplanders (Sami People) and their relationship with the essentially wild herds of reindeer in northern Europe. These herdsmen remain hunter-gatherers, but instead of pursuing the herds, they have in effect joined the herds. They switched from being simple hunters to becoming herders.

Almost universally, these Lower Neolithic herds remained essentially wild herds; the shift to actual domesticated breeds will take another few thousand years (with the exception of Mouflon mountain sheep that make the transition to domestication quite easily).

And, over the course of the next few thousand years, stage-one agriculture spreads across the Middle East. This is agriculture using wild plants. For the first time, we see intentional sowing of wild grains and fruit trees. Now, wild grains do not usually yield enough to support life on their own, and fruit trees yield only a seasonal bounty. But now they form an increasingly important supplement to the diet of the hunter-gatherers as they follow their herds on annual migrations. We are going to associate this with the Bible's garden story.

However, the Lower Neolithic is limited only to the Middle East from soon after the beginning of the Younger Dryas glacial period.

THE GARDEN STORY

(Gen 2:5-6 STV) And, all domesticated plants were not yet on the earth, and all domesticated greens had not yet grown, because Yahweh-Almighty God had not rained on the earth and man was not plowing mannish-soil. And a fog went up from the earth and watered all the sphere of the mannish-soil . . . This in essence says, "Once

upon a time, there was no such thing as domesticated plants, since the climate was wrong and mankind didn't farm." So, while we tend to view the garden story as being about the fall of man and Original Sin, or maybe even Freudian sex, the story itself says, "Nope, it's about agriculture." The Bible tends to be uncooperative and stubborn like that quite a lot.

Notice the statement about the lack of rain, one of the hallmarks of any glacial period. The extremely cold glaciers suck all the moisture out of the atmosphere as snow. Furthermore, the cooler climate means that the cooler equatorial oceans don't produce anywhere near as many clouds. For many parts of the earth, the main, if not the only, fresh water supply comes from summer melt off of the glaciers.

The only other source of moisture would come from nightly fogs off lakes and marshes fed by that runoff, which is exactly how the Bible describes the setting for the Garden of Eden. Since both the Paleolithic Revolution and the Lower Neolithic Revolution happen during glacial periods, either period fits this verse. (This is one of many details that make even the most dogmatic skeptics wonder, at least, how in heaven Moses could know that!)

Another part of the garden story ties it to a glacial period. The story mentions four rivers that flow into the garden: "The name of the first is the Pishon: it winds through the entire land of Havilah, where there is gold . . . the Gihon: it winds through the entire land of Cush . . . the Tigris . . . and the fourth river is the Euphrates. (Genesis 2:11–14)

The last two, the Tigris and the Euphrates, are quite familiar to most of us. The second, while not familiar to most of us, was never much of a mystery. Traditionally, the Gihon has been tied to a confluence of ancient rivers that flowed out of western Iran, the Bible's second Cush. All three of those rivers flow into what is now the western-most Persian Gulf, an area that was then a marsh just above sea level.

It was the first river, the Pishon, which was something of a poser. Havilah had long been identified as the gold-bearing area of northern Saudi Arabia; however, no river was known to exist there. But now, modern geological surveys have established that a major river did indeed once flow out of that area. However, it had been reduced to only a seasonal trickle since the last ice age ended and had completely dried up at about 2,200 BC at the very latest.[31] During the last ice age, all four of these rivers emptied into what is now the western Persian Gulf.

In choosing between the two events—the Paleolithic Revolution of 40,000 BC or the Lower Neolithic Revolution of 10,900 BC—we would tend to think "Adam = first man, therefore Paleolithic!" But, whatever very important theological themes we see in the story of the Garden of Eden, it is, after all, set in a *garden*. And, gardens are what the Neolithic is all about, not the Paleolithic.

Also, consider the story of Cain and Abel. Cain is a farmer, and Abel is a herdsman (as opposed to a huntsman.) With the death of Abel, Cain is sentenced to take his brother's place (by implication) in following the herds. Adam's third son, Seth, presumably takes up the mantle of farming left by Cain. Again, the theme here is herding and farming, the very themes that define the Lower Neolithic.[32]

Note also that Abel's herds are specifically referred to as sheep and not goats or cattle. Most domesticated breeds of livestock— goats, pigs, cattle, and horses—date to thousands of years later. However, the wild Mouflon sheep of the mountains of Iraq easily made the transition to becoming man's first domesticated herd animal in the Lower Neolithic.[32] Since men have bred sheep for domestication longer than any other form of livestock, these sheep are now unable to make the transition back into the wild. You can find areas with feral horses, cattle, goats or pigs, but feral sheep just simply can't survive on their own.

If we grant, however grudgingly, that the story of the Garden of Eden is, at least, about the dawn of agriculture, this would set it at the dawn of the Neolithic Revolution, about 10,900 BC at the very earliest.

---

31. Kitchen pp. 429–430.
32. Budiansky, p 39–40.

And, this in turn would indicate that Adam was not the first modern man. Now, before you choke on that concept, consider the following:

REEXAMINING AN OLD TRADITION: Many people think that Genesis begins with two creation stories: the first contained in chapter one and the second in chapter two, the garden story. And others then take great delight in showing the contrasts between the two stories, crowing that they have found an example of the Bible contradicting itself.

However, notice that verse 2:5 above doesn't say, "There was no man created yet to plow the ground," but rather that "no man plowed the ground." Just because nobody plowed the ground doesn't mean nobody was there. Nothing in the garden story indicates that it is simply an expansion of verse 26 of the creation story. Creation has already happened; this is a brand-new story.

(Genesis 2:7 STV) And Yahweh Almighty God pressed man out of a mannish dusty-coated-animal, and blew into his nostrils frisky breath. And man became a frisky breather. And, Yahweh-Almighty God planted a fenced pleasure garden to the east, and put there the man whom He had formed. . . (Note that the word for dust here is literally *gray*. On occasion, even the KJV translates it as "fawn," a reference to a small animal's dusty gray coat.)

Bible critics who see the garden story as a second creation story point to this verse and claim that the author simply borrows the Greek myth that has Zeus form humanity from mud figurines. And then they use this to claim proof that the garden story must date to the Greek occupation of Palestine. (Actually, the verse mentions gray/dust, not mud, and the Greek mythology dates to at least five hundred years after the Exodus. Any copying would have gone the other direction.)

On one hand, the question arises whether this passage (Genesis 2:7) refers to a creation at the time of the garden story, or to a simple and elliptic summary of what takes place in the creation story. If you follow the creation story's steps, all of humanity is created from the dust, step by step. Do we have here a second creation of man, or simply a reference to the dusty coated animal that God made man from in Genesis 1:25-26, and that man is in his carnal nature? Taking the word for dust in this sense, the curse following the fall of man becomes, "A dusty [coated animal] you were, and to a dusty [coated animal] you will return" {Genesis 3:19).

On the other hand, down through the ages, virtually all the narratives presenting the garden story present Adam as a full grown adult. (For instance, Michelangelo painted Adam in the Sistine Chapel as a full grown adult with a child's genitals.) However, nothing in the story itself indicates that Adam had no childhood, no infancy, and no birth. If mankind has already been around for at least 30,000 years by the time of this story, then God pressing an infant Adam from a "mannish dusty" would have an entirely different implication. Again, the imagination goes into overdrive.

Next, you may count the garden itself as a creation. But even then, all God does is plant a hedge around a pleasant garden. Any competent human gardener could do the same. And, while it requires creativity, it hardly rates as miraculous creation. And, while God brings animals to Adam, the story never says he creates them on the spot.

Next, you may settle on Eve, since God clones her from Adam's side, something that modern science speculates we will be able to do ourselves in a few years. Now, this does rank as at least preternatural by modern standards. However, Eve may not be something essentially new, especially if modern man already exists on the earth from day six of the creation story.

On the other hand, if the garden story is the equivalent of the sixth day of creation, and if we take day six to be one twenty-four-hour day and the same day as our story, then God goes though making all the listed mammals, then makes man male and female, and gives them dominion over all the earth. God being God, we can stipulate this.

However, Adam, created late in the day, has time to move into the garden and invent a language (remember, God waits to see what Adam says, not vice versa.) Then, God parades all the species of creation before Adam so he can name each species, and then Adam takes an apparently very, very short but deep nap and wakes up to find a wife—maybe an easy task for God, but definitely a hectic day for Adam.

Some try to explain this by claiming that Adam was a super-intelligent, super-speed-talking superman. This, of course, raises the question of why he then fell for the super-dumb apple routine.

Finally, nothing in the garden story actually says that Adam is the first modern man. In fact, the interlude between the creation story and the garden story that we looked at earlier implies the opposite.

However, if Adam is not the first modern man, but rather a specific man selected for a specific task, does this mean that the Bible goofs when it implies so clearly that he is the ancestor of us all, and not just the Semites?

Once again, this fits mainstream paleontology. The answer to this came from a new science called genetic paleontology.

MURDER IN THE NEOLITHIC: Two announcements from the science of genetics shook the scientific world in the last decades of the twentieth century.

The first announcement, in 1988, was of the "Mitochondrial Eve." Human cell structure contains a relatively simple DNA strand called mitochondrial DNA, which we inherit only from our mothers. This strand is not involved in sexual pairing or admixture and therefore stays virtually unchanged from generation to generation. However, it does slowly change at a theoretically steady rate.

By examining the differences between mitochondrial DNA samples drawn from groups all around the world, and then by estimating the rate of change, geneticists concluded that all modern humanity is descended from a single female genotype dating to about 170,000 BC.[33]

Next, geneticists set out to do the same thing with a strictly male strand of DNA, the Y chromosome. However, this strand is part of the cell's nucleus and much more complex. Therefore, it took over a decade for their study to yield results. However, it wasn't the confirmation of the 170,000 BC date they were looking for. Instead, they concluded that all humanity was descended from a single male genotype, dating to about 60,000 BC.[34] As a side issue, both these announcements initially raised fierce opposition from evolutionary theorists. According to traditional evolutionary doctrine, species evolve—not individuals. That either the female or male lines could spring from a single genotype was rankest heresy. Worse yet, genotypes occur first in only one individual. Groups don't all mutate at once.

The dust from the debate over these findings has still not settled. In particular, paleontologists and geneticists disagree about the rate of change, the measuring stick used by the geneticists.

Many paleontologists note that the ratio of the genetic female line to the male line of 170,000 BC over 70,000 BC is roughly similar (sort of) to the ratio of the Upper Paleolithic at 40,000 BC over the Lower Neolithic in 10,900 BC. This has led some to suspect that the geneticists' initial estimate of the rate of change may be off by a factor of three or four. This would make the female line date to the dawn of the Paleolithic Revolution (Genesis 1:26) and the male line date to the lower Neolithic Revolution in the Younger Dryas glacial period (the garden story). (Also, keep in mind; it's unlikely that either of those genetic markers originated in those respective eras. It simply means that the lines from both the Upper Paleolithic and the Lower Neolithic all descended from the respective originators of those markers.)

---

33. *Newsweek*, 1988.
34. Spencer Wells, p. 159.

In the wake of the garden story, the Bible may indicate something similar: "The sons of God saw the daughters of men that they were fair: and they took them wives of all which they chose." (Genesis 6:2).

Now, one traditional view of this verse supposes that these "sons of God" were randy angels. However, it is much more likely that the phrase refers to the descendants of either Seth or Cain, or both. Plausible supports have been given for any of those positions.

> There were giants [choppers] in the earth in those days: and also after that, when the sons of God came in unto the daughters of men, and the bare children to them, the same became mighty men which were of old, men of renown." (Genesis 6:4)

Here, the word the KJV translated as "giants" literally means "Choppers."[35] It implies beefy wielders of axes. Think of Alley Oop and not men of unusual height. This passage, coupled with others in the same chapter, tends to hint that all those "sons of God" went out and slaughtered all other male lines from the Paleolithic Revolution, stealing their daughters.

Couple this with the fact that Cain's very name means "spear." Furthermore, in the genealogies following Adam, several other men have names incorporating the words for either arrows or slender throwing spears (Strong's). We get the impression that a superiority of weapons in addition to the agricultural advantage played a role here.

"For the earth [was] filled with violence." (Genesis 6:13) This certainly seems to be the very thing that geneticists have told us in saying that only one male line survived the Neolithic Revolution, while about eight of the female lines survived. (Many genetic paleontologists explain the disconnection in a less bloody fashion, but the rest of us Neanderthals think they are just wimps.)

In summary, this leaves us associating the "mitochondrial Eve" with the dawn of modern humanity, both male and female, in the

---

35. Strong's 5303.

creation story's day six. We would then associate both Adam and Eve with the "Y-chromosome Adam" at the dawn of the Lower Neolithic Revolution.

As a side issue, the fact that at least eight female lines survived from this time may indicate that, while we can say all modern humanity is descended patri-linearly from Adam, not everyone is matri-linearly descended from Eve.

This in turn raises a whole different set of issues. For instance, be aware that some racist groups have historically said something similar. So keep in mind that we are statistically certain to have all descended from all eight of the female lines, Eve's included, through their many grandsons. For another instance, this may underline the Bible's emphasis on the fall of Adam, as opposed to the fall of Adam and Eve. Some had thought that this was just a bit of theological sexism—Eve doesn't even get the credit for rebelling first. However, these particular rabbit trails threaten to meander through thorn bushes thicker than we have time to trim here.

THE MYSTERIOUS UPPER NEOLITHIC REVOLUTION

EVENT # 3: The Upper Neolithic Revolution is marked by the sudden spread of certain domesticated breeds of plants and animals. On one hand, these domesticated plants and animals give a much higher yield than wild varieties. On the other hand, they require constant attention, and much more labor to maintain. This means that men no longer have time to hunt and gather; instead, they must stay relatively near one place to tend their crops and protect their flocks, and incidentally build cities. The dawn of domesticated agriculture parallels the dawn of civilization.

But, this Upper Neolithic Revolution has always presented something of a mystery. Suddenly, with no evidence of transition forms, modern domesticated breeds of crops and animals explode out of the Middle East. Domesticated wheat kernels are very different from wild wheat kernels, and bones of domesticated goats, sheep, and cattle are very different from the bones of wild sheep, goats, and cattle. However, to breed domesticated crops and herds is the undertaking of many generations. Yet, when archeologists dug around ancient village fire pits, they found no transition between the wild and the domesticated wheat kernels or bones. Somewhere, there had to be remains of that original civilization, at least one major village where the slow miracle of domestication had taken place.[36]

For two decades this became the holy grail of Middle Eastern archaeology. Ancient villages were dug up; fire pits and their debris were meticulously dated. Over the last couple of decades of the twentieth century, the data began to accumulate and a pattern began to emerge. No matter where you started in Europe, Asia, or Africa, the older the domesticated agricultural remains, the closer you drew to one location. Surprisingly enough, that location was not in Africa or the fertile crescent of the Middle East. No matter where you started, the trail went cold on the banks of the Black Sea.[37]

AN OLD CONTROVERSY: For especially the last century, men have long debated whether Noah's Flood, if it happened at all, was a local or a worldwide event. Within evangelical Christianity, the controversy centered on Genesis 7:19–20:

> And the waters prevailed exceedingly upon the earth; and all the high hills that were under the whole heaven, were covered. Fifteen cubits upward did the waters prevail; and the mountains were covered.

Does this phrase *under the whole heaven* refer to all the planet earth, or all the earth being viewed by the protagonist? For instance, if Johnny holds out a handful of marbles and I say, "Johnny placed

---

36. Ryan.
37. Ryan pp. 171–187.

all the marbles in the tray," this obviously means that Johnny put *all* the marbles under current discussion in the tray, not *all* the marbles on the entire planet earth.

Furthermore, in Genesis 4:20 & 21 we see the interesting reference to the descendants of Cain, "Jabal... the father of such as dwell in tents" and "Jubal...the father of all such as handle the harp." The present tense of the verbs "dwell" and "handle" seems to imply that at least some of Cain's descendants survived the flood.

While this debate has been around for many centuries, two things have brought it to the foreground in this last century.

First, lots of evidence from geology has undermined the idea of a planet wide flood. While, yes, many, if not most, mountains showed fossil signs of marine life, these tended to be signs of many generations of sea life, not just a one-year-flood interval. Furthermore, every objective dating system used indicates that those fossils are millions of years old. Finally, too many ancient but easily dissolved land formations were clearly much older than humanity itself and could not have survived a universal flood.

Second, archaeology unearthed the famous Sumerian story, *The Epic of Gilgamesh*, which contained striking parallels to the story of Noah's flood. Suddenly, it became fashionable to view the flood as simply the overrunning of the Euphrates River during some exceptional series of rainstorms.

Probably you've seen the PBS special that depicts a Sumerian merchant and his family on a large reed-barge loaded with livestock, grain, and beer that gets swept out to sea during a heavy rainstorm. By the time they get back to land, everyone—animals and all—are drunk from having to drink all that beer they had been planning to sell. This of course runs counter to the feel of the story as described in Genesis. That story describes a huge catastrophe that wipes out the world's first civilization, changing the course of human history. However, the beer-barge trivialization of the Bible story still plays on the Science Channel, with the actors keeping straight faces and no laugh track in the background.

In spite of all that, since 1997 many secular paleontologists routinely refer to the largest catastrophe in all the history of human civilization as "Noah's Flood" (much to the aggravation of die-hard secularists). This event, which initially threatened to destroy all of human civilization, miraculously kicked off the Upper Neolithic Revolution instead in 6,200 BC.

Just as the Younger Dryas glacial period began with the Clovis Catastrophe, the Upper Neolithic begins with its own catastrophe, which we will deal with in chapter eight: "Noah and the Upper Neolithic."

The STV: The Garden Story Table

King James Version of the Bible	Transliterated Pronounceable Bible	Literal Bible with Vertical Strong's #s "Bolded Quotes are from Strong's Hebrew Lexicon" {Alternate information in braces}	The Science Teacher's Version
2:4 These	'Eeleh	|0428| These	The following *are*
are the generations of	towldowt	|8435| the generations **"from [to bear young; causatively, to beget;]; (plural only) descent, i.e. family; (figuratively) history: --birth, generations."**	the family histories *from* when
the heavens	hashaamayim	|8064| the heavens	the whirling flows
and of the earth	whaa'aarets	|0776| and the earth	and the solid earth
when they were **created,**	bhi**baar'aam**	|1254| when they {were} created	*were* **created,**
in the day	byowm	|3117| on the day of	*given* on the day
that the Lord	`sowt	|6213| the making of	Yahweh-
God made	Yahweh 'Elohiym	|3068| Yahweh |0430| God's *(Mighty Ones)*	Almighty God showed
the earth	'erets	|0776| earth	the earth
and the heavens,	wshaamaayim.	|8064| and heavens.	and the whirling flows.
2:5 And every	Wkol	|3605| And every	And, all
plant of	Siyach	|7880| shrub of **"from [to ponder, i.e. (by implication) converse (with oneself, and hence, aloud)]; a shoot (as if uttered or put forth), i.e. (generally) shrubbery: bush, plant, shrub"**	domesticated plants
the field	hasaadeh	|7704| the field **"from an unused root meaning to spread out; a field (as flat): country, field, ground"**	

before	Terem	|2962| not yet	**were not yet**
it was	yihyeh	|1961| it was	
in the earth,	baa'aarets	|0776| on the earth	**on the earth,**
and every	wkaal-	|3605| and every	**and all**
herb of	`eeseb	|6212| plant of	**the**
the field	hasaadeh	|7704| the field	**domesticated greens**
before	Terem	|2962| not yet	**had not yet**
it grew:	yitsmaach	|6779| it had sprung up,	**grown,**
for	kiy	|3588| because	**because**
the Lord God	lo'	|3808| not	**Yahweh-**
had not	himTiyr	|4305| had rain sent	**Almighty**
caused it to	Yahweh	|3068| Yahweh	**God had not**
rain	'Elohiym	|0430| God	**rained**
upon	`al-	|5921| on	**on**
the earth,	haa'aarets	|0776| the earth,	**the earth**
and there was	w'aadaam	|0120| and a man	**and man**
not a man	'ayin	|0369| was not	**was not**
to till	la`bod	|5647| to till	**plowing**
	'et-	|0853| -	
the ground.	haa'daamaah.	|0125| the ground **"reduplicated from [to show blood (in the face), i.e. flush or turn rosy: be (dyed, made) red (ruddy)]; reddish: (somewhat) reddish."** {Homograph: the word for red is written the same as the word for man. So reddish could just as easily be mannish}	**mannish-*soil*.**
2:6 But there went up a mist	W'eed	|0108| and a mist **"from the same as [to rake together] (in the sense of enveloping); a fog: mist, vapor"**	**And, a fog**
	ya`leh	|5927| went up	**went up**
from	min-	|4480| from	**from**
the earth,	haa'aarets	|0776| the earth	**the earth**
and watered	whishqaah	|8248| and watered	**and watered**
	'et-	|0853| -	
the whole	kaal-	|3605| all	**all**
face of	pneey-	|6440| the surface of	**the sphere of**
the ground.	haa'daamaah.	|0125| the ground.	**the mannish *soil*.**
2:7 And the Lord God formed	Wayiytser	|3335| And formed **"probably identical with [to press (intransitive), i.e. be narrow; figuratively, be in distress:] (through the squeezing into shape); ([compare 3331]); to mould into a form; especially as a potter; figuratively, to determine (i.e. form a resolution)"**	**And, Yahweh-Almighty God pressed**
	Yahweh	|3068| Yahweh	
	'Elohiym	|0430| God	
	'et-	|0853| -	
man	haa'aadaam	|0120| the man	**man**
of the dust	`aapaar	|6083| {out of} dust **"from [to be gray]; dust (as powdered or gray)"** {Homograph: |6081| "gazelle"; Homograph |6082| "a fawn (from the dusty color)"}	***from* a mannish dusty-*coated-animal*,**

of	min-	|4480| from	
the ground,	haa'adamaah	|0125| the ground,	
and breathed	wayipach	|5301| and blew	**and blew**
into his nostrils	b'apaayw	|0639| into his nostrils	**into his nostrils**
the breath of	nishmat	|5397| {the} breath of	**frisky**
life;	chayiym	|2416| life.	**breath.**
and man	wayhiy	|1961| And became	**And, the**
became	haa'aadaam	|0120| the man	**man became**
a living soul.	lnepesh	|5315| a soul.	**a frisky**
	chayaah.	|2416| living	**breather.**
2:8 And the	WayiTa`	|5193| And planted **"to strike in, i.e. fix;**	**And**
Lord God		**specifically, to plant"**	**Yahweh-**
planted	Yahweh	|3068| Yahweh	**Almighty**
	'Elohiym	|0430| God	**God planted**
a garden	gan-	|1588| a garden **"from 1598 [to hedge**	**a fenced**
		about, i.e. (generally) protect: defend]; a	**pleasure**
		garden (as fenced)":	**garden**
eastward in	b-`Eeden	|5731| in Eden **"[{to be soft or pleasant;**	
Eden;		**figuratively and reflexively, to live**	
		voluptuously}; pleasure: delicate,	
		delight, pleasure] (masculine); Eden"	
	miqedem	|6924| to the east,	**to the east,**
and there he	wayaas	|7760| and put	**and put**
put	emshaam	|8033| there	**there**
	'et-	|0853| -	
the man	haa'aadaam	|0120| the man	**the man**
whom	'sher	|0834| whom	**whom**
he had	yaatsaar.	|3335| He had formed.	**He had**
formed.			**formed.**

THE COMPLETE SCIENCE TEACHER'S VERSION OF THE CREATION STORY

GENESIS1:1 In the beginning, and most importantly, Almighty God created whirling flows, and *then* solid matter.

1:2 And, the solid matter was empty desolation. And, darkness wrapped a turning sphere deep in a surging mass. And, the breath of Almighty God fluttered like a nesting hen on the turning sphere of waters.

1:3 And, Almighty God said, "Be light," and it was light.

1:4 And, Almighty God saw the light, "That's good." And *then*, Almighty God separated the light from the darkness.

1:5 And, Almighty God called the light day, and the darkness He called *the* twist away. [And was evening and was morning, Day One.]

1:6 And, Almighty God said, "Let an open space split the flows. And, let it divide flows from the flows."

1:7 And, Almighty God showed the open space separating the flows under the space and the flows above the space. And, it was so.

1:8 And, Almighty God called the open space whirling flows. [And was evening and was morning, Day Two.]

1:9 And, Almighty God said, "Gather the flows under the whirling flows into one place and expose bare land." And, it was so.

1:10 And, Almighty God called the bare land earth, and the gathered flows He called roaring seas. And, Almighty God saw, "That's good."

1:11 And, Almighty God said, "Earth, sprout tender sprouts, plants seeding seeds, fruit trees showing fruit, reproducing its sort in itself on the earth." And, it was so.

1:12 And, the earth brought out tender sprouts, glistening greens seeding seeds of its sort, solid plants showing fruit reproducing its sort in itself. And, Almighty God saw, "That's good."

1:13 [And was evening and was morning, Day Three.]

1:14 And, Almighty God said, "Be lamps in an opening of the whirling flows to distinguish between the day and the twist away, and let them be for beacons, and for formal assemblies, and for days, and annual cycles.

1:15 And, be for lamps in an opening of the whirling flows to shine on the earth." And, it was so.

1:16 And, Almighty God showed two great lamps: the greater lamp to rule the day and the lesser lamp to rule the twist away and the stars.

1:17 And, Almighty God presented them in an opening of the whirling flows, to shine on the earth,

1:18 and to rule over the day and over the twist away, and to distinguish between the light and the darkness. And, Almighty God saw, "That's good."

1:19 [And was evening and was morning, Day Four]

1:20 And, Almighty God said, "Let the water swarm with swarming, breathing, frisky *beasts*, and shrouds flapping on the earth, and on the turning sphere of the open whirling flows

1:21 every shroud with flaps of its sort." And, Almighty God saw, "That's good." And, Almighty God created huge long monsters and all sorts of breathing, frisky scampering-*beasts*, breeding in the water to their sorts.

1:22 And, Almighty God blessed them, saying, "Be fruitful and multiply, and fill the waters of the roaring sea, and shrouds multiply on the earth."

1:23 [And was evening and was morning, Day Five.]

1:24 And, Almighty God said, "Earth, bring out breathing friskies of their sorts, large mammals, and scampering-*beasts*, and frisky-*herds* of the earth of their sorts." And, it was so.

1:25 And, Almighty God showed frisky-*herds* of the earth to their sorts, and large mammals of their sorts, and all mannish scampering-*beasts* of their sorts. And, Almighty God saw, "That's good."

1:26 And, Almighty God said, "Let Us make a man in Our image to be like us, and to rule over the fish of the roaring seas, and over shrouds of the whirling flow, and over the large mammals, and over all the earth, and over all scampering-*beasts* scampering on the earth."

1:27 And, Almighty God created the man in His image. In the image of Almighty God He created him. Male and female He created them.

1:28 And, Almighty God knelt to bless them. And, Almighty God said to them, "Be fruitful and multiply, and fill the earth, and tread on it. Rule over the fish of the roaring sea, and over the shrouds of the whirling flows, and over the frisky *beasts* scampering on the earth."

1:29 And, Almighty God said, "Look! I have presented to you every glistening green seeding seed, which *is* on *the* turning sphere of all the earth, and every solid plant which has in it fruit, solid plants seeding seed, to you it will be for food.

1:30 And, to all the friskies of the earth, and to all *the* shrouds in the whirling flows, and to all the scampering-*beasts* on the earth which are frisky breathers—all the green glistening greens for food." And, it was so.

1:31 And, Almighty God saw all that He had showed, and, "Look! Very Good!" [And was evening and was morning, Day Six.]

2:1 And so, the whirling flows and the earth and all their troops were finished.

2:2 And, on the seventh day Almighty God finished His angelic message which He had showed. On the seventh day He stopped all His angelic message which He had showed.

2:3 And, Almighty God knelt to bless the seventh day, and made it special; because He stopped on it from the entire angelic message which Almighty God created to show.

2:4 The following *are* the family histories *from* when the whirling flows and the solid earth *were* created, *given* on the day Yahweh-Almighty God showed the earth and the whirling flows.

2:5 And, all domesticated plants were not yet on the earth, and all the domesticated greens had not yet grown, because Yahweh-Almighty God had not rained on the earth and man was not plowing mannish-*soil*.

2:6 And, a fog went up from the earth and watered all the sphere of the mannish-*soil*.

2:7 And, Yahweh-Almighty God pressed the man from a mannish dusty-*coated-animal*, and blew into his nostrils frisky breath. And, the man became a frisky breather.

2:8 And, Yahweh-Almighty God planted a fenced pleasure garden to the east, and put there the man whom He had formed.

8

Noah and the Upper Neolithic Revolution
Bible Passage: Genesis 6:1-8:14

Before we begin, I want to highly recommend the book *Noah's Flood* by William Ryan and Walter Pitman, 1998, published by Simon and Schuster. This is not any kind of a Bible study aid, but rather an informal record of the expedition and research that led to uncovering the ancient disaster that many in the mainstream scientific community now commonly refer to as "Noah's Flood." Much of the material in this chapter refers to this book.

NOAH'S NEW RESPECTABILITY

For a decade scientists have noted that the onset of the Upper Neolithic coincided with another North American catastrophic event, the collapse of Lake Agassiz-Ojibway in 6,200-BC, in what has come to be called the 8.2 Kiloyear event. (A Kiloyear is a measure of thousands of years before the present.)

> Hudson Bay and Hudson Strait were the sites of a rapid deglaciation that culminated in the catastrophic drainage of proglacial Lake Agassiz-Ojibway into the North Atlantic at ~8.47 cal kyr BP. It has previously been suggested that this sudden outburst of freshwater may have weakened the thermohaline circulation and triggered the 8200 cal BP cold event recorded in Greenland ice cores.[38]

This basically says that in about 6,200 BC this huge North American lake broke through a glacial ice dam and drained though Hudson Bay and into the Atlantic Ocean, raising sea level about five feet and drastically cooling the climate. Two aspects of this have set some to wondering if they had a candidate for the event that precipitated Noah's flood.

First, for some it raised an immediate question. "Was it possible that this collapse may have been sudden enough to precipitate a major tsunami in the North Atlantic? Was this the breaking of the fountains of the deep?" However, this wave would only have affected the North Atlantic, and no evidence was ever found of a major tidal wave at that time. Furthermore, this would not have affected the Middle East, the arena of the Upper Neolithic and the setting for the Bible story.

However, while the 8.2 Kiloyear event reduced overall rainfall in the long term, intense debate surrounds speculation about how those huge currents of cold fresh water, bearing thousands of massive icebergs, would have affected the normal sea currents and the earth's weather patterns. Either the onslaught, or the recovery 600 years later may have set off gigantic but temporary El Nino effects,

---

38. Lajeuness, P., St-Onge, G., http://adsabs.harvard.edu/abs/2007AGUFM.C51A0075L.

Figure 8.1

The 8.2 Kiloyear Event-Lake Ojibwy drains through Hudson Bay

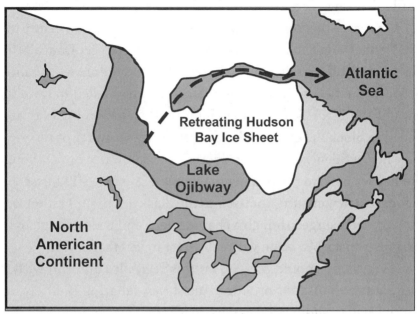

precipitating gargantuan volumes of clouds and volley after volley of heavy rainstorms sweeping eastward across Europe and the Middle East. (Can you say, "Forty days and forty nights"?)

THE 1999 BLACK SEA STUDY: Then, in 1999, in the wake of the fall of Communism in the Soviet Union, an international effort of mainstream scientists began a survey of the floor of the Mediterranean, and perplexed by what they found there, they turned their attention to the floor of the Black Sea. That expedition's conclusions, and the resulting book, *Noah's Flood*, plunged the Bible's story into the realm of scientific orthodoxy.

During past warm interglacial periods, fresh water would pour from the retreating glaciers into the Black Sea and then spill into the Mediterranean Sea. What the expedition found was that in the warming period just after the Younger Dryas ice age, the water from the retreating glaciers had found another outlet to the northern

Baltic Sea instead. This cut off the water supply to the Black Sea. Instead of resurging back upward, its water levels continued to fall until it had shrunk to three hundred feet below its current level.

However, other research since has indicated that well before this the Mediterranean had already risen one hundred feet from all that glacial melt-off, certainly high enough to access the ancient channel between the two bodies of water. Since this had failed to raise the level of the Black Sea, this may indicate that something had happened to block the channel, holding the salty sea water back.

Then suddenly, at about 5,600 BC, the salt water broke though the barrier blocking the ancient channel. (Or, some still insist that it gouged a new channel for itself to the Black Sea basin.) Either way, the salt water surged though a channel deep and wide enough to fill the entire Black Sea basin with salt water in less than a year.

(Hollywood should pick up on this seed idea and run with it. Just picture thousands of Stone Age slaves, laboring franticly under the lash to shore up a massive half-mile long, 70 foot high dike across the Bosporus strait's southern sill, in a doomed attempt to hold back the storming sea. Yah, I know; I watch way too many movies.)

Ryan then went on to document a series of ancient myths from the eastern Mediterranean that connected Tiamat (Tehom, Tehomat, a mythical giant sea serpent) with catastrophic flood stories associated with the straights of Bosporus. He pointed out that for many months the water flume spouting from the gorge into the Black Sea basin would have certainly looked like a roaring, smoking, giant sea serpent to Stone-age witnesses.[39]

Despite actual vitriol Ryan's research has garnered from diehard secularists, for the last ten years his research has held up fairly well. For instance, Robert Ballard, the deep sea explorer famous for finding the Titanic, explored the bottom of the Black Sea, and . . .

---

39. Ryan. p. 250.

Figure 8.2

The Black Sea Shoreline-before and after the flood

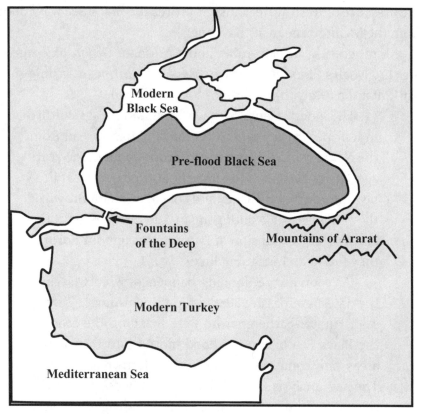

. . . Identified what appeared to be ancient shore-lines, freshwater snail shells, drowned river valleys, tool-worked timbers, and man-made structures in roughly 300 feet (100 m) of water off the Black Sea coast of modern Turkey . . . radiocarbon dating of freshwater mollusk remains indicated an age of about 7,500 years.[40]

Both Ryan and Ballard used the radiocarbon dating of the shells of coastal freshwater mussels in the Black Sea. These mussels only live and die near the water's surface at the shoreline. Dating those

40. http://en.wikipedia.org/wiki/Black_Sea_flood, accessed 3/16/2010

mussels gives a fairly accurate picture of where the shoreline was at any given date. Also, since the Black Sea currently has salt-water, the presence of fresh-water mussels proves the Black Sea was cut off from the Mediterranean at that time.

More recently, in November 2007, *National Geographic* ran an article "'Noah's Flood' May Have Triggered European Farming" by Anil Ananthaswany that referenced Noah's Flood.

> The flood seems to have kick-started agriculture in Europe, Turney said. After farming had spread from the Near East to southeastern Europe about 9,000 years ago, the growth of agriculture in Europe had inexplicably slowed. When Turney and colleague Heidi Brown of the University of Wollongong in Australia looked at the dates for the expansion of farming throughout Europe, they found an intriguing link.

> "As soon as the flooding happened, what we see in the dates is a massive acceleration [in farming]," Turney said. Hunter-gatherers who were living on the coast of the Black Sea before the flood moved into the interior areas, only some of which were being farmed at the time. The new analysis showed that the number of sites in the coastal and inland regions of the Balkans grew rapidly from about 8,200 years ago to about 7,300 years ago.

Granted, those in favor of the more catastrophic interpretation of the data don't care about any ark or divine intervention in human affairs, but they now insist that the Bible story refers to the greatest catastrophe in all the history of human civilization, and the preservation of the domesticated crops and animals—ark or not—as the most significant save in the history of civilization.

Notice in passing that this perspective on the Bible story changes our view of the story's message. Historically, many have tended to view the story of Noah's flood as the triumph of back-to-nature pastoralists over the evils of civilization. However, by tying the flood to the preservation of the world's only major stock of domesticated animal breeds, the story's whole point shifts to saving civilization.

However, we have to remember that we definitely don't have the proverbial "smoking gun" here. The fact that Ryan's findings fit the Bible story perfectly doesn't actually prove anything. It has, though, been perversely fun watching the disloyal opposition thrash around on this one.

THE DESPERATE DEBUNKERS: The reaction in most of the scientific community has been "Oh, how interesting! I wonder what else will turn up." However, secularist ideologues, for whom science is just a tool to beat back Christianity, obviously have not received Ryan's news well. The fun part of this debate is listening to the angry sputters of those pushing to minimize the research's impact. The bare thought that those "ignorant Bible thumpers" might be encouraged by the turn of events sets them to clutching their chests and making strange noises—a truly objective and scientific reaction.

Predictably, they put their own expedition together trying to find something, anything, to minimize the damage. *National Geographic News* printed their findings on February 6, 2009, in an article titled "'Noah's Flood' Not Rooted in Reality After All?"

> Marine geologist Liviu Giosan and colleagues carbon-dated the shells of pristine mollusk fossils, which the researchers say bear no evidence of epic flooding. . . . Found in sediment samples taken from where the Black Sea meets the Danube River, the shells "weren't eroded, agitated, or moved," said Giosan, of the Woods Hole Oceanographic Institute in Massachusetts. "We know the mud is exactly the same age as the shells and so can determine what the sea level was about 9,400 years ago." . . . The results suggest the Black Sea rose 15 to 30 feet (5 to 10 meters), rather than the 150 to 195 feet (50 to 60 meters) first suggested 13 years ago by Columbia University geologist William Ryan and colleagues.

Sound's impressive, doesn't it? But notice two glaring flaws in what they say.

First, they point out, "Looky-looky! No erosion!" This could probably be best answered with a succinct word used by our younger generation: "Duh?!" The ocean's waters flooded in from the *other side* of the Black Sea, not the Danube River. And, that salt water took at least six months to raise the sea level to its current position. How would that erode anything? Furthermore, "calculations made by Mark Siddall predicted an underwater canyon that was actually found."[41] This showed exactly the kind of erosion that Ryan's hypothesis called for.

Second, they dated the mussels to 1,800 years *earlier* than Ryan's date for the flood. Once again, "Duh?!" The whole conclusion of Ryan's research was that the water level of the Black Sea had steadily declined during the preceding warming period. In his own research, he had already documented and dated coastal freshwater mussels getting steadily younger as he went down the slope until he got to the final pre-flood coastline.

What this boils down to is that they simply replicated one piece of what Ryan's group had already documented. This had indicated that the waters of the Black Sea had steadily receded during the interglacial period before the Flood. It is hard to believe that any competent scientist could trumpet this as a major revelation. But then, the article closed with a telling quote:

> Tony Brown, a paleo-environmentalist at the University of Southampton in the U.K., said he fully supports Giosan and colleagues' new findings. "This seems to be a further nail in the coffin of the Ryan hypothesis," Brown said. "I hope this will counter some recent catastrophist and misguided accounts of the spread of farming across Europe by what is likely a mythical flood."

41. http://en.wikipedia.org/wiki/Black_Sea_deluge_theory#cite_note-6, accessed 4/23/2010. Cites Nature 2004.

Obviously, to Mr. Brown, this is not about science. Science doesn't care who gets what ideas; science just cares about facts. However, those trumpeting this study don't care about science, or apparently even basic logic. They just can't stand watching all those scientists read Ryan's study and start giving credence to another one of the Bible's "myths."

(Chuckle-chuckle, chortle, gloat-gloat)

VISUALIZING THE STORY OF NOAH'S FLOOD

THE SETTING: Let's re-visualize the story, even toning down the volume of the flood to something that reasonable naysayers would have to grudgingly stipulate.

When we visualize the story of Noah, we tend to imagine an immense tidal wave crashing through the countryside, gouging up trees and houses, crushing the hapless populous. But if we are looking at the Black Sea catastrophe as Noah's flood, then that probably isn't what happened.

Think of Death Valley, only much, much larger, and you have a good idea of what the Black Sea basin was like. However, a trickle of water from the north feeds the much smaller lake in the center of the desert. Around the lake, you have the world's first civilization. Its isolation at the middle of the almost uncrossable desert has provided it the perfect setting to exterminate all larger predators and settle down to the task of breeding ever better strains of several different grains and more placid and useful strains of animals native to the mountains surrounding the Black Sea basin, like mountain goats, aurochs (seven-foot-tall wild cattle, recently extinct), pigs, and the already domesticated Mouflon sheep.

Even though the ice age has ended, like Death Valley today, rain remains relatively rare, though gully washers do happen occasionally. Any settlement would have sought high ground and yet have pressed as close to the lake as possible.

Also, the words *hills* and *mountains* mean entirely different things to different people. As a child visiting my father's hometown in a plains area, he pointed out Cane Hill to me. I looked where he pointed in vain until I figured out that he meant that little seven-foot rise in the middle of a field. And when he took me into the mountains, I kept waiting for the "mountains" to loom on the horizon. I didn't know he meant those little thirty-foot hills we were already in. Likewise, a visitor from Nepal to California (where I grew up) couldn't help but be amused by my idea of what constitutes a mountain. Beneath twenty feet of the waters of the Black Sea are lots of formations that would have constituted mountains to its former inhabitants.

THE STORM: The Bible mentions "forty days and forty nights" of rain, something the collapse of an ice barrier, spilling of a pro-glacial lake, and the attendant shifting and then re-shifting of the oceans' currents would likely have precipitated. With that kind of a soaking, all the populous would simply have hunkered down with their flocks in their compounds on low hills surrounding the lake, waiting out the miserable weather. Probably, the storms were already approaching their conclusion before the sea broke through the "fountains of the deep (*Tehome*)."

THE FLOOD: This brings us to Genesis 7:20-21, 24: *And the waters prevailed exceedingly upon the earth; and all the high hills, that were under the whole heaven, were covered. Fifteen cubits upward did the waters prevail . . . And the waters prevailed upon the earth an hundred and fifty days.*

This doesn't mean the water covered the land for 150 days. Instead, it means the water slowly and steadily rose, until after 150 days it had reached the tips of the hilltops' trees—no tidal waves. (Twenty feet is about the height of trees that could grow in that kind of biome. The upper branches of hilltop trees sticking out of the water would have provided the last measuring stick. Once the last twig had disappeared, the chronicler would have had no way of knowing how much further the water rose. And, this use of a tree-top marker would in turn further support the idea of a local flood, unless we want to believe that the ark floated by Mt. Everest's trees-tops.)

Now certainly, if you happened to have been standing in the pathway when the Fountains of Tehome breached, then you would have had all the Hollywood-style drama you could ever hope for. However, the Black Sea basin stretches for eight hundred miles. From most of the shores of the then existing lake, the event was well below the horizon. (A few hundred feet seems like a long drop if you're looking straight down it; however, from miles away it doesn't look like much at all.) Most likely, the event went unnoticed by the populous huddled out of the rain on the hills around the lakeshore. Even if the weather had been clear, most likely the dust and mist kicked up by the event would have merely shown as another cloud on the horizon.

Probably, the record rains and the suddenly swollen rivers feeding the lake did cause its water to rise a few yards to meet the runoff coming to its shores. I'm sure it produced much conversation, but few if anybody in the early stages would have felt inclined to flee. It was many days' journey across the surrounding desert in the best of times. Who in their right mind would have made the attempt in those awful conditions? Besides, only a fool would try to run away from rain. It rains everywhere! It would have made much more sense to simply wait it out. "After all," I'm sure people kept saying, "it has to stop any time now."

And stop it did. By that time, their low hills had become widely separated islands. Certainly, at first they would have settled down to simply wait for the fresh water to recede. They had lots of goats to eat, and they would have wanted to thin their herds anyway to match the temporarily reduced grassland. Imagine their alarm when the water suddenly began surging upward over three feet a day. (While overall the waters would rise an average of only one or two feet a day, depending on who you listen to, at first the smaller diameter at the bottom of the lake's bowl would cause a faster rise.)

By the time the water became too salty to drink and panic set in, it was far too late. Who would have thought to store water for themselves and their flocks during all that rain and sitting next to a lake? Possibly, a few who had had the foresight to store some fresh water managed to paddle on reed rafts the many miles to what is now the coast of the Black sea. However, it is unlikely they would have had much in the way of domesticated grain or livestock with them. For most it was far too late; those who didn't die of thirst drowned, along with that treasure of domesticated crops and animals developed over the previous few thousand years.

THE ARK: Nothing in Ryan's study had anything to say either pro or con about any ark. And, barring one of those strange expeditions actually finding the remains of a petrified boat with "Noah was here" written on the wall, it's unlikely that archaeology ever will provide evidence of such a thing.

The best we can do is to consider the plausibility of the concept. And, that concept poses two major, if not to say incredible, challenges.

First, the main challenge of the story has always centered on the inherent problems of acquiring and accommodating seven breeding pairs of all the kosher animals in addition to a pair of every other species of animal on the face of the entire earth.

However, if the story actually concerns itself only with the unique domesticated animals of the Black Sea basin, then the number of species to be saved shrinks tremendously. Fitting this more limited range of animals into the ark along with enough food to last everyone a couple of years would have been very doable. All those headaches about accommodating large carnivores, elephants, and rhinos—not to mention thousands of other species—simply fade away.

Second, the dimensions of the ark itself seem preposterous, especially in the light of what we know about shipbuilding today.

On the negative side, shipbuilding from wooden planks is a highly advanced technology, and it took a couple thousand years of cumulative knowledge before we could build large, wooden-plank ships. Even then the largest wooden ship ever built did not measure up to Noah's ark. There is an intrinsic limit on how large a wooden plank ship can get before the torque motion of waves begins to tear it apart.

(In passing, some contend that nobody really knows what constituted a "cubit" in the time of this story. In the time of the Exodus, a cubit ranged from elbow to fingertip. However, other systems used the distance from the tip of the extended thumb to the opposite extended pinky, about half the standard cubit. But even with a smaller cubit, it was still a big boat.)

Could God have given Noah some knee-up in an as-yet-undiscovered technology? Well, sure, but why bother? Despite the visuals we got in the movie *Evan Almighty*, the Bible story never mentions saws or hammers or pegs and wooden planks. What it does mention is "gopher wood" and pitch—not pitch, as in the gummy stuff on the outside of some trees, but pitch as in tar, like the La Brea Tar Pits in Los Angeles, or the tar pits known to exist around and under the Black Sea.

In the Middle East, the oldest boat technology was not the wooden-plank ship. The oldest boat technology consisted of weaving large bundles of reeds into rafts or even bowls. You may have seen a PBS special that outlines the process. While tradition has guessed that "gopher wood" was cedar, again nobody really knows what it was. If gopher wood was not cedar but rather some thin and flexible wood or reed, the same technology could have been used on it.

Note this phrase: *rooms shalt thou make in the ark, and shalt pitch it within and without with pitch.* Usually, the cute pictures don't show the ark as black with tar. But, more to the point, if the ark was a woven, ten foot thick, tar-soaked barge with walls, the phrase *within and without* becomes much more literal. (In passing, note that the "rooms" would have provided cross-bracing and buttressing, and the bowl shape easily achieved by laying the bundles against earthen banks.)

In fact, in 2001, the British archaeological expedition to Kuwait at a site called H3-As-Sabiyah unearthed the remains of what is now considered to be the world's oldest boat, dating to around 5,500 BC. They found fifty pieces of an inch-thick crust of tar (called "bitumen") that was used to coat a reed boat. Saltwater barnacles coat the outside of the pieces while the insides have the clear impressions of the bundled reeds that made up the body of the boat.

This is clear evidence that the oldest (to date) sea-faring boat technology used tar as noted in the Bible story. Furthermore, a clay boat model found at the site shows a typical reed-bowl kind of craft.[42] Researchers noting the sophisticated construction of the boat have concluded that even in 5,500 BC the technology was already old. They fully expect to find much older examples in the future. Again, "How in heaven could Moses have known about *that?*"

(Remember, Ryan has dated the Black Sea flood to 5,600 BC, virtually contemporary with the As-Sabiyah fragments. For all we know, the ark became a popular tourist spot and the tar pieces and reed boat model dug up in Kuwait were souvenirs.)

Could a tar, reed ship/barge as large as the Bible describes be feasibly built in that era? And, would it have had the flexibility and strength to hold together for a year on the open water? Actually, I don't know. I first heard this proposed forty years ago, and I got the impression at the time that the idea was an old one then. But, I have yet to find any serious, unbiased engineering study of the matter, either pro or con. So, all I can say is that, for now, it seems plausible to me.

---

42. Dr Harriet Crawford and Dr Robert Carter, http://www.ucl.ac.uk/archaeology/kuwait/index.htm, accessed June 15, 2009.

THE LANDING SITE: The Bible says, "And the ark rested . . . upon the mountains of Ararat." We have all seen that image of the ark teetering on the top of Mt. Ararat, the tallest mountain in the picture. Furthermore, you have probably seen photos of intrepid explorers clambering around the rocky slopes and glaciers of Mt. Ararat looking for old cedar planks.

However, all along the southeastern shore of the Black Sea, the mountains Ararat leap out of the water and climb into the highest peaks. Nothing in the Bible says the ark rested on the peak of the highest mountain in the range. Any one of the ridges or shelves that extend out from the mountainous southeastern shoreline of the Black Sea would still fit the Bible's description. Any of those ridges would have been in the mountains of Ararat at the time from the story's point of view.

Also, when we view the flood as the filling of the Black Sea basin, our view changes of what the Bible means by saying the waters receded. That much shifting of water mass would likely have caused some shifting of the tectonic plates, setting off swarms of earthquakes, possibly lowering sea level slightly, causing the Black Sea to recede a few feet from the flood's high-water mark. Instead of a mile of water seeping away, we get a water-soaked subcontinent shedding about six feet of water into the Black Sea basin and back out into the Mediterranean through the straits of Bosporus.

The ark would most likely have run aground on a ridge a few hundred yards offshore. In that case the retreating waters would have left the ark suspended a yard or two above the waterline on a peninsular ridge extending out from the shore. Once the ark was beached, it could have still made an impressive walled compound for several generations, giving its inhabitants time to adjust to dealing with new classes of predators and other hazards the civilized populous of the Black Sea basin had not dealt with for many generations.

As a final note, if I wanted to waste my time looking for the ark, I would focus on a ten to twenty-foot mound on some low ridge projecting from the coastline. Then, instead of looking for cedar planks, I would spend my time pulling up shallow core samples, looking for a large patch of tar mixed with vegetation where none should be.

So, what's the verdict on the story of Noah's Flood? Like the popular TV show, *Myth Busters*, I would have to say that while many of the details are merely PLAUSIBLE, overall it is CONFIRMED.

9

The Creation Story's Structure

In chapter one we mentioned the possible colophon structure of the "It was evening and it was morning, Day #" endings of six sections of the creation story. That such a cuneiform grammatical convention would find its way into an alphabetic document would indicate that the creation story dates to the earliest fusion of the cuneiform and hieroglyphic traditions that gave rise to the alphabet and the dawn of the age of literacy. This in turn helps to date the writing of the creation story to somewhere around 1,450 BC, the traditional date of the Exodus.

In this chapter we are going to focus on how the structure of the creation story ties into the structure of the Mosaic Law in general. Then we will look at a symbolic layer over the events of the creation story that may have an additional prophetic message. Now, before you bail out, fleeing from an impending beast of tedium, I assure you that this will lead to some very non-tedious conclusions.

CHIASTIC STRUCTURE OF THE LAW

In 1999, David A. Dorsey published "The Literary Structure of the Old Testament." This straightforward and relatively dry literary textbook arrived with a bomb blast that has seminary windows still shaking. This is one of those books that every serious student of the Bible absolutely *must* read at least once. And, it should sit within arm's reach of every pastor's desk, right next to their concordance and Bible dictionary. Until recently, this was sold primarily as a seminary textbook for about triple any reasonable price. (Publishers generally follow the long-standing tradition of gouging college students.) However, the price has come down drastically, and I currently see paperback copies offered on Amazon.com for about $34.

Many people over the years have published outlines and structures of the various books of the Bible, so it didn't at first seem like one more would be such a big deal. However, tucked away in its second unit, Mr. Dorsey fairly conclusively demonstrated that the first six books of the Bible—Genesis through Joshua—make one of the world's largest known single chiastic poems.

From this Dorsey came to the conclusion that the Law was initially a single work. However, since no single scroll could practically hold such a large work, at some point the Law had been arbitrarily broken into six equal scrolls just to make it lift-able.

Dorsey points out:

> the seven parts of the historical introduction (Gen. 1:1–Exod. 19:2) appear to be matched in chiastic order by the seven parts of the historical conclusion (Num. 10:11–Josh. 24); and at the center is the treaty itself (Exod. 19:3–Num. 10:10, which forms its own sevenfold symmetry).[43]

---

43. Dorsey, p. 97.

Now, I know that many of you are scratching your heads, wondering what "chiastic order" is. A chiastic poem, also called a chiasm, refers to the poetic structure of A-B-C-D-C-B-A. The "rhyming" parts are tied together, not by repletion of sounds, but rather with either a repetition of a clear theme or by repetition of a unique key phrase when the themes seem a little weak.

Section One: Historical Introduction to the Treaty at Sinai

A Nations receive their territories, **Genesis** 1:1–11:32

  B Abraham promised Canaan, 12:1–21:7

    C Isaac, death of Abraham, the first founding father, 21:8–28:4

      D Jacob-family injustice, 28:5–37:1

        E Joseph-faithful obedience, 37:2–50:17

          F Exodus-victory over foreign Egypt, **Exodus** 1:1–13:16

            G Failure and grace in the wilderness, 13:17–19:2

Section Two:

              H The Treaty at Sinai, 19:3–**Leviticus–Numbers** 10:10

Section Three: Historical Conclusion to the Sinai Treaty

            G' Failure and grace, 10:11–21:20

          F' Victory over foreign Moab, 21:21–**Deuteronomy** 3:30

        E' Call to obedience, 4–12

      D' Laws on family justice, 12–27

    C' Death of Moses, the second founding father, 27–35

  B' Conquest of Canaan, **Joshua** 1–12

A' Tribes receive their allotted territories, 13–24 [44]

Dorsey goes on to demonstrate that each of those seven parts is itself a poem, usually a chiasm, and occasionally each of those subparts are themselves poems, and so on, sometimes down to a fourth or fifth layer, sometimes down to each single phrase in a verse.

---

44. Dorsey, p. 101.

This structure is so detailed and formal that he even shows us that the single verse cursing Canaan (Genesis 9:25) is clearly two verses out of order. Is this an example of a minor scribal error of accidentally switching the similar verses 25 and 27? Or, is it a poetic device to emphasize the jarring nature of the curse itself, which is so important to the story of the invasion of the land of Canaan?

THE OVER LAYERING OF STRUCTURES: Dorsey also points out that many passages have over layering structures. For instance, the step E above—"Joseph-faithful obedience"—in the overall structure, may provide the best example of this. Like most of the Law's chiasms, it uses one of several variations of seven steps—in this case, seven steps in and seven steps out. (Usually, the seventh step forms a single middle, but sometimes the seventh step is repeated, as in this example.)

E Joseph-faithful obedience (basic single chiastic structure)

　1 *introduction to boy Joseph*

　　2 *grievous mourning in Hebron*

　　　3 *reversal of elder and younger sons of Judah*

　　　　4 *Joseph's enslavement to Egyptian*

　　　　　5 *disfavor at pharaoh's court*

　　　　　　6 *Joseph's revelation of pharaoh's dreams*

　　　　　　　7 *brothers come to Egypt for food*

　　　　　　　7' *brothers come to Egypt for food*

　　　　　　6' *Joseph's revelation of his identity to brothers*

　　　　　5' *favor at pharaoh's court*

　　　　4' *Joseph's enslavement of Egyptians*

　　　3' *reversal of elder and younger sons of Joseph*

　　2' *grievous mourning near Hebron*

　1' *conclusion and death of Joseph*

Looking closer, we find that two additional structural schemes overlay that first basic structure—first a double chiastic over layering structure, and then second, a double linear over layering structure.

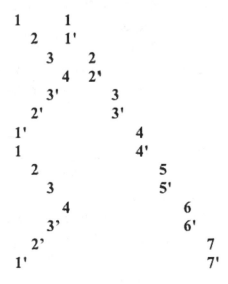

Each of these structures rhymes different themes or key phrases, which all had to be inserted into their corresponding passages. This often forced the author to use widely differing internal structures to get the right three themes or key phrases to fit into each passage in the right order. And, it was just that artistic structural variety that the JED-P crowd had historically pointed to in their scholarly ignorance to say that different authors had written different side-by-side passages.

THE SIGNIFICANCE OF THE STRUCTURE: This rediscovery of the Law's overall structure has far more than poetic significance.

First, this settled a long-standing debate among orthodox scholars as to whether Joshua itself was part of the book of the Law. Many had noted for some time that the flow of the story of Joshua seems to continue the ongoing narrative of the first five books.

---

45. Dorsey, pp. 59–62.

Second, it settles the question of Deuteronomy. Deuteronomy uses spellings of words that don't come into the Hebrew language until well over five hundred years after the writing of the other five books. Furthermore, those spellings in Deuteronomy closely resemble the spellings in the book of Jeremiah.

Therefore, the JED-P crowd had always claimed that Jeremiah or one of his contemporaries had written his own new and improved version of the Law to deal with issues of concern to Judah just before the Babylonian captivity.

However, this ignores the fact that, since such scrolls in the ancient world were usually read out loud, it was common for scribes recopying older books to update the text into the current styles of printing and spellings as they went.

Now that we see Deuteronomy as part of the overall structure of the Law, it slides right into place without missing a beat, and is obviously contemporary to the other sections. It had to have been in place from the beginning, and any revisions at the time of Jeremiah would have messed up its intricate structure. Furthermore, while a scribe might update a document's print and spelling to his current era, the same scribe would have found it more difficult to guess at the styles of print and spellings from the distant past. In other words, it's vastly more likely that Deuteronomy was updated than that the other sections of the Law were back-dated.

Third, orthodox theologians have debated for millennia whether Moses himself actually penned the Law. Many have pointed out that the book itself implies that Moses, Aaron, Miriam, and Joshua all had a hand in commissioning the work, yet nowhere does it mention whose hand did the actual writing. Furthermore, by viewing all six books as a single unit, this strongly implies that a single hand held control of the overall structure.

On one hand, the fact that the book of Joshua concludes with the burial of Joshua some thirty years after the death of Moses strongly suggests that that guiding hand probably didn't belong to

Moses, or Aaron, or Miriam, and maybe not even Joshua. On the other hand, we will see later that internal evidence has coupled with literary archaeology to establish that the Law could only have been written at the time of the individual stories themselves. Furthermore, Joshua closes leaving obvious questions unanswered, questions that could have been easily answered just a few years later. It is highly unlikely that any Hebrew scholar even one century later could possibly have written the work with the detail and form we have here.

The obvious solution is simply to say that God himself organized and guided the writing of the Law. However, this doesn't get around the fact that someone's actual hand did the writing. This would have to have been someone with the equivalent of an advanced degree in Egyptian literature and law, someone with an exceptional intellect and artistic bent. We have to remember this incredibly complex opus dates to the dawn of literacy. (Remember the discussion of literacy from chapter two.) In composing this gigantic poem, the author achieved something of a magnitude that no other piece of literature since has ever quite matched.

For now, we will leave this question hanging, but keep it in the back of your mind as we go through the next section: "The Creation Story and the Exodus."

THE CREATION STORY AS A TABLE OF CONTENTS

THE GENERATIONAL SECTIONS OF GENESIS: Most, if not all, Bible scholars recognize that the book of Genesis divides into twelve very distinct sections. With the lone exception of the creation story itself, each section begins with a variation on the phrase *these are the generations of (so and so)*.

Since the creation story doesn't follow this pattern, some have suggested that it is a separate work artificially pasted onto the beginning of Genesis. However if we look closely at the creation story's first three days, we see what looks like a detailed outline of the entire book of Genesis using Egyptian symbolism.

DAY ONE: In the first day of creation we see a very Egyptian theme, that of light versus chaos. In Egyptian mythology, creation begins with chaos, and powerful gods rebel to organize and drive it back and bring light. Chaos stands for death and social confusion. Light stands for life and human intelligence and civilization. Chaos comes first.

It is interesting that the first story after the creation story also deals with the theme of turning away from light into darkness, the story of the garden and the fall of man. In this context, the first day becomes a symbol for the creation of the image of God in man, followed by the human choice to turn away from the light into the darkness.

Also remember, in chapter six we pointed out that Genesis 2:4 may directly state that God revealed the garden stories on the same day as day one of the creation story, tying it even more closely with day one.

DAY TWO: At the time of the Exodus, both Egypt and the Middle East had a very well-known flood myth about Tehomat, a goddess of chaos, the giant sea serpent of the watery abyss.[46]

> It was Maraduch, the last born of the gods, who entrapped Tehomat . . . clove her into two pieces, and controlled the rains from heaven above and the floods on earth below with her split body stretched from pole to pole. Maraduch . . . to the Sumerians he was the arch engineer, the Pontifex Maximus of the gods.[47]

So, when the second day refers to divided waters, above and below, we have a plain literary allusion to a catastrophic flood myth,

---

46. Ryan, p. 50.
47. Willcocks, p. 32.

without actually confirming the Sumerian version. So, here we see the creation story's day two stand for the second section of the book of Genesis—Noah's flood. In the creation story, we have a great expanse dividing water below from water above. In the flood story, we have a great flood of water divide a vast expanse of unrecorded human history (before it) from a great expanse of unrecorded history (after it).

DAY THREE: To the Egyptians and to the Hebrews, the roaring sea stood for the surrounding uncivilized, or Gentile, world, always raging, always battering against the land. The land stood for civilization as opposed to chaos. To the Egyptians, the sacred land of Egypt was the very bastion of civilization. And, the Hebrews sought their own Promised Land, where they too could be civilized. Without a land of their own, they were merely uncivilized wanderers (a possible meaning of the very word "Hebrew"). To the Hebrews, and through the entire Bible, land symbolized the patriarchs and the Promised Land.

To the Egyptians, crops stood for the life of the nation. As crops thrived, the nation thrived. As crops failed, the nation withered. Similarly, throughout the Old Testament, the plant often symbolized the nation of Israel.

Plainly, the first three days of the creation story stand as a clear outline of Genesis. Each created item in the three days combine to function as a table of contents for the sections of the entire book of Genesis. Furthermore, notice that the parallels are clear and organic. While we can certainly see some repetition of key phrases, these are actually not needed to make the associations plain.

Examine the following chart to see how each of the "generations" sections pairs in exact order with the things shown in those first three days of the creation story.

Figure 9.1

Genesis Sections		Section Stories	Creation Story Outline
1:1–2:3,		The Creation Story	"In the beginning"
			Day One, Gen 1:2–5
2:4–4:26	"the generations of the Heavens and the Earth"	Adam & Eve, Fall of Man, Cain & Abel,	light, day and night
			Day Two, Gen 1:6–8
5:1–6:8,	"the generations of Adam"	Genealogies to Noah, the Nephilim, judgment pronounced, Noah finds favor	"the waters below the expanse"
6:9–9:28,	"the generations of Noah"	the flood to death of Noah	"the expanse"
10:1–11:9,	"the generations of the sons of Noah"	Genealogies of nations, Tower of Babel	"the waters above the expanse"
			Day Three, Gen 1:9–11
11:10–26,	"the generations of Shem"	Genealogies to Abraham	"the roaring sea"
11:27–25:11,	"the generations of Terah"	the stories of Abraham, to his burial	"the solid earth"
25:12–25:18	"the generations of Ishmael"	Genealogies of Ishmael to his line settled	"the tender shoot"
25:19–35:29,	"the generations of Isaac"	Life of the shepherds, Jacob to Isaac's death	"grass"
36:1–36:8,	"the generations of Esau"	The marriages of Esau to his settlement in Seir	"seeding"
36:9–37:1,	"the generations of Esau"	The dynasty of Esau in Seir	"seed"
37:2–50:26,	"the generations of Jacob"	The story of Joseph	"tree bearing fruit"

THE CREATION STORY'S OTHER PARALLELS: The association of the creation story's first three days with an outline of the twelve sections of Genesis is not particularly controversial. However, from day four onward, the associations have given rise to several competing interpretations.

DAY FOUR: On one hand, we see the phrase *the sun and the moon and eleven stars* used in Joseph's dream in Genesis 37:9. This would indicate that day four stands for the collected seed of Abraham, the Hebrew people themselves.

On the other hand, the Egyptian moon god, Ah, stood for law and civilization. We see this reflected in Jeremiah 31:35's phrase *the ordinances of the moon.* Since the Law ties all the major feasts to either new or full moons, the moon itself often stands for the Law of Moses.

Traditionally, the moon and the stars it rules has symbolized what the rabbis called "the Law of Moses and the prophets." For instance, in Daniel 12:3 we see that "they that turn many to righteousness [shall shine] as the stars forever and ever." Here, we see this part of day four stands for the Law of Moses and the institution of the prophets that give us all the rest of the Old Testament.

But, what about the symbolism of the sun? In Egyptian symbolism the sun god, Ra, stood for life and death and resurrection. Also, we find verses like Psalm 89:35–36: "I will not lie unto David. His seed shall endure forever, and his throne as the sun before me."

Since the sun is greater than the moon, it is mentioned first. However, we have to remember that the Hebrew day begins at sunset. So, chronologically, the moon comes before the sun, announcing its arrival.

Therefore, to the rabbis, the sun in day four stood for the throne of David and the golden age of the nation of Israel. On the other hand, resurrection is the overwhelming theme of the Christian New Testament. So, for Christians, the sun plainly symbolized Christ and the New Testament. Both of these approaches view day four's symbolism as prophetic, since both the Jewish and Christian interpretations deal with things future to the writing of the Law.

Here we have three different perspectives on what day four stands for. If we go with just the repetition of a key phrase, it stands for the Hebrew people, struggling through the night of their Egyptian captivity, into the open light of the liberated nation. If we go for the stronger, organic Egyptian symbolism as used in the first three days, it prophetically stands for either the Law and the prophets and the kingdom of God, or for the Old and New Testaments, the written Word of God. However, none of these points of view actually contradict each other, and nothing prevents us from taking day four as standing for all three things. A dual or triple-duty symbolism is more, not less, artistic.

DAYS FIVE AND SIX AS PROPHECY: Since the first four days of the creation story plainly symbolize historical events, Bible scholars for millennium have naturally expected that the remaining two days would also have symbolic meanings. And, initially, the most logical place to look would be the last half of the Hexateuch—the first six books of the Bible.

Unfortunately, while some parallels have been found, they tend to be simple repetitions of key words and phrases, and not the clear and organic parallels we see in the first four days.

Therefore, down through the centuries, the faithful have looked for prophetic meanings for the seven animals of days five and six—even St. Augustine tied days five and six to events in his time to try to make predictions. Generally, these systems apply the symbolism only in terms of local concerns and issues. We human beings naturally tend to see ourselves and our own times as central to the universe.

Never-the-less, one prophetic system has remained popular since the Reformation. It points to organic and strong parallels between the animals of days five and six, and uses a much larger perspective. Many church leaders over the last few centuries have referred to this system.

Now, I know that some will glibly think in terms of psychic predictions, reducing God to the level of showmen like Nostradamus. However, the Bible is not really big on psychics. The Old Testament prophets never pretended to have ESP. The most they would say is that God said he would do such and such.

Great theological minds for thousands of years have debated the foreknowledge of God. For what little my opinion is worth, I don't think that the Bible necessarily teaches that God *sees* the future so much as it teaches that God *creates* the future. He sees what he plans to do, and then he does it. Biblical prophecy may not psychically envision the future so much as it announces God's intent to act.

174

THE CURRENT POPULAR PROPHETIC SYSTEM: In essence, this system combines the seven animals of days five and six with the seven churches of Revelation 2:1–3:14, which are themselves taken to stand for seven distinct ages of church history.

So as we consider this system, we have to ask ourselves how natural the correlations are between the details of the days of creation and the details of recorded church history. Are we forcing the pattern; are we seeing something that isn't really there? Follow along and judge for yourself.

Whole books have been written analyzing the seven-churches passage of Revelation and pointing out its detailed correlations with the last two thousand years of church history. However, this Bible passage actually doesn't need much exposition; even a cursory reading brings detailed events to mind. As we proceed here, I am only going to mention the church that each animal of days five and six corresponds to, and an interpretation of each church's name.

DAY FIVE AND THE CHRISTIAN CHURCH'S FIRST THREE SYMBOLS: Day Five presents three animals: the water creature, the shroud, and the long-monster.

Correlation number one: In its earliest days, the Christian church used a common acrostic, "Jesus Christ God's Son our Savior," in Greek: "Iesus Kristos Theon Uyoo Soterior." This spelled out IK-ThUS, Greek for fish. If you know much about church history, you know that we call the first church age the Apostolic Church Age, and its symbol has always been the fish, the life from the sea. (Compare this to the Ephesian [Foundation] Church in Rev. 2:1–7.)

Correlation number two: Historians call the second church age the Church of the Martyrs. If you go into the catacombs under Rome where Christians buried their dead, you will often find tombs painted with a human figure raising outstretched arms and sporting a pair of wings. Today, some would think this is a picture of an angel guarding the soul of the dearly departed. But in actuality, the painting depicts the deceased in an attitude of prayer. At the time, wings conventionally symbolized a martyr's death. Throughout western history, birds (shrouds) have symbolized death. The symbol of the Church of the Martyrs has always been the wings of the shroud. (Compare this to the Church of Smyrna [City of Myrrh, the Embalming Spice] in Rev. 2:8–11.)

Correlation number three: This brings us to the third church age. Since most of us descend from the western Catholic Church, many of us forget that the original Catholic Church founded under the Emperor Constantine was based in Constantinople before the Dark Ages descended. Generally, historians refer to this as the Byzantine Empire. This Catholic Church stretched from Ireland through southern Europe to the Near East, then back across the top of Africa, a huge, long, stretched-out monster. (Compare this to the Pergamum [The Fortified Tower] Church in Rev. 2:12–17.)

In day five we see symbols of the first three church ages, laid out in order. The parallels here are organic and clear. Furthermore, remember that to both the Egyptians and the Bible, the sea symbolized the chaotic heathen world. Likewise, these first three church ages rise out of the pagan world.

DAY SIX AND THE CHRISTIAN CHURCH'S LAST FOUR SYMBOLS: Day Six presents four animals: The behemoth, the wild beast, the herd animals, and the beast-man. Again, you can judge for yourself whether the symbols fit.

Correlation number four: The next church age deals with the divided Roman and Greek Orthodox Catholic churches, where brown-robed silent monks plodded the halls of the Dark Ages like shaggy, speechless behemoth. (Compare this with the Thyatiran [Crown and Tiara, or Crown of Tyre, or derivation unknown] Church of Rev. 2:18–29.)

Correlation number five: This next age is not the church's finest moment. In the violent upheavals of the Reformation and Counter-Reformation, the branches of the church tear and savage each other like wild beasts. (Compare this with the Sardis [Dark Stones] Church of Rev. 3:1–6.)

The word-by-word parallels between this passage and the traumas leading up to and including the Reformation and Counter-Reformation debacle practically grab the reader by the scruff of the neck and shake him.

Correlation number six: The violence subsides, and Christianity settles into denominational church herds, grouped by common cultures and social classes. (Compare this with the Philadelphian [Brotherly Love] Church of Rev. 3:7–13.) Interestingly enough, even William Penn's naming of the city of Philadelphia reflected the then popular belief that the emerging American colonies represented the promise of a coming Philadelphian church age, an age of many different denominational church herds living in relative harmony.

Correlation number seven: This brings us up to our modern humanistic church, man-centered and materialistic, the spiritually brutish beast-men. (Compare this with the Laodicean [People's Diocese] Church of Rev. 3:14–22.)

Thus, in day six we see symbols of the last four church ages laid out clearly. Just as day five's churches were the three churches rising out of the roaring sea of the pagan world, day six's four churches all rise out of the solid earth of Christendom.

Now, I am aware that it's not difficult to take any whole and then find a way to divide it into seven parts. However, this sevenfold division of church history has been generally recognized by even secular historians who have no interest in any symbolism in the creation story.

The following chart summarizes some of the correlations between the creation story's days five and six, the seven churches of Revelation, and church history as it unfolded.

Figure 9.2a

The Seven Church Ages in Genesis 1 & in Revelation 2 & 3		
Day Five, The Church Rising Out of the Sea of Paganism		
The Fish	The Shrouds	The Long Monster
2:1–7	2:8–11	2:12–17
Ephesus	Smyrna	Pergamos
Name Means Foundation City	Death Spice City	Fortified Tower
Historic Church The Apostolic Church	The Martyrs' Church	The Byzantine Church
Christ's Character Holds the stars and walks between the candlesticks	The first and the last, was dead but is now alive	Has a sharp two-edged sword
The Church's Virtues Hard work, endurance, orthodoxy, hate the "Laity Conquerors"	Good work, tribulation, poverty	Dwells in Satan's seat, holds fast, faithful martyr "Anti-fathers"
The Church's Flaws Have lost their first love	None	Pagan compromises, idolatry, syncretism, the hateful "Laity Conquerors"
Church's Penalty Extinction	None	Will face the "sword of my mouth."
The Church's Remedy Go back to doing your first works	Be faithful unto death	Repent
The Church's Reward Will eat of the tree of life	Crown of Life	He that overcomes eats hidden manna and gets a new name

Figure 9.2b

The Seven Church Ages in Genesis 1 & in Revelation 2 & 3			
Day Six, The Church Rising Out of the Solid Earth of Christendom			
The Behemoth	**The Wild Animals**	**The Herds**	**The Mannish-Beast**
2:18–29	3:1–6	3:7–13	3:14–19
Thyatira	**Sardis**	**Philadelphia**	**Laodicea**
Name Means Crown and Tiara*	The Dark Gems	City of Brotherly Love	People's Church
Historic Church The Two Catholic Churches	Reformation and Counter Reformation	Denominational Church	The Humanistic Church
Christ's Character Eyes like flame, feet of brass	He who has seven spirits and seven stars	He that is holy and true, has the key of David	The faithful and true witness, the beginning of the creation of God
The Church's Virtues Good work, charity, service, patience, last works even better	Has a remnant near death. A few have not defiled their garments	Good works, open doors, hast a little strength, kept His word, not denied His name	None
The Church's Flaws Pagan Lady worship, and pagan syncretism, allowed to repent but refused	Are already dead, evil works	None	Mediocrity, materialism, are wretched, miserable, poor, blind and naked
Church's Penalty Tribulation, plague, shame	Christ will come like a thief	None	Christ will spit them out of his mouth
The Church's Remedy Those who avoid the sin, just have to wait it out	Overcome, do not defile your garments	Overcome	Buy gold and clean raiment, anoint your eyes, be extremists and repent
The Church's Reward Those who endure receive power over the nations, receive the morning star	I will not blot his name out of the Book of Life	Jews will worship at your feet. You will be kept from temptation, and be pillars in the temple of God	Will sup with Christ, and will sit with Christ on his throne

*Or Crown of Tyre, the fortified, isolated island city, or of uncertain derivation

BISHOP USSHER AGAIN: Finally, note that the symbolism of the six days of creation breaks history into the same six historical eras that Ussher's six one-thousand-year intervals of genealogical dates did.

This actually makes sense. If we say that the Bible's genealogical dates arbitrarily skip generations to give us neat and tidy patterns, then we have said that we see those patterns as deliberate. The very artificiality of the genealogies may make them part of the message. So, while Ussher's dating system may not make good science, it may offer a good literary analysis.

THE SYMBOLISM OF DAY SEVEN: You probably have noticed that if we take the creation story as a prophecy, then almost all the prophecy has been used up. What used to be a sweeping outline of thousands of years of the coming future is now almost all in the past. It's like the movie cliché that shows the timer counting down to the last few seconds on the doomsday bomb.

The Bible once contained vast and detailed prophecies about the future. Now, virtually all that prophecy has become history, with only a very few rather lurid prophetic details remaining. Naturally, most of our minds automatically go on to doom, gloom, and the end of the world.

But, before we start running in circles, dodging pieces of falling sky, we should consider that the symbolism of the creation story has one more day to go.

Now, the following statement may sound trite, given all the significance that the Sabbath has played in the history of both Judaism and Christianity. But, since the last of the symbolism of the creation story is contained in the seventh day, we need to point out that this passage treats the seventh day as something very positive indeed.

The Sabbath symbolizes God's communion and Joy in his creation. It does *not* stand for the destruction of that creation. So, when we contemplate the complete fulfillment of the symbolism of day six and the trauma we may think that implies, we should remember that God has been working persistently and deliberately toward this goal for many thousands of years. He labels the end product as something "very good."

> And God saw everything that he had made, and, behold, it was very good. And the evening and the morning were the sixth day. Thus the heavens and the earth were finished, and all the host of them. And on the seventh day God ended his work which he had made; and he rested on the seventh day from all his work which he had made. And God blessed the seventh day, and sanctified it: because that in it he had rested from all his work which God created and made. (Genesis 1:31–2:3)

Section Four:

The Creation Story and the Exodus

10

The Exodus Theater

The Revelation Days approach to the creation story ties it closely to the first week of the Exodus. However, until recently, we had only the vaguest idea of where exactly that took place. On the bright side, the book of Exodus gives us specific names of quite well known places in the decades near the event.

Unfortunately, over time most of these cities and fortresses were abandoned, or renamed. Finding and identifying these places has been the subject of intense debate for the last century and a half. Only in the last few years has archaeology arrived at a consensus on many of them.

In this chapter we will look at the Egyptian locations mentioned and consider how this clarifies our understanding of the story. For lack of a better system of organization, we will follow an outline suggested by the bolded words in the following verses:

And **Pharaoh** spake unto Joseph, saying . . . **The land of Egypt** is before thee; . . . make thy father and brethren to dwell in **the land of Goshen**. . . . And Joseph placed his father and his brethren . . . in the best of the land, in **the land of Rameses**, as Pharaoh had commanded. (Genesis 47:5, 47:11)

And the children of Israel journeyed from Rameses to **Succoth**, about **six hundred thousand on foot that were men**, beside children. (Exodus 12:37)

And it came to pass, when Pharaoh had let the people go, that God led them not through **the way of the land of the Philistines**, although that was near . . . but God led the people about, through the way of **the wilderness of the Red sea**. . . . And they . . . encamped in **Etham**, in the edge of the wilderness . . . and the Lord spake unto Moses, saying, Speak unto the children of Israel, that they turn and encamp before **Pi-hahiroth**, between **Migdol** and the sea, over against **Baal-Zephon**: before it shall ye encamp by the sea . . . and the Lord caused the sea to go back by a strong east wind all that night . . . and the sea returned . . . and the Lord overthrew the Egyptians in the midst of the sea. (Exodus 13:18, 20; 14:1, 21, 27)

PHARAOH: Pharaoh is simply Egyptian for "Great House," and refers to the head of any royal family or kingdom. Egyptologists have long divided Egyptian history into the Old and New Kingdoms, with a period of civil war and chaos dividing the two called the Middle Kingdom. Both the relatively stable Old and New Kingdoms kept good historical records. However, the Middle Kingdom, also called the Intermediate Periods, was less organized.

Egypt had fallen into a series of civil wars and lacked any strong leader. Around 1700 BC, foreigners from Asia, eventually called the Hyksos, migrated into the eastern Egyptian Delta. It was once thought that they had invaded, but current opinion suspects a local ruler invited them in, because they brought important new technologies with them—things like more advanced metallurgy, better weapons, and the chariot.

Then, according to most geologists, around 1628 BC the Minoan eruption blasted Eurasia. Many insist that its volcanic ash and the resultant dimming of the sun's light caused a series of bad growing seasons and famines that destroyed several ancient civilizations. Although the debate on that has yet to settle, by 1620 BC the Hyksos did own the entire eastern Delta, and from the city of Avaris went on to economically dominate the rest of what we today call Egypt.

Of course, this scenario bears striking resemblance to the story of Joseph. So, many people identify Joseph's pharaoh as this as yet unnamed early Hyksos king. Other groups place Joseph's pharaoh in the Old Kingdom, since they believe that either the Hebrews themselves were the Hyksos kings or that the Bible indicates a much earlier date.

In the Bible story, Joseph and his family seem to function as a kind of civil service for the government—actually, a fairly common pattern in world history. A small group becomes a privileged ruling caste. They have lots of power and money and want to spend their time doing fun and flashy things like party, hunt, and go to war. What they don't want to do is the drudgery of actually running the country. For that, they hire a civil service to hold the reins of domestic power.

However, this poses risks. On the one hand, if they draw that civil service from the oppressed majority, then that same civil service could organize a civil uprising and kick the ruling caste out. On the other hand, if they draw that civil service from the lower levels of their own caste, they run the risk of a palace coup.

So, they solve the problem by bringing in a third group that nobody respects. We saw this happen in recent history with the Sandinistas in Nicaragua. The people were restless and not to be trusted, and the Sandinistas wanted to spend their time partying. Therefore, they brought in nearly a thousand Cubans to run their civil service.

Under the Hyksos the eastern Delta prospered, and under their economic domination the rest of Egypt began to settle into its own prosperity. Yet, reading the Egyptian documents from the time, you would think the Hyksos liked to eat Egyptian babies. All the rest of Egypt hated them.

Why? Apparently, their very technological and economic superiority didn't sit well. Egyptians had always viewed themselves as intrinsically better than all the rest of the world. Notice that in the Bible story the ruling caste (either Hyksos or Egyptian) will not even eat at the same table with those not of their caste. Any perceived arrogance on the part of the Hyksos would have caused automatic outrage.

So, around 1550 BC, the pharaoh of the Egyptian Upper Kingdom finally conquered the Hyksos and expelled them from the Delta (Upper Kingdom, as in at a higher elevation; i.e., the up-river, southern part that has all those pyramids and things). To accomplish this, the young pharaoh placed a blockade around the center of the Hyksos' civil service, the city of Avaris, and finally captured it, pressing that entire, possibly Hebrew, civil service into slavery.

While the Hyksos worried about the loss of their civil government, Ahmose led an elite force north along the eastern edge of the Delta and captured the Hyksos fortress of Tjaru that guarded their trade route to their natural allies in Canaan.

With their supplies cut off, the remaining Hyksos negotiated a deal. They agreed to leave Egypt forever if the new Pharaoh would let them take their families and all the possessions they could carry with them. (Some think they just ran with no formal deal involved.) Regardless, about 100,000 of them fled into Canaan, with Ahmose pursuing them to make sure they left.

Those who think the Hebrews were the Hyksos civil service, but not themselves Hyksos, believe that the Egyptians enslaved the Hebrews in the fall of Avaris. Furthermore, this may imply that the Hyksos sold the Hebrews out, preferring to keep their gold rather than include the Hebrews in the escape deal. Possibly, this may have been one of many reasons the Law reflected such a grudge against the Canaanites. The universally despised caste of civil servants had been left behind to the tender mercies of the "new king over Egypt, which knew not Joseph. . . . And the Egyptians made the children of Israel to serve with rigor" (Exodus 1:8, 13).

Those who believe the Hyksos were the Hebrews (the ancient historian Josephus among them) believe that the Hyksos' flight itself was the Exodus. However, internal evidence from the Exodus story itself, and mounting evidence from archaeology, has shown this to be unlikely. We do know that thousands of "Asiatics," as Egyptians called them, had indeed been left behind by the Hyksos' flight, and pressed into slavery.

THE LAND OF EGYPT: You have to understand that the Egypt referred to in Genesis and Exodus is not the Egypt we think of today. When we think of Egypt, we think of that big square country sitting on much of the Nile River in northern Africa, the land of the pyramids and the sphinx. However, in the Bible stories, Egypt was only the eastern Nile Delta where the Nile spills into the Mediterranean Sea—no pyramids, no sphinx. Couple this with the fact that the Nile Delta is a flood plain made up of mud washed down from higher elevations. Rocks are very hard to come by, so everything is built of mud brick. If you see a stone, someone had to go to all the trouble to carry it in from somewhere else—something they didn't bother to do very often.

This means that most buildings and monuments melted back into the landscape within a few centuries and had to be rebuilt, usually on top of the remains of the old buildings. Old stonework was often recycled and incorporated into new buildings, often miles away. And, understandably, very few papyri survived burial in the

Delta's soggy mud. Nobody wanted to spend lots of money just to trace the foundation outlines of dissolved mud-brick houses.

Consequentially, until recent decades, very little archaeological excavation had taken place in the eastern Nile delta. All the really exciting stuff was in the desert far to the south. Worse yet, for most of the last century the area has been the stage for a series of wars, both WWI & II, and then the Arab-Israeli conflicts. Despite all the Indian Jones films you've seen, most archaeologists try really hard to avoid getting shot.

Therefore, for many years critics of the Bible were able to claim that we had no evidence that the Hebrews were even in the Nile Delta during that period. As Kitchen points out,[48] this was perfectly true, mostly because there was no evidence of much of anything at all from that period of the Nile Delta. However, a couple of developments have prompted new research.

First, when Israel seized the Sinai for a while in the 1970s they began a systematic program of excavations tentatively identifying ancient sites mentioned in the Bible.

Second, the relative peace between Egypt and Israel for the last few decades has allowed those excavations to continue. However, since this is now under the control of the Egyptian government, it places some practical restrictions on what the local researchers actually say. When you see an Egyptian archaeologist speaking on a PBS program, remember that if he ever said anything to support the idea that an Exodus actually occurred, he would probably lose his job, if not his life. (While Islam in theory accepts the Exodus, the gun-toting Radical Islamists, especially the Palestinians, have been working hard to deny it.)

THE LAND OF GOSHEN, THE LAND OF RAMESES: The land of Goshen is a triangle of all the grassy plain between the northern half of the Delta and the Suez trough. Its grassland's water comes

---

48. p. 246.

Figure 10.1

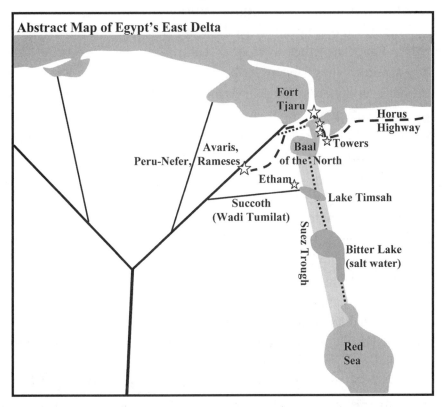

Abstract Map of Egypt's East Delta

from nightly dews swept off the humid Delta by evening breezes, and seasonal rains off the Mediterranean. The land is fertile, and produces good crops when canals bring water to it. This open landscape is the only significant grassland near the Egyptian Delta.

In contrast, all the rest of Egypt was the land of the river. Given its narrowly defined limits, the Egyptians had thoroughly tamed the inner Delta. Virtually every inch was surveyed and plotted; circular fields crowded in honeycomb fashion over every square foot (with the exception of each field's six corners, which were allowed to grow wild and support birds and small game for the dinner table.)

The only significant wild threats remaining were those of the river—the crocodile and the hippopotamus. The few remaining lions had been largely exiled to the Upper Nile, where they could steal down to the river to drink and hunt at night, and then return to the desert to hide from human hunters during the day.

This affected Egyptian attitudes toward herding cultures in general. In Egypt, livestock was not just allowed to wander—otherwise they would trespass on a neighbor's land and incur both wrath and fines. But, shepherds? Shepherds just let their flocks wander all over the place, eating whatever was in their path. Furthermore, given the ready access to water, Egyptians usually bathed at least once every day. But, stinking shepherds? Egyptians doubted that shepherds ever took a bath.

Not only that, Egyptians were civilized and didn't generally walk around their neighborhoods brandishing a weapon. While shepherds? Shepherds had to deal with lions and raiding thieves all the time, and therefore were famous for walking around armed to the teeth and spoiling for a fight.

All in all, Egyptians of all eras have viewed Goshen's shepherds as uncivilized louts. So, while to the Egyptians this borderland "beyond the river" was marginal at best, to the Hebrew shepherds, this was "the very best of the land."

Notice that Genesis uses the phrases *land of Goshen* and *land of Rameses* interchangeably. Occasionally, we find phrases like this intended to update the names in both Genesis and Exodus. At the time of the final edit of the Law, this area was called the land of Rameses. However, Rameses the Great gave his name to Goshen centuries after the time of Joseph.

Archaeologists searched for many years for the ancient Hyksos city of Avaris, the center of the Hyksos civil service.

> The name (also spelled Auaris) originates from Egyptian Hatwaret, specifying an administrative capital (cf. Hawara at the entrance to the Faiyum). Avaris is the city where in the times of the Middle Kingdom the main settlements of the Habiru in Egypt were situated (the biblical Goshen).[49]

49.http://www.history-book.net/?e=1064.

Eventually, they thought they had located that city, based on marks on brickwork found at Tanis. (Remember *Raiders of the Lost Ark*? "The Nazis have found Tanis!"—cue ominous music.) However, at that site they were unable to come up with any useful information on even the Hyksos, let alone the Hebrews.

However, just a few years ago, they found a new site and discovered that the bricks they had found at Tanis had simply been mined from the old capital and used in a new location. Ancient Avaris turns out to have been located about fifteen miles south of Tanis on what was then the eastern bank of the easternmost branch of the Nile. This placed the ancient Hyksos civil service capital at the center, western edge of Goshen.

Interestingly enough, one of the prominent features of the oldest levels of Avaris is its many gigantic granaries—enough granaries to suggest that Avaris served as a grain distribution point for all of Egypt. (Hmm, what does this remind us of?) Also, within the first couple of years at the site archaeologists found evidence of a New Kingdom Eighteenth-Dynasty palace:

> Ahmose I, (Moonborn) the founder of the Eighteenth
> Dynasty, captured Avaris just before the Hyksos were fi-
> nally expelled from Egypt, after a water-borne siege. The
> Hyksos capital was razed to the ground in the aftermath
> of the Egyptian triumph. Soon after, however, a palace
> compound was constructed in the early 18th Dynasty. It
> consisted partly of mud bricks from the Hyksos citadel
> and seems to have functioned as a royal residence.[50]

Soon after this, Avaris disappeared from Egyptian written records. Archaeologists assumed the site had been abandoned, but Manfred Bietak, the archaeologist in charge of the current Avaris project, asserts it was just renamed.

> After the conquest of Avaris, the 18th Dynasty Kings
> immediately started to construct military camps and

---

50. http://www.history-book.net/?e=1064.

storage facilities for troops. . . . The Excavations of cemeteries of soldiers show that Nubian Kerma people were stationed there, probably many of them archers. Specific burials reveal that military discipline was enforced obviously by executions and grim execration rituals. . . . this site should be identified with the naval and military stronghold of Peru-nefer, hitherto localized at Memphis.[51]

Next to the old Avaris summer palace, which his aunt/stepmother, the Pharaoh/Queen Hatshepsut, had abandoned twenty years earlier, Thutmose III built this harbor for up to three hundred boats and facilities to receive goods and foreign dignitaries, which he named Peru-nefer, "Happy Journey," or "Bon Voyage." Given the location, Thutmose III most likely built Peru-nefer using "Hyksos/Asiatic" brick-making slaves, diverted from the ongoing fortification of Tjaru directly down-river, overseen by a demonstratively harsh Nubian military force, also probably drawn from Tjaru.

This marina figures prominently in Egyptian records, and was well known except for its lost location. Thutmose III turned the last stages of the project over to his teenage son, Amenhotep II, who remained strongly associated with the site for the rest of his life.

Bietak also adds, "South of the palace a whole town started to spread out. This was abandoned entirely after Amenhotep II."[52]

Significantly, many conservative Christians have traditionally identified this pharaoh as the pharaoh of the Exodus. After the sudden, unexplained death of both Amenhotep II and his heir in 1400, Peru-nefer is abandoned. For one-hundred-twenty years, palace, fortress, and town lay deserted melting into the landscape. This may prove a fitting epitaph to what may be the Egyptian side of the Exodus story.

---

51. Bietak; 2006, http://www.deltasinai.com/uwsegyptfort/speakers.htm.
52. Ibid.

However, the identification of Peru-Nefer as Avaris is a quite recent proposal; we should probably give the archaeologists a few years to squabble over it before we lean on it too heavily. Never the less, since this has apparently held up to debate well so far, it has huge implications. Peru-nefer was a major port and the base of diplomatic embassies for the early Eighteenth Dynasty. Until now, scholars had always thought it to have been located many miles further south at Memphis, far from the land of Goshen.

Before deciding that Avaris was the site of Peru-nefer, archaeologists had already established that Avaris was also the site of the Rameses the Bible identifies as the starting point of the Exodus.

> The removal of the monuments of Pi-Ramesses to Tanis led early archaeologists to erroneously identify Tanis as the site of Pi-Ramesses . . . However, more recent and thorough excavations . . . have identified the true site of both the Hyksos capital Avaris and the Ramesside capital Pi-Ramesses. . . . The discoveries here include the foundations of palace buildings, temples, arsenals, storehouses, and tombs. Pi-Ramesses was spread over a vast area of about 18 square kilometers. . . . This makes it one of the largest cities of ancient Egypt, (Biblical Ramses).[53]

A new dynasty had arisen in Egypt, and Rameses the Great was not concerned about a 120-year-old curse on the previous dynasty. He chose the deserted site for his new capital and expanded it northward, renaming it again after himself. However, a few years after he died the Egyptians finally abandoned the site for good when the river shifted course.

So, when the Bible says the Hebrews leave from the city of Rameses, this means either that Rameses was the pharaoh of the Exodus, or he was the pharaoh when the Book of the Law went through its final edit sometime during the early book of Judges.

---

53. http://en.wikipedia.rog/wiki/Avaris, accessed December 12, 2009.

SUCCOTH: A seasonal canal connected the Nile River to the Suez Trough. This canal follows the route of a naturally occurring stream, today called Wadi Tumilat. If you picture the V of the Nile Delta, Wadi Tumilat is a narrow finger that juts straight east (more or less) from the middle of the eastern leg of the V.

This shallow, fertile valley cuts right through the south end of the land of Goshen about ten miles south of Avaris and empties into the largest continually freshwater lake in the Suez trough, Lake Timsah, about ten miles north of Bitter Lake. Archaeologists have confidently identified Wadi Tumilat as the Succoth the Bible identifies as the place where the fleeing Hebrews first gathered.

Any mass exodus from the land of Goshen would naturally flow into the valley of Wadi Tumilat, taking them down slope toward the freshwater Lake Timsah and the marshy edge of the Suez trough. This offered a chance to stock up on drinkable water before striking into the wilderness (assuming they could find a way across the marshes and canals).

Archaeologists still debate which of the garrisons/towns along Wadi Tumilat actually is the specific Succoth mentioned in the Bible. However, for the purposes of the story, it doesn't make much difference. Since Wadi Tumilat was a waterway into the Delta, it was fortified with several garrisons, especially at its eastern end.

No matter what plans Moses would try to make, this is where the scattered populous of Goshen would naturally congregate, especially after plundering the eastern delta. They would want to go the opposite direction of Pharaoh's army.

SIX HUNDRED THOUSAND ON FOOT THAT WERE MEN: Here we have an area where we may need to revise our traditional understanding of the Bible. In Exodus 12:37 we read, "The Hebrews journeyed from Rameses to Succoth. There were about six hundred thousand men on foot, besides women and children." Adding in the women and children inflates the number involved in the Exodus to about two million people. If you have ever considered this story, you know the problems inherent in that number, not the least of which is "how on earth did the Hebrew women have that many babies in that much time?" Our problem may stem from a misunderstanding of the word the KJV translates as thousand:

> In Hebrew, as in English (and elsewhere), words that look alike can be confused when found without a clear context. . . . The same applies to the word(s) *lp* in Hebrew. (1) we have *'eleph*, "thousand," . . . (2) there is *'eleph* for a group—be it a clan/family, a (military) squad . . . And (3) there is *'lp*, a leader, chief, or officer, giving *'alluph* . . . So the question has been asked by many: Are not the "six hundred three thousand five hundred fifty people" in such passages as Num. 2:32 actually 603 families/squads/clans, or leaders with 550 members or squads commanded . . . 20,000 early Hebrews.[54]

Again, in the context of the story, twenty thousand makes much more sense than two million. This would answer many of the objections of those who insist that the Sinai Peninsula could never physically hold such a hoard plus their flocks, with or without manna and miraculous supplies of water; the fire marshal would never allow it.

This also enhances the story's message. If as a child you heard the traditional rendition, you may have found yourself thinking, "What a bunch of cry-baby cowards! Two million of them and they still jump at every shadow." By better understanding what the Bible says, we can see why the Hebrews would be so terrified of Pharaoh's six hundred chariots. Facing that kind of threat, you and I probably would have been right up there with the elders, screaming "We're all gonna die! We're all gonna die!" Real faith and courage trusts in the face of real dangers.

---

54. Kitchen, pp. 264–265.

THE WAY OF THE LAND OF THE PHILISTINES: The Horus (Hawk) Highway was the only passable roadway east out of Egypt. We now know that the Horus Highway actually went as far south as Avaris, since archaeologists have uncovered a massive collection of stables for (so far) well over 400 horses, despite the city's location in the middle of an intricate network of marshes and canals. This lends plausibility to the Bible's reference to Pharaoh's 600 chariots, something critics had scoffed at in the past.

From there the highway swung northeast into Goshen's relatively higher ground, proceeded north up the western side of Goshen, and just south of the Mediterranean shore crossed a bridge over an eastward flowing branch/canal off the Nile. It then followed that canal eastward to wind its way through a series of interconnected lakes, bridges and fortresses before heading northeast into what later came to be called the Land of the Philistines in the time of the early Judges of Israel.

Since we now know that "The Way of the Philistines" literally began at the Hebrews' front doorstep, this slightly changes how we interpret the rest of the verse. The Bible says God avoided leading them that way "Lest perhaps the people change their minds when they see war and return to Egypt." This may have been referring to war with Pharaoh and not with the Canaanites.

Remember, all Pharaoh had ever agreed to was for them to "go three days journey into the wilderness and sacrifice to the Lord." Pharaoh himself had qualified this with "not very far away." (Exodus 8:27-28) If the people had taken the Horus Highway right off, bolting for the only door out of Egypt, all deals would have been off, and Pharaoh would have reacted instantly, plagues or no plagues.

Now you might wonder, "So what? God could just zap 'em in some other way." However, the problem would not be Pharaoh; it would be the Hebrew slaves. At the first hint of war chariots, they would have likely all scattered and fled back to their compounds, to pretend they had never left in the first place.

THE WILDERNESS OF THE RED SEA: A few miles east of the Delta, on the other side of the grasslands of Goshen, a low marshy trough runs north and south between the Mediterranean Sea and the Gulf of Suez at the northern tip of the Red Sea. In 1869, the famous Suez Canal was opened, draining a trickle of salt water from both the north and south into a great salt lake below sea level in the middle, called Bitter Lake, at a carefully controlled pace to balance the water lost to evaporation. The process of digging that canal gave us our basic information about the wilderness of the Red Sea.

In digging the canal between Bitter Lake and the Gulf of Suez in the south, they found the remains of a similar canal dating back to the Twelfth Dynasty, in the mid-1800s BC, long before the time of the Exodus. Then they found that from Bitter Lake in the center, another canal went directly north to connect with Lake Timsah and then directly east through the seasonal Wadi Tumilat canal to connect with the Nile during flood season.

Thus, water commerce could flow north from the Indian Ocean, be drawn or poled on up to the Nile, and then flow back down to the Mediterranean Sea, giving Egypt a lucrative monopoly on water traffic between the two seas.

Likewise, from Bitter Lake, the modern Suez Canal cuts north and slightly west to intersect the alternately saltwater and freshwater estuaries of the northeastern corner of the Nile Delta. In the process, the canal drained a series of freshwater lakes along its route. And, as they dug between those lakes, they discovered other ancient canals linking those lakes to the Mediterranean Sea.

According to Hoffmeier, this northern system of lakes and canals may actually themselves have joined to Lake Timsah[55] and thus on to Bitter Land and on to the Suez Gulf on the Red Sea. The canal system itself meandered through broad marshes and served as a barrier to discourage invaders from the east. The logistics of moving thousands of civilians across this barrier would have been a nightmare.

55. p. 260.

Furthermore, recent findings have called into question the traditional understanding of the crossing of the Red Sea. In the Hebrew Bible, the story is the crossing of the *Suf* (Reed) *Sea*. However, the Greek translation of the Bible made a couple of centuries before Christ translated this as the Red Sea, and this translation stuck. Actually, the Hebrew Bible would more likely have been referring to any of the reed-filled lakes of the Suez trough.

Unfortunately, this information came out at about the same time that the JED-P crowd was on the upswing. So, most evangelicals, including me, continued to resist this, thinking it was just another attempt to trivialize the Bible. Our sarcastic response was usually, "Look, another miracle! All Pharaoh's soldiers and horses decide to lie down and drown themselves in three feet of water!"

However, the Bible clearly names a series of locations to identify the specific site of the crossing. In the surge of archaeological data gathered in the last generation, evidence has begun to mount identifying some of these locations and narrowing the options for the crossing. The data and logic involved is much too complex for me to go into here; however, suffice it to say, I have been reluctantly pried away, kicking and clawing, into the Suez trough away from the traditional Red Sea locations.

ETHAM: As of now, the specific place called Etham, where they first camped, is still under debate; however, majority opinion feels it had to be close to one of two lakes: most likely the freshwater lake at the eastern end of Wadi Tumilat, Lake Timsah. Note that this location perfectly fits the agreement with Pharaoh. They have indeed gone "three days into the wilderness," at a location "not very far away." Now all that remains for them to keep their agreement is to make those sacrifices, and then turn around and come back to work making bricks.

TURN: However, once Moses has all the Hebrews in one place, he can establish some kind of order. The Bible says in Exodus 14:1, after they take on water, God tells Moses to "Speak unto the children of Israel, that they *turn* and encamp before Pi-hahiroth," Tradition viewed this as a simple instruction to turn south and head for the Red Sea—a logical and obvious course of action.

However the word for turn used here is (Strong's) |7725| *shuwb* "to turn back . . . not necessarily with the idea of return to the starting point." But, turning back would be such an illogical, if not downright stupid course that the KJV translators figured that could not possibly be the correct translation. After all, the Red Sea was in the other direction. Certainly, if the gathering bands of Hebrews had gotten such a command earlier as a secondhand message, nobody would have believed it. "You've got to be kidding! God couldn't possibly have said anything so dumb. You must have misunderstood."

So, God waits until they are all gathered and confronted by Moses and the scary cloud to give the command to turn back and bolt for the north along the west edge of the Suez trough. The mob has no choice but to obey. Reluctantly, they follow Moses north towards what was then one of Egypt's most heavily fortified zones. Taking this route forces the mob to stay together. They have the barrier of the marsh on their right, nobody would want to stray to the left, lest soldiers on the Horus Highway spot them, and the very timidity that poses such a problem in the first place would keep anyone from wanting to lag behind. You can just see them scurrying north, getting more nervous with every step, chanting, "Chariots and soldiers and arrows, oh my!"

Furthermore, by taking off north from this location instead of Peru-Nefer they give themselves at least one full day's headstart. Before Pharaoh can respond, someone has to gallop back to Peru-nefer and tattle. When Pharaoh does finally get word, we now know that Pharaoh's "six hundred chosen chariots, and all the chariots of Egypt" (Exodus 14:7) were already poised and ready to go at the head of the Horus Highway. Their natural assumption would be that the Hebrews would attempt to cross the Horus Highway bridge across the canal near the Mediterranean. Pharaoh races to "head them off at the pass." When the passage says that Pharaoh "pursued after" this would indicate that while the Hebrews fled along the east side of Goshen's ridge, Pharaoh parallels their flight using the Horus Highway on the west side of that same ridge.

PI-HAHIROTH: From this location's name, Pi-hahiroth—the Mouth of the Canal, or simply the Canal[56]—and the Bible's description of the site, we would need to look for some cul-de-sac abutting where a canal joins a lake, not the Red Sea. We have already mentioned that a small branch of the Nile shot eastward in the far north. Satellite imagery has shown that a major canal augmented it and fed its waters into the eastern lobe of the El Ballah Lake system.[57] On its way, it paralleled the northern edge of a western lobe of the El Ballah Lake.

Now, Pharaoh expects that the Hebrews intend to bear left when they get to the canal, cross the Horus Highway bridge, destroy it once they pass over it, and further delay the pursuit. Instead, Moses bears to the right, turning his back on the bridge and heads into the cul-de-sac between the canal and the lake. This delights Pharaoh; who thinks, "They are bewildered by the land: the wilderness has closed them in." So, he turns his army off the highway and follows them into the dead-end corridor, blocking off all reasonable chance of escape.

Over the years, many have insisted that in this story Moses actually lies to Pharaoh. The deal with Pharaoh was to go into the wilderness, make sacrifices, and then return. However, notice here that the Hebrews have still technically kept their end of the agreement. They did not go over the bridge. They are indeed still in the wilderness of the Red Sea, not very far away, where they said they would be. However, Pharaoh, by leading his army on the attack down the corridor has now breached the agreement himself, making it null and void.

56. Hoffmeier, p 105
57. Ibid, p. 105

MIGDOL: A century earlier, after expelling the Hyksos, Ahmose I had settled comfortably in his new palace at Avaris. However, the following pharaohs, Thutmose I, II, and III, didn't feel quite so secure. They remembered that the fall of Fort Tjaru at the northernmost end of Goshen heralded the fall of the Hyksos, and visions of the same thing happening to them haunted their dreams. Therefore, the Thutmoses diverted much of the Avaris labor force (probably Hebrew) that had built the palace and set them to the century-long task of making bricks for a massive expansion of Fort Tjaru.

In recent years, archaeologists have finally discovered this long-looked-for Fort Tjaru. Here are some excerpts from a National Geographic News article on Fort Tjaru by Dan Morrison published on July 27, 2007:

> The largest known fortress from ancient Egypt's days of the pharaohs has been unearthed near the Suez Canal. . . . The massive fortress, discovered at a site called Tell-Huba, includes the graves of soldiers and horses and once featured a giant water-filled moat, scientists said. The discovery dates back to ancient Egypt's struggle to re-conquer the northern Sinai Peninsula from an occupying force known as the Hyksos . . . "The bones of humans and horses found in the area attest dramatically to the reality of such battles," said Zahi Hawass, director general of Egypt's Supreme Council for Antiquities (SCA) . . . The fort dates from the 18th and 19th Dynasties (from 1560 to 1081 B.C.).
>
> Tjaru's mud brick walls were 42 feet (13 meters) thick, enclosing an area 546 yards (500 meters) by 273 yards (250 meters). Twenty-four watchtowers loomed over the parapets. A deep moat ringed the entire complex. It was the biggest in a chain of 11 fortresses that stretched from Suez to the present-day city of Rafah on Egypt's border with the Palestinian territories.

I hope you caught that part about the forty-two-foot-thick walls, and the twenty-four watchtowers. As of now, Fort Tjaru is considered the largest mud-brick structure up to that point in Egyptian history. Modern mud core surveys have established that in the early Eighteenth Dynasty the coast of the Mediterranean Sea lapped much further south from where it does now, bringing it up to within one-half-mile of Fort Tjaru, which sits on a low stone ridge that curved gently around the northwestern edge of the eastern lobes of the El-Ballah Lake.

The giant fortress guarded the point where the Horus Highway turned south and crossed over a bridge (or ferry) across the one-half-mile wide band of water that joined the western and eastern lobes of the El Ballah Lake system. Hoffmeier points out[58] that the south end of that bridge was guarded by a smaller, second section of Fort Tjaru that sat at the northern tip of a peninsula of higher ground. Apparently, the Egyptians considered this southern edifice the main Fort Tjaru despite its smaller size, since it contained parade grounds and review stands. In addition, it was here that travelers and goods crossed the main Egyptian border.

Proceeding south down the peninsula and then turning east around the lake, the Horus Highway after three miles passed by a second and third fortress, that Hoffmeier suggests[59] may have been the Migdol mentioned in Exodus.

From a vantage point on a cul-de-sac at the northeast edge of any of the western lobes of the lake one could look due east across a shallow, one-half-mile wide band of water. The massive twin fortresses of Tjaru would have been clearly visible only a mile or two to the north, on the other side of the canal/river. Furthermore, the third fortress would have loomed on the horizon a mile or two directly east. Even if it turns out that Hoffman is wrong, and none of these fortresses was specifically named Migdol (Towers), certainly the word "Towers" well described the area.

---

58. Hoffmeier, pp. 96-108
59. Ibid, p. 104

BAAL-ZEPHON: While the Bible names *Baal-Zephon* as the actual site of the crossing of the *Suf* Sea, it has not yet been definitely located. However, its name translates as "Baal of the North." Since it plainly lies within the boundaries of Egypt, we would naturally suppose the "north" mentioned here is the Egyptian's north—one more reason to favor the El-Ballah Lakes near the northern Fort Tjaru and not the Red Sea to the south as the site for the crossing of the *Suf* Sea.

Keep in mind that Baal was a Semitic god, not an Egyptian one. We would suspect that the name must date back to the time of the Semitic Hyksos of the northeastern delta. The southwestward turn of the Horus Highway after passing to the west of Fort Tjaru would serve as a logical place for weary Semitic merchants to stop at some Semitic temple to give thanks for surviving the journey and to pray for good prices for their goods. Interestingly enough, Hoffmeier sites an Egyptian document from that era that actually refers to one of the western lobes of El Ballah Lake as "The waters of Baal."[60]

Notice that here we have all three things the Bible mentions combine to make a cul-de-sac. A canal, "Pi-hahiroth," blocks their left side on the north, a lake associated with Baal blocks off their right side on the south, and they stand faceing a collection of towers, "Migdol," that loom over the east side of a one-half-mile wide strip of shallow sea, leaving Pharaoh snarling and snapping at their backsides.

Since the Exodus takes place in spring, the Nile waters would have been at their lowest ebb. Furthermore, the presence of a passageway between a canal and the lake implies that a ridge of slightly higher or more solid ground divided the two. Reasonably, we would expect that ridge to continue across the band of sea, creating shallower waters with more solid footing for a ford. The high east winds

---

60. Hoffmeier, p. 106

mentioned in the story could have easily blown water out El Ballah's northern channels into the Mediterranean Sea and dropped the water level to expose such a solid ridge extending to higher ground on the eastern side.

(In Cecil B. DeMille's movie, *The Ten Commandments*, we see magical, towering walls of water standing on both sides of the crossing, something suggested by the KJV translation of the story. However, the Bible's Hebrew just says the water formed "barriers" on both sides of the crossing, with no "walls" implied. Just think a minute; how suicidally stupid would an army have to have been to venture between the water-walls depicted in the movie?)

However, even given all of this, the story suggests a tidal wave off the Mediterranean hit at the right time to drown Pharaoh's army. The song of Miriam composed the next day celebrates "heaps" of

Figure 10.2

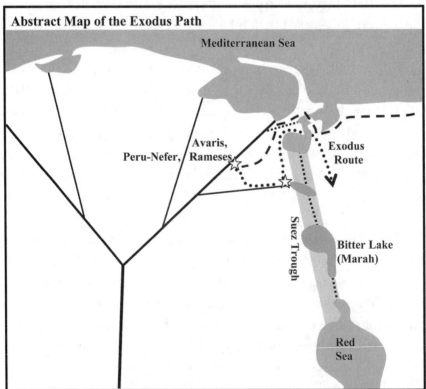

206

water [Exodus 15:8] that apparently caught Pharaoh's army by surprise and drowned every one of them. Given the local terrain, such a wave would rush in from both the north and northwest splitting around Fort Tjaru to spill into both the eastern and western lobes of the Suf Sea at the same time, slamming turbulently together at the narrow band in the middle. Furthermore, according to Jewish tradition, the force of that wave washed the debris of that army onto the shore at the foot of the Hebrews. This allowed them to plunder the bodies of the soldiers and arm themselves with better weapons than simple slings and staves.

(In fact, archaeology has recently found evidence of such a wave, which we will look at in the next chapter.)

SO HOW DEFINITE IS THIS? Notice that the titles of both the maps in this chapter contain the word "abstract." In reality, very little in the Egyptian delta follows neat and tidy lines like those that the maps indicate. Rivers squiggle like dying worms, and the lakes have convoluted shores like insane jigsaw puzzle pieces. Only man-made objects like canals and roads maintain straight lines and smooth curves. In particular, the western lobe of Lake El Ballah consisted of many jagged pieces, not the one compact body like the map presents. So far as I know, archaeologists haven't yet pulled up anywhere near enough core samples to determine where its many shorelines stood. And, even though we know for certain that a canal in the far north shot eastward from the Nile like the map suggests, we don't yet have any idea how many other canals did the same thing.

On my map I place the crossing at the extreme northern edge of the lakes. Kitchen does not like this position for the Suf Sea crossing. "We should not look any further north; otherwise we . . . would end up in an ancient Egyptian militarized zone."[61] However, perversely, that is exactly why I do like it. Moses heads for the single most stupid place he could possibly lead the fleeing Hebrews. This would

---

61. Kitchen, p. 260.

make the elders' famous exasperation with Moses' generalship quite understandable. In addition, the evidence for a New Kingdom tidal wave around Fort Tjaru came out in 2007, a few years after both Kitchen and Hoffmeier published their books. Factoring in a tidal wave off the Mediterranean would tend to push us further north.

Remember, in the story Moses deliberately baits Pharaoh. It's not as if he makes a stupid mistake and God says, "All right, dummy. Since you've got yourself in this pickle, I'll go ahead and part the waters for you and then drown Pharaoh's army." If you read the story, you see that God has already scheduled the waters to part at that very time and place. He has had Moses hurry up the crowd, even marching for some portion of the nights (Exodus 13:21), to make sure they are there before Pharaoh, in time to bait him into the scheduled death trap at the "Mouth of the Canal."

11

The Exodus Jigsaw Puzzle

The Revelation Days approach to the creation story has it play out in the Egyptian theater during the first week of the Exodus (goat's milk and crackers only, since soda and popcorn hadn't been invented yet), and it may have repeated weekly for some time after that to make sure everyone got the message.

In the last chapter, we looked at the geographic theater where the revelation of the creation story took place, a picture only now coming into focus after centuries of debate and eyestrain. However, in this chapter we will look at the ongoing debate about exactly when the Exodus story played out.

ASSEMBLING THE EXODUS JIGSAW PUZZLE: Dating the Exodus continues to be something like a small group putting together a very large jigsaw puzzle. Usually, one person begins by dumping the box on a cleared table, spreading out the pile of pieces, then turning pieces face up as fast as they can, exposing a myriad of unorganized details. Archeologists have been running all over the Middle East for the last couple of centuries doing just that.

Next, a couple of other people begin picking out edge pieces and assembling them into a frame—the outermost boundaries of the picture. By now, archaeology has done this. We know the outermost limits of when the Exodus could have happened. Some date it as early as the early date for the Minoan Eruption, about 1628 BC; some date it as late as sixty years before the first appearance of Hebrew stone houses in the hills of Palestine, about 1270 BC. Giving us an extreme range of about 353 years (?!).

Third, the puzzle-solving group settles into piling together pieces of similar shades, colors, and details. One person looks for the pieces with the blue flowers, the next person may look for pieces that have traces of a house of a particular color, while another looks for leaves of a certain shade against a certain shade of sky. For the last century, archaeologists have compiled hundreds of books with photos cataloging examples of types of pottery, styles of art, fire pit bone fragments, grave goods, and so on.

Occasionally, someone will carefully lift an assembly of five to ten pieces, and set it with more or less confidence somewhere inside the previously assembled framework, proclaiming, "There, I think, that house goes!" As time goes on, more and more assembled objects get placed in the framework, until they begin to crowd each other, taking up far too much space, covering areas that someone else declares absolutely must be the place for their jumping dog.

This is where Middle Eastern archaeology stands today—lots of very carefully assembled groups of details that don't quite make room for all the other groups of details. One archaeologist insists, "No, your treatise on the ash layer of Jericho absolutely must move back a bit," while another insists, "But that's absurd! If I move it back fifty years, then I lose that very clear connection with the pottery from such and such an era."

Eventually, the group begins shifting individual objects around, making clear connections to other objects, finding in the process that this or that object was misplaced or misassembled. Archaeology has just begun that process, but as of now it is far from finished.

And, we are a long way from that final stage where we connect all those tediously similar sky or ocean pieces and finish the puzzle. So, to finish off our puzzle metaphor, this chapter will simply list some of the key objects that now overlap and crowd into our time span for the Exodus.

Warning: While the following material is lots of fun, trying to bring order to it will most likely fry your brain. Believe me; I TRIED, and my ears are still smoking.

THE LITERARY STYLES OF THE INTERNAL DOCUMENTS: When Wellhausen published his documentary hypothesis, his big idea was to analyze the Old Testament as secular literature. He then proceeded to show how the different literary styles of the OT had evolved to give us our present Bible.

When he did this, we have to note that he made no comparisons with ancient documents from the time and no references to archaeological data. He just made the whole thing up. After all, he pointed out, there simply was no data to reference, and the logic of capable minds (i.e. anyone who agreed with him) was all that was needed.

But now, the situation is entirely different. Archaeology has turned up many volumes of documents from the time frames in question. We are now in a position to compare the OT to other works and see where it fits in.

K. A. Kitchen in 2003 published an excellent book, *On the Reliability of the Old Testament*. Hopefully, those of you with some background in college-level Middle Eastern history followed the advice at the beginning of this series and rushed out, bought a copy, and have already read through it twice by now.

However, since Kitchen's book is not light reading, most of you illiterate barbarians probably did no such thing. Never fear, we will try to summarize some of what Kitchen has to say in a few words, hopefully butchering it only a little bit.

Among the many things that Kitchen does in his book is to summarize the literary styles of the various historical periods and show how the Bible fits solidly into each of them

He points out that Genesis through Joshua contains a number of formal treaties, all with slightly different formats. Kitchen examines each of these formats and compares them to other legal documents from those periods of history:

> Thus in two thousand years ancient Near Eastern treaties passed through six different time phases, each with its own format of treaty or covenant; there can be no confusion (e.g.) of a treaty from the first phase with one the third phase, or of either with one from the fifth or sixth phases, or these with each other. Based on over ninety documents, the sequence is consistent, reliable, and securely dated. Within this fixed sequence biblical covenants and treaties equally find their proper places.[56]

Kitchen lays these all out for us to see in their proper order in great detail. (You *really, really should* read the book.)

Also, Kitchen points out a host of details in the patriarchal stories specific to the period from 2000 BC to 1500 BC, which he summarizes on pages 352–353. Kitchen concludes that the bulk of the material of the patriarchal stories had to predate 1600 BC (page 359). However, the materials probably were put together around the time of the Exodus, since some of the connecting narrative has explanatory material from that period. Then, a few centuries later, some transcriber did things like update some city names. (For example, the only reason to specify Ur of the Chaldees was to distinguish it

---

62. Kitchen, p. 4.

from other cities named Ur that didn't exist at the time of Abraham and yet did when the editor finalized the stories.)

Kitchen concludes:

> We are compelled, once and for all, to throw out Wellhausen's bold claim that the patriarchs were merely a glorified mirage of/from the Hebrew monarchy period. For such a view there is not a particle of supporting factual evidence . . . the main features of the patriarchal narratives either fit specifically into the first half of the second millennium (BC) or are consistent with such a dating. . . . In contrast, the old Wellhausen-type view is ruled out by the horde of contrary facts unearthed since 1878 and 1886. . . . The oft-stated claim of a "consensus" that the patriarchs never existed is itself a case of self-delusion, and . . . in fact a "con-nonsense-us".[57]

THE DEVELOPMENT OF A STABLE EGYPTIAN CHRONOLOGY: An important factor in dating Biblical events has been the establishment of clear dates for the reigns of all the Egyptian Pharaohs. Egyptian politics often impinged on Bible stories, and when it did we can then confidently (more or less) date that story. Until recently, this Egyptian chronology was settled with a margin of error of only about 20 years, depending on whether a particular lunar observation was taken at one latitude or another. These were called the high and low dates. However, evidence from geology has challenged this, and it remains to be seen what will remain when the volcanic dust settles.

THE MINOAN AND OTHER ERUPTIONS: The Minoan eruption on the island of Santorini, also called the Santorini eruption or the Thera eruption, had a huge impact on the eastern Mediterranean. Some have blamed this eruption for the fall of several ancient civilizations, including, eventually, the Minoans themselves. Others have tied this eruption to the myth of Atlantis.

---

63. pp. 371–372.

However, in the archaeological community, it became the focus of a huge debate. The problem was that both Egyptologists and geologists have quite confidently dated the eruption, each with convincing evidence. Unfortunately, the two dates disagreed initially by nearly 300 years, which has recently narrowed to about 125 years. And so, a battle royal has ensued for the last decade. The two sides may be beginning to come to a compromise involving speculation that the Minoan eruption may have actually have been a series of events spanning several centuries, but so far as I know, they still haven't agreed yet.

One of the interesting recent developments is the ongoing discovery of chunks of pumice lava from the Minoan eruption scattered around the northeastern Delta and many miles inland, along with evidence of tsunami damage up and down the coast. This has stirred quite a bit of excitement, since it would indicate that a tidal wave swept the material inland.

The debate centers on when it washed inland past Fort Tjaru. Some think it swept in at the time of the original eruption, placing it at about 1628 or 1500 BC, depending on whose dating system you pick. It either happened as the Hyksos came to power, or it happened as they were expelled from Egypt.

Most doubt that any wave from Santorini itself could actually sweep floating lava that far. (Deepwater waves go under floating objects and don't propel them forward.) Instead, they propose that ocean currents had deposited the lava on the Egyptian coast, and that a tsunami at a much later date swept the lightweight lava inland. In any case, the inland pumice offers evidence that at some time in the early to mid-Eighteenth Dynasty a tidal wave swept past Fort Tjaru and into El-Ballah Lake in northeastern Egypt.

Then, other factors have gotten tossed into the mix. In the same time frame, an even larger volcano has been found to have erupted in Alaska, possibly affecting the climate. While others claim that the Sinai Peninsula itself saw some volcanic eruptions. This means that throwing volcanism into the mix of visualizing the Bible stories is easier to do, but harder to date—for now.

THE NEW KINGDOM: With the fall of the Hyksos, the Egyptian Upper and Lower Kingdoms are united under the rule of Ahmose. So, although Ahmose is a direct continuation of the southern Seventeenth Dynasty, historians mark him as the founder of the Eighteenth Dynasty. With the Eighteenth Dynasty Egypt enters a "New Kingdom," an era of stability and prosperity in which they reach the peak of their civilization's power.

THE OLDEST ALPHABET: When Wellhausen presented his JED-P documentary hypothesis, he insisted the Law could not have been written until centuries after the time of Moses.[58] However, like virtually every other "fact" set forth by Wellhausen, this one too turned out to be completely false. In chapter two we mentioned that archaeology has established that the written Hebrew alphabet goes back to at least 1450 BC, with roots going back to at least 2,000 BC.

So, while the Law was written using literary structures that aided the process of memorization, and some Hebrew scholars did indeed memorize the entire Law, they did so off of written documents from the very beginning. There is NO evidence to support any "oral tradition."

THE SLAVERY QUESTION: In DeMille's movie, we see teams of slaves toiling under the lash to build Egypt's great monuments. However, recent studies have established that the Egyptians considered that kind of monument work a religious privilege. So, that work was done by relatively well cared-for, free artisans.

For a while much was made of the Egyptian distaste for slavery. Nevertheless, as Kitchen points out, the use of Middle Eastern slaves in private households is well documented, although Egyptian slaves did have it relatively easy compared to slaves in other nations.

---

64. Wellhausen, Chapter X.

The Egyptian public tended to frown on either cruelty or neglect. An Egyptian slave in a private household could generally count on not being unduly overworked, beaten, or starved.

However, in the New Kingdom from 1540–1170, we see troops of foreign slaves making bricks for the state. This would be an entirely different matter than household slaves. Social pressure to not appear cruel would have had no effect. For instance:

> In brick making, the most famous example comes from a scene in the tomb chapel of the vizier Rekhmire of circa 1450. I shows mainly foreign slaves "making bricks for the workshop-storeplaces, of the Temple of Amun at Karnak in Thebes" and for a building ramp. Here, labeled "captives brought-off by His Majesty for work at the Temple of [Amun]," hence serving as forced labor, Semites and Nubians fetch and mix mud and water, strike out bricks from brick molds, leaving them to dry and measuring off their amount. And all is done under the watchful eye of Egyptian overseers, each with his rod. As many have observed, it offers a vivid visual commentary on part of what one may read in Exod. 1:11–14 and 5:1–21. Close account was kept of number of bricks produced, and targets were set, as in the Louvre leather scroll, Year 5 of Ramesses II, 1275. The forty "stablemasters" (junior officers) of this document had each a target of 2,000 bricks, clearly to be made by men under them with group foremen. These officers fulfilled the role of the *noges'im*, "overseers," of Exod. 5:6.[65]

Probably, when the Hebrews each had to serve regular tours of duty on the brick-making force, they had off time to return home to deal with their households in compounds on the south side of Avaris. By allowing the Hebrews to retain families in the land of Goshen

---

65. Kitchen, p. 247–248.

and time to tend their own flocks, the Egyptians would have been freed from the need to feed, clothe, or even replace their slaves.

THE MEDJAY: You may have seen pictures of palace scenes in ancient Egypt with a preponderance of black-skinned guards wearing pharaoh-style headdresses. Those are Medjay.

The Medjay came from the nomadic Nubian tribes that occupied the hilly desert between the Nile and the Red Sea, seasonally migrating with their herds north and south. They had always enjoyed a reputation as fierce warriors, and were often a major thorn in the side of the Old and Middle Egyptian Kingdoms.

During the campaign to expel the Hyksos, Kamose, the last Pharaoh of the Seventeenth Dynasty, and the elder brother of Ahmose (the first Pharaoh of the Eighteenth Dynasty), enlisted the aid of a mercenary army of Medjay. Somehow either Kamose or his mother managed to forge a much more permanent bond with that army. So, after the death of Kamose, that Medjay army settled in Egypt permanently, becoming the personal bodyguard for the pharaoh, Ahmose I. In his late twenties, Ahmose uses this elite fighting force to take the key Hyksos fortress of Tjaru, winning the war.

That victory sealed the Medjay as Pharaoh's personal enforcement arm. From that point forward in Egypt, the very word for police officer was Medjay, whether the individual was Nubian or not. We see this referenced in the popular action-adventure *Mummy* movies. The fictional army with facial tattoos that fight against the evil mummy army call themselves Medjay.

One important thing to remember about the Medjay—after taking Fort Tjaru, that fortress becomes the Medjay's permanent base. Medjay troops man its walls, and Medjay troops supervise it and the land to the southwest of Fort Tjaru, an area the Bible calls "the Land of Goshen."

Also, when Thutmose III rebuilds Avaris as a major port—which he then renames Peru-Nefer—the fortress that guards it is also manned by Nubians, probably Medjay.

It is most reasonable to assume that the thousands of brick slaves employed to build both those fortresses would have been drawn from the local Goshen area. So, while the rest of Egypt's slave overseers were always Egyptians, very probably the taskmasters who actually beat on the Hebrews were black.

If the Medjay become famous for anything, it's for the thoroughness of their beatings, usually administered to offenders on the spot without the benefit of trial. Pictures from the time often show a victim lying face down on the ground while one Medjay sits on his hands, another sits on his feet, and a third uses a long rod to systematically bruise every inch of flesh from the shoulders to the calves. In fact, that waist-high rod became virtually the official emblem of the Medjay.

Furthermore, this all took place in an Egyptian fringe land, out of sight of the general Egyptian public. At this early date, the Medjay aren't really fully assimilated Egyptians yet, and don't particularly share the popular Egyptian distaste for cruelty.

This would go a long way toward explaining why Aaron and Miriam were so upset that Moses had taken a black wife in that incident in Numbers 12:1: "And Miriam and Aaron spake against Moses because of the Ethiopian woman whom he had married."

In the Bible, this story has something of a humorous ending. God strikes Miriam, Moses' elder sister, with temporary leprosy, bleaching her skin pure white, in effect saying, "You like white so much? Here, I'll give you white!"

THE PLAGUES: It is interesting to note that the first nine plagues of the book of Exodus are specifically Egyptian plagues. The plagues of Egypt all fit clearly documented events, all fitting clearly into the seasonal crops from July through April, interconnecting in a logical fashion from a too high a seasonal flood with the possible exception of the 10th plague.

What happened in the tenth plague if treated as at all historical would be regarded as a miracle by believers of any stripe, and as an exaggeration or 'strange event' by nonbelievers of any kind; but it cannot be used to prejudge the preceding nine plagues—they are too closely tied to tangible realities to permit any such pranks.[66]

What this means is that the Exodus story is an authentic Egyptian story, since it contains details whose natural sequence a foreigner wouldn't know. Furthermore, if it was concocted by a native Egyptian, it would have required someone with a grasp of Egyptian physical and natural history far beyond normal education levels. As the proverb goes, "Ya couldn't make this stuff up."

Note the reference above to a "too high seasonal flood." The seasonal flood marked the beginning of summer, and the nature of that flood virtually determined what kind of year—feast or famine—Egypt would have. A too high flood was a rare but well-documented disaster. It stirred up so much mud that its waters would turn red, and the Egyptians would say the river "turned to blood":

> The Middle Kingdom work, Admonitions of an Egyptian Sage (its modern title), (which) describes Egypt's woes in a time of misery under an inept king, and remarks, "See, the River (Nile) is blood, one shrinks . . . and thirsts for water." So, such concepts—and phenomena—were not unknown to ancient Egypt.[67]

From the story it's clear that Pharaoh thinks it's all a trick. To Pharaoh, the annoying thing is that Moses and Aaron stand up in front of the court and pretend, he thinks, to call the plagues down as if on cue. When Moses turns the Nile into blood, certainly Pharaoh suspected that the sneaky Hebrews had spotted a high Nile making its way into the Delta and simply alerted Moses in time for Moses to stand there waving his rod dramatically and take the credit.

---

66. Kitchen, p. 250, cites G. Hort.
67. Kitchen, p. 250.

Next we have the plague of frogs. Moses knows that Pharaoh will think it's all a trick. So Moses has Pharaoh choose a time for the frogs to all die. "Ah-ha!" Pharaoh thinks, "Moses knows the frogs are all sick from the high Nile and will die at any moment. Here's my chance to mess up the show!" Possibly prompted by one of the more clever magicians, Pharaoh doesn't say, "Right now!" Instead he says, "Tomorrow!" giving us the comic line, "One more night with the Frogs! Croak!"[68]

As the plagues progress, in the story we see Pharaoh always more than half convinced that he's simply being outsmarted by his step-uncle. Yet, his confidence gets shakier and shakier as matters progress. After all, the plagues are all natural and previously well-known events, even up to and including the volcanic ash fall and fiery hail. But how on earth is Moses getting ahead of each event in time to wave around his cursed rod?!

It isn't until the appearance of the fiery cloud, and the selective death of the firstborn—something without any natural precedent—that we see Pharaoh capitulate. Even then, he suspects that he's simply being tricked. So, when he sees his enemies trapped and vulnerable, he absolutely must attack. Yet even then, he gets slammed by Moses' anticipation of another natural disaster. "How on earth did Moses know a strong east wind would come up right now and expose a land bridge?" You can just imagine Pharaoh's last thought was something along the lines of, "And how, by all the Gods of Egypt, did Moses know a tidal wave would come just now?!"

THE WORD HEBREW: Throughout Middle and New Kingdom history, we find references to "Habiri," and "'Apiru." In some contexts, these refer to Asiatic mercenary troops assigned to do particularly violent and nasty jobs, sort of like Special Forces. In other contexts they just refer to wandering bands outside normal society—homeless outcasts or hobos, either as bandits or as seasonal

---

68. "One More Night with the Frogs" ©Johnny Flanagan 1981.

laborers. We find this word also used in the same sense in Canaan through the same periods. Most think that the Hebrews took that name to themselves to emphasize their nomadic family history. The Bible simply uses the word but never explains it.

Those who identify the Hebrews with the Hyksos, like the PBS special, point at the similarity between that word and the name of the city Avaris, the old Hyksos capital, since the sounds of b and v are so similar. They take the word Hebrew to be the (Ha'-) Avaru; i.e. those from Avaris, "the official departments or wards." However, most linguists think this is far too much of a stretch.

On the other hand, the similarity of the words could reasonably give rise to a deliberate cross-language pun, using the Hebrew word for *wanders* as a euphemistic substitution for a possibly pejorative Egyptian word, 'Avaru, the despised "Warders."

THE AMARNA LETTERS: A store of cuneiform tablets written by Canaanite mayors to the current pharaoh was found in the ruins of Amarna, the brief capital of the famous "monotheistic" pharaoh, Akhenaten. Given the issues and events mentioned, the letters fall within a twenty-year window, stretching from Akhenaten's father to Akhenaten's son, the famous boy-king Tut. The most famous of these letters, EA 288, comes from a mayor/king of a Canaanite city who writes to complain about Pharaoh's refusal to help while Canaan is under attack from a hoard of 'Apiru.

> May the king give thought to his land; the land of the king is lost. All of it has attacked me. I am at war as far as the land of Seru and as far as Ginti-kirmil. All the mayors are at peace, but I am at war. I am treated like an 'Apiru, and I do not visit the king, my lord, since I am at war. I am situated like a ship in the midst of the sea. The strong hand (arm) of the king took the land of Nahrima-(Mittani), and the land of Kasi, but now the 'Apiru have taken the very cities of the king.[69]

---

69. http://en.wikipedia.org/wiki/Amarna_letters, accessed July 26, 2009

While this seems to be a fairly clear reference to the Hebrew (`Apiru`) conquest of Canaan under Joshua, most scholars refuse to concede this, since most believe that the Exodus took place under Rameses the Great, who won't be born for another sixty years yet. However, this letter still makes the imagination work overtime.

This letter also refers to the fact that both Eighteenth and Nineteenth Dynasty Egypt considered the land of Canaan as their personal property. If outsiders came in to plunder it, we would expect Egypt to react promptly. Yet, so far as we can tell, the pharaohs of this period ignored those pesky `Apiru`. (I wonder why.)

THE MERENPTAH STELE: About a century and a half after the Amarna letters, Pharaoh Merenptah, the successor to Rameses the Great, raided the area in 1210 BC and bragged about decimating Israel, noting it in a stone tablet monument called the

> Merenptah Stele, widely known as the Israel Stele, which makes reference to the supposed utter destruction of Israel in a campaign prior to his 5th year in Canaan: "Israel has been wiped out . . . its seed is no more." This is the first recognized ancient Egyptian record of the existence of Israel—"not as a country or city, but as a tribe" or people.[70]

This tells us that by 1210 BC, the Hebrews had already been established themselves as a recognized people/group in Canaan. And, they had already gained enough of a reputation that the pharaoh felt compelled to exaggerate based on winning (maybe) one battle.

THE HEBREW SETTLEMENT OF THE HILLS OF PALESTINE: Once the early Eighteenth Dynasty under Thutmose III had conquered Canaan and placed it under merciless taxation, its population steadily declined. Intense surveys of settlements from that pe-

---

70. http://en.wikipedia.org/wiki/Merenptah_Stele, accessed July 26, 2009.

riod show that the population steadily declined until by 1200 BC barely five thousand people remained in the hill country of Canaan. But then, virtually overnight the population suddenly jumped to more than five times that number. The pottery remains of this group at first matched that of the lowlands of Canaan, but soon shifted to something simpler. Also, unlike earlier Canaanites, these fire pits included no pig bones.[71] This clearly indicates that a new group had moved into the area *en masse*, and this new group initially obtained all their pottery from the natives.

This marker gives us the latest date for the conquest of Canaan mentioned in the book of Judges. The only question is how long did the Hebrews camp at Gilgal, huddled together for protection and living on tribute from the cowed Canaanites until they finally settled into stone homesteads in the hills? Estimates range from one generation to six generations, depending on who you identify as the pharaoh of the Exodus.

In this chapter we have looked at a dozen of the assembled objects that crowd our puzzle board. Together these have conclusively shown that Israel definitely began in a real, not a fictional, Egypt and definitely migrated as a group into Canaan. The old JED-P claim that the Exodus story was total fiction with no basis in fact has been conclusively squashed.

However, right now, we don't suffer from a lack of evidence of the Exodus; we suffer from too much evidence. We have too many choices, too many unconnected objects. In the next chapter we'll look at the three main attempts being made to match up the objects and give us a clear picture of the event that gave us the creation story.

---

71. Kitchen pp. 225–226.

12

Three Versions of the Exodus

The Trouble with Blind Dates

Two key Bible verses have traditionally directed us in dating Israel's sojourn in Egypt and the Exodus:

> Now the sojourning of the children of Israel, who dwelt in Egypt, was four hundred and thirty years. (Exodus 12:40)

> And it came to pass in the four hundred, and eightieth year after the children of Israel were come out of the land of Egypt, [that Solomon] began to build the house of the Lord . . . So was he seven years in building it. (1 Kings 6:1, 38)

Since archaeologists currently date the completion of Solomon's temple to 960 BC, a straightforward understanding of these verses would place the Exodus at 1440 BC and the entry into Egypt at about 1870 BC.

This of course immediately raises questions about the margins of error in this system. Recently, geologists have been giving Egyptologists some grief; however, this may not mean much here. We can discount the margin of error in Egyptian history back to the completion of Solomon's temple, since moving that date moves all the other dates and makes no difference to our discussion. Any disconnect between the date of Solomon's temple and the Egyptian markers would apparently be minor—a few years at the most.

Egyptologists express lots of confidence that their kings' lists leave room for only a small margin of error during that 480-year stretch between 1440 and 960 BC. Although, the stretch between 1870 and 1440 BC is a lot less secure. So, this of course requires us to have to have a measure of confidence that the Egyptologists have tied down the sequence of events in Egyptian history rather firmly. However, Egyptologists still have significant disagreements with both geologists and tree-ring dating experts about dating both eras. We would do best to simply sit back and let the titans fight this one out.

DATING JOSEPH'S FAMINE: Theologians have long disagreed about what the Bible means by the 430-year "sojourn in Egypt." For instance, one rabbinic traditional identified the entry into Egypt as not when Jacob showed up with his whole family to take advantage of Joseph's invitation. Instead, those rabbis dated it to the first time Abraham and Sarah stayed in Egypt a couple of hundred years earlier. They did this because of their belief that since Israel was Abraham's seed, they were therefore anywhere Abraham was at that time.

This is so alien to modern thought that I for one simply can't quite wrap my mind around it. However, if we examine that, then we find that Joseph's famine dates right at the geologist's magic date of 1628 and the Minoan eruption, which in turn would validate that the pharaoh of the famine was the Hyksos leader that came to directly dominate the entire eastern Delta, and economically dominate all of both the Lower and Upper Kingdoms.

So, I've shrugged my shoulders and gone with it. I may not understand it, but it fits. However, nothing says we absolutely must tie Joseph's famine with the Minoan eruption. I like it just because it makes for such a nice dramatic story.

DATING THE EXODUS: Currently three mainstream approaches to dating the Exodus dominate the field:

A—the early date: This view places the Exodus between 1546 and 1535 BC. The Hebrews don't serve *under* the Hyksos, they *are* the Hyksos, and Moses is the last great Hyksos general. In this view the Hebrews were never slaves in Egypt; they ruled Egypt. And Moses' "Let my people go!" is actually about avoiding having the surviving Hyksos being pressed into slavery, or cutting that period of slavery to only a few years.

The PBS special, "Exodus Decoded," takes this view. What makes this so popular is the discovery of volcanic ash and pumice around Fort Tjaru and westward into the Delta at about this period. Also Egyptian records speak of a mass Exodus of about 100,000 Hyksos after their defeat.

In this view, the Bible story is a bit of historical fiction. The broad details and big characters are historical; however, the story's drama is a fictional attempt to focus on that last spectacular escape, to hide the fact that their ancestors were actually refugees from a lost war.

B—the late date: In this view, the pharaoh of the Exodus is Rameses the Great, who ruled Egypt between 1279 and 1213 BC. This is the most popular view and even K. A. Kitchen in his book I've already recommended to you supports that view and does a good job of presenting its case. Given Kitchen's stature, I have to give this view very serious consideration.

Kitchen points to several factors that he feels require us to view Rameses the Great as the pharaoh of the Exodus.

First, and not least, Rameses the Great moved the Egyptian capital from the south down to the northern site of Aravis/Peru-Nefer, naming his new capital Rameses. When Rameses dies, the new pharaoh moves back south and abandons the site, which is then no longer called Rameses. Since this Rameses is obviously the city of Rameses referred to in the Bible, this would seem to make Rameses the Great the pharaoh of the Exodus.

Those who oppose the late view say that this just means that when the Law goes through its final edit early in the book of Judges, the city name of Aravis/Peru-nefer is updated to Rameses.

Second, Kitchen points out that material evidence of a Hebrew occupation of Canaan first appears around 1,200 BC, which would also fit making Rameses the pharaoh of the Exodus. Kitchen goes into great detail to establish that the Bible story does not have the Hebrews rush in and conquer Canaan. Instead, he documents that they simply raid a few cities to eliminate the Canaanites' defenses. The Hebrews then return to Gilgal and do not occupy the devastated cities or areas. In this, Kitchen expands on Judges 1:28 that states: "And it came to pass, when Israel was strong, that they put the Canaanites to tribute, and did not utterly drive them out."

Likely such tribute came in the form of just the kind of material culture that archaeologists look for, which would make the Hebrews look Canaanite in the material record. Kitchen does all this to buy twenty years to further support Rameses as the pharaoh of the Exodus.

(Here his position is much stronger that the traditional view I support, since the traditional position needs to add in another century of the Hebrews living off the Canaanites before they settle down, build actual houses of stone, and start providing for themselves.)

One problem with the late Exodus view is the fact that it is a minimum of 120 years later than what seems to be indicated by 1 Kings 6:1. Kitchen does have an explanation for this:

> The 480 years may have in fact one of two origins. First, it could be an era date made up of twelve 40-year "full generations," such that 12 x 40 = 480; . . . In the ancient Near East . . . such procedures were almost cer-

tainly in use. . . . Or else, second, the 480 years are in fact a selection from . . . years aggregate.[72]

Kitchen means here that the scribes would look at the many official genealogies, average them, count the number of ancestors, and then multiply by twenty. A "full generation" refers to the average age a man could expect to be when his eldest grandson was born—forty years old. He goes on to document this dating scheme in other cultures in the Middle East, and then gives a series of examples in the Bible where eras are marked off in tidy multiples of twenty years. If we accept this, then we would have to accept that the average age a typical Hebrew had his first son was more like 14 than 20. On one hand this tends to raise our eyebrows a bit. On the other hand, I have to concede that Romeo was 15 and Juliet was 13.

His second possibility, which he doesn't particularly like, is that often the years of parallel rulers are calculated "in aggregate." For example, X rules one area from 1050 to 1010—forty years. Meanwhile, Y rules a neighboring area from 1040 to 1000—another forty years. We would say they each ruled forty years, or they ruled for fifty years (1050 to 1000). However, an aggregate calculation would say the two of them ruled for eighty years. He gives examples from surrounding cultures that did just that.

This is like a TV commercial that says, "Our Company has 25 years of combined experience!" Of course this just means that their 50 employees have only been doing this for six months. I get the impression that Kitchen would accept this only if he had to.

However, to me, the main problem is that the reign of Rameses the Great is one of the better documented periods of Egyptian history. And the story of the Hebrews' Exodus simply doesn't figure in it at all. Minor details may dovetail with the Exodus, but the ties are, at this time, weak. Even allowing for Pharaoh's censorship, we would expect to see more parallels in the record.

---

72. p. 307.

Kitchen would, of course, answer this with his famous dictum, "Absence of evidence is not evidence of absence." Which means that just because we haven't found evidence yet, it doesn't prove anything.

Finally, what we know about Rameses the Great doesn't make him quite stupid or villainous enough to be the pharaoh of the Exodus. Granted, this isn't *evidence*. But if you look at the overall story, it would certainly make you wonder, set you to looking for other options.

Kitchen is writing as an archaeologist first and a Bible scholar second. Given the nature of his target audience, both by circumstance and character, he cannot allow himself to speculate on other choices that lack material evidence.

C—the traditional date: Given my track record so far in this book, you may be surprised to see me come down on the side of tradition, especially given the fact that the physical evidence all seems to hover just before and just after that date.

It reminds me of when I once woke up from a blow to the head, only to find some annoying person wagging a pair of blurry fingers in front of my face asking me to count them. After a few confused moments, the blurry pair of fingers resolved into one clear finger halfway between the blurry originals.

Also, both the early and late dates have one glaring deficiency—they seem to make no allowance for the *story*. The glory of the Exodus story lies in its rich characters. There is an internal consistency to all the people that only a historical event could provide. And, everything they do seems to me to make sense only in the context of the traditional view. If we go with the traditional date, we find people and a rhythm of events in the historical record that very neatly fit the story.

In any case, I have no particular scholarly reputation to uphold. And the phrase, "could be," doesn't make me shudder, as long as I stay within the boundaries of the facts I happen to think I know. And, if it turns out I missed the target, I can just say, "Oh, well," and move on. It's actually lots of fun.

A STORY THAT FITS

The traditional view ties the life of Moses to the mid Eighteenth Dynasty. To help you visualize that, take a moment to look at the timeline below. Note that this also provides some translations of the Egyptian names. On one hand, this may make things more complicated. On the other hand, I hope it helps you visualize the story.

PHARAOH'S DAUGHTER: This then brings us to consider "Pharaoh's daughter." This is a formal title applied to whichever female currently carried the ancient bloodline, regardless of her age. Her father could be dead and she the reigning queen of Egypt and she would remain Pharaoh's daughter until she had a daughter of her own reach puberty and qualify to carry on the bloodline.

The Egyptians at this time used a matrilineal inheritance system, on the theory that no matter what question you raised about the identity of a child's father, you always knew who the mother was. To be Pharaoh you had to marry Pharaoh's daughter. If a pharaoh had a son by a wife "not of the blood" that he wanted to inherit the throne, then that son *had* to marry his own sister, Pharaoh's daughter, to make him legitimate.

If the current pharaoh had no son, then Pharaoh's daughter could marry some worthy noble instead, bringing much-needed fresh genes into the pool every few generations. Understandably, after thousands of years of incest, the pharaohs often suffered from bad health and died young.

You need to understand this to understand the situation of the story's "Pharaoh's daughter." Her name is Hatshepsut, the "Lady Noblest," and she is the reigning queen of Egypt. Her father was not of the royal blood, since her grandfather, Amenhotep ("Windpeace"), had died sonless. Since she had no brothers of the blood, she has been raised with the finest education available in the ancient world, groomed to be pharaoh in her own right, since only she bore the divine bloodline.

Timeline of the Early 18th Dynasty of Egypt (standard chronology)

Key: rYear = year regency begins   dYear = year of death   f. = female

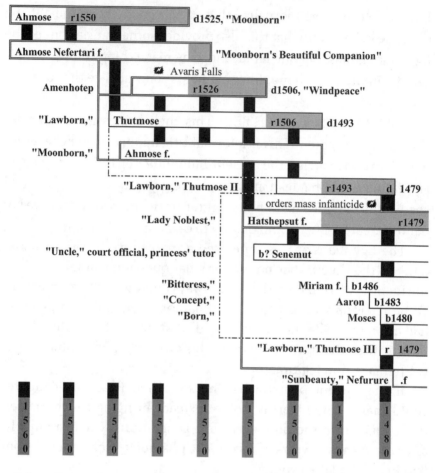

Ahmose   r1550   d1525, "Moonborn"

Ahmose Nefertari f.   "Moonborn's Beautiful Companion"

Avaris Falls

Amenhotep   r1526   d1506, "Windpeace"

"Lawborn,"   Thutmose   r1506   d1493

"Moonborn,"   Ahmose f.

"Lawborn," Thutmose II   r1493   d 1479

orders mass infanticide

"Lady Noblest,"   Hatshepsut f.   r1479

"Uncle," court official, princess' tutor   b? Senemut

"Bitteress,"   Miriam f.   b1486

"Concept,"   Aaron   b1483

"Born,"   Moses   b1480

"Lawborn," Thutmose III   r   1479

"Sunbeauty," Nefurure   .f

1 5 6 0   1 5 5 0   1 5 4 0   1 5 3 0   1 5 2 0   1 5 1 0   1 5 0 0   1 4 9 0   1 4 8 0

Gods used in Royal Names:

Aah   = The moon god, in charge of natural law and order

Amun = The god of air, in charge of breathing, life, wind, and eventually fertility

Ra   = The sun god in charge of creation, death, and resurrection

Thoth = The ibis headed god of social law, associated with the moon god.

Timeline of the Exodus (standard Egyptian chronology)

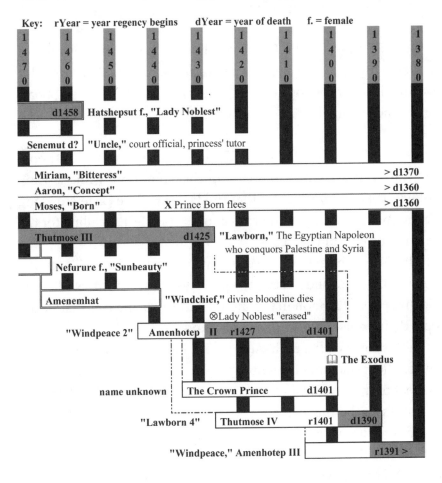

Key: rYear = year regency begins   dYear = year of death   f. = female

| 1 4 7 0 | 1 4 6 0 | 1 4 5 0 | 1 4 4 0 | 1 4 3 0 | 1 4 2 0 | 1 4 1 0 | 1 4 0 0 | 1 3 9 0 | 1 3 8 0 |

d1458 | Hatshepsut f., "Lady Noblest"

Senemut d? | "Uncle," court official, princess' tutor

Miriam, "Bitteress"   > d1370

Aaron, "Concept"   > d1360

Moses, "Born"   X Prince Born flees   > d1360

Thutmose III   d1425   "Lawborn," The Egyptian Napoleon
who conquors Palestine and Syria

Nefurure f., "Sunbeauty"

Amenemhat   "Windchief," divine bloodline dies
⊗Lady Noblest "erased"

"Windpeace 2" | Amenhotep II   r1427   d1401

📖 The Exodus

name unknown | The Crown Prince   d1401

"Lawborn 4" | Thutmose IV   r1401   d1390

"Windpeace," Amenhotep III | r1391 >

233

However, when her father, Thutmose ("Lawborn"), faces death, he marries her to Lawborn II, his only son by a low-level concubine. The boy is sickly but had unexpectedly lived long enough to reach puberty. So, the Lady Noblest finds herself married to her barely pubescent, sickly, and not very bright younger stepbrother.

However, in the eyes of Egypt, the Lady Noblest is the focus of the Egyptian worship of the divine bloodline. This bloodline alone had the right to approach the gods in the myriad of religious ceremonies that defined Egyptian life.

THE SETTING: The Egyptian capital has moved south out of the Delta; however, the pleasure palace at the ruins of Avaris is still a favorite place for the royal family to escape the summer heat, boating around its canals.

THE INFANTICIDE DECREE: As Lawborn II nears adulthood, his health doesn't much improve. In this condition, while visiting the Avaris palace, he decides that the Hebrew slave caste crowding around Avaris is far too numerous and issues a decree calling for the mass infanticide of the males.

This is not the act of a towering tyrant; instead, it is the act of a peevish and sick child. Notice the patronizing scorn with which the midwives treat Pharaoh in the Bible's narrative. The fact that he accepts their excuses points to a weak mind.

In this context, Pharaoh's sister/wife, Lady Noblest, the queen of Egypt, titled Pharaoh's Daughter, goes down to bathe and cool off in the heat of the day. She has heard of her incompetent step-brother/husband's barbarous decree, and, given what we know about her future conduct, is undoubtedly disgusted. While all nobility in the ancient world is of necessity accustomed to blood and violence, this act is worse than bloody; it is ugly and degrading.

However, as the symbol of all that is beautiful and good in Egypt, she also cannot be seen to publicly contradict her foolish brother/

husband. Something indirect yet potent is called for. When she reaches the water, the answer is handed to her in a basket.

When the baby's six-year-old sister, Miriam ("Bitteress"), runs up to the Lady Noblest and offers a "nurse" for the newfound infant, it is likely that Pharaoh's Daughter was highly amused. First, who could have resisted the charmingly transparent precocity of the baby's older sister? Second, she would have loved the fact that a woman had found a way to do exactly what a domineering man had said, and yet completely avoided the intention.

Her stupid stepbrother/husband says, "Throw your baby in the river!" So this desperate and brave slave woman puts the baby in a basket, throws him the river, and sets a six-year-old guard. In that lighthearted mood, she names the baby Moses, "Born," ostensibly because he was born out of the Nile, but at the same time it may have been a subtle mockery of her husband/brother's name, Thutmose: "Lawborn."

By adopting the Hebrew baby, the Lady Noblest publicly presents the perfect picture of loving femininity. And, she has not even contravened the letter of the decree. The baby, after all, *has* been thrown in the Nile. The law *has* been fulfilled, and now she takes him out of the water, and makes him a member of the royal household. How *nice* of Pharaoh to go to *all that trouble* just to provide her with such a *cute* baby boy, since her brother/husband so *unfortunately* is not well enough to do so by *normal* means.

She then blithely hands off the baby to its natural mother, and waits for the word to spread. And, undoubtedly, word did spread of the Lady Noblest's charming defusing of an ugly situation. We hear no more about Hebrew babies being thrown into the Nile. From what we know of Lady Noblest from history, this potent sweet indirection remained her style.

THE CHILDREN: Soon after this, possibly taking the hint, Lawborn II fathers a child with his sister. Lady Noblest bears him a daughter, which she names Neferure: "Sunbeauty." In the same short period, Lawborn also fathers a son by a minor concubine, who ends up named Lawborn III. Different versions of this story give the three infants various relative ages. However, given that Moses is eighty at the time of the Exodus, following the royal genealogy backward would make him very near the same age as Lawborn III. This would indicate that his impending birth may have provided Lady Noblest with further motive to goad her husband/brother.

Furthermore, different versions give the Lady Noblest various ages. I tend to favor making her about twenty-six, since examination of her probable mummy indicates she died at about fifty years old. This means she takes over as Pharaoh at the age of twenty-nine. Some view her as young as nine years old; this comes from strictly adhering to the standard relationship between the Egyptian and biblical chronologies. I just tend to be a little more skeptical that Egyptologists have tied the edges down so firmly.

As nurse to Lady Noblest's adoptive son, it would have been in Moses' (Born's) natural mother's best interest to keep her son in view of Pharaoh's daughter as much as possible. Most think she and her other children become part of the palace household, since both of Born's two natural siblings become famous for their training in the arts, pointing to a palace education.

When Lawborn III is three years old, his invalid father finally dies. The Lady Noblest takes over as regent at first, but gains such approval of her reign that she soon rules as Pharaoh herself, going on to become one of greatest pharaohs in all of Egyptian history. In war she was famously effective, yet rarely went to war. In peace she launched the golden age of Egyptian art and architecture. Under her rule Egypt experienced unprecedented prosperity. And, in her lifetime she was arguably the most beloved pharaoh Egypt ever had.

One more figure enters the mix—a famous genius with the simple name of Senenmut, "Uncle." Historians know several things about Uncle. First, he very competently administers many of the civil functions of the Egyptian government. Second, gossips claimed he was Lady Noblest's lover. Third, he achieves fame as the project manager that builds what was for a millennium the most beautiful monumental structure of the ancient world—the famous colonnaded monument, *Dejeser-Dejeseru*, the Sublime of Sublimes. For centuries following, pharaohs scorned pyramids and chose to be buried in stone tombs behind this most beautiful of monuments. We now call this area the Valley of the Kings.

However, officially, Uncle's primary job was to tutor Sunbeauty, Lady Noblest's daughter. Statues of Uncle from the period often show him with Sunbeauty on his lap. In a household like that, you can't tutor one child without incidentally tutoring the others, even if two—like Born's siblings, Bitteress and Concept—are only attached as servants.

THE NEW SETTING: Soon after assuming power, Lady Noblest moves her court back up south to Karnak and stays there. This would imply that the bulk of the famous abuse of the Hebrews happens hundreds of miles out of the sight of Born as he grows up. He could easily acknowledge his Hebrew parentage, but not really understand what that meant. (*Nobody* calls a member of a royal court a bad name, at least not more than once.)

SUNBEAUTY: She has been groomed to co-rule with Lawborn III when Lady Noblest retires or dies. However, while we hear lots about her as a child, we don't hear much about her as an adult. Many feel that she married Lawborn in her early teens, and then dies, possibly in childbirth, possibly bearing Lawborn's son and intended heir, Windchief.

LAWBORN III: For a while historians tended to think that the young Lawborn chaffed under the usurping authority of his evil stepmother/aunt. However, few believe this anymore. To begin with, Lawborn III is too well trained to support any idea that his stepmother is holding him down. Second, she puts him in charge of the army while he's still a teenager, something she would hardly do if any tension existed between them. Third, she handles the long boring ceremonies and the politicking with the priests, something a young man couldn't help but be relieved to avoid. Lawborn was manifestly delighted with his stepmother. He got to do all the fun stuff; she got to do all the boring stuff.

When Lady Noblest dies, after a reign of twenty-one years, the twenty-four-year-old Lawborn truly mourns her passing. Things progress well for Lawborn after that. He continues a series of military campaigns and decisively conquers all of Canaan. He places the survivors under heavy taxation and expands Egyptian territory and wealth to its greatest extant. Historians call Lawborn III the "Egyptian Napoleon."

FORTY YEARS LATER: The Bible narrative picks up when Born is forty years old. By now, both the Lady Noblest and her daughter Sunbeauty have died, and Lawborn has been well established as king for up to sixteen years. As an elder member of the royal household in Karnak, Born may have been closely bonded to Windchief, the son and heir of Lawborn III and the deceased Sunbeauty, especially since Lawborn spent so much time away on military campaigns while Windchief was a child.

Quite likely, as Windchief grows to be a young man, Born would have retained his beloved status in his nephew's heart. However, just when Born turns forty years old, Windchief dies in his early twenties, leaving Lawborn III having to select a new heir.

(Another version of this story thinks this Windchief is the firstborn who dies in the tenth plague, and shifts all the events back forty years. This more closely matches the standard relationship between the Biblical and Egyptian chronologies. However, it lacks any other striking parallels with known events, and requires that Pharaoh not die in the Red Sea crossing.)

However, Lawborn III has a problem. He himself is not of the blood, and all the direct bearers of the divine royal blood have now died. He now has no member of the royal bloodline to stand with him in official ceremonies. Life has suddenly become much less secure for Lawborn III.

Worse yet, any heir he selects will not be of the blood, and will face the real possibility of civil unrest. He settles on his fifteen-year-old son by a concubine, Amenhotep, "Windpeace II." Since Windpeace was the name of the last male Pharaoh of the blood, it's likely that the name was newly selected for the occasion, to superficially tie him to the royal blood in the public eye.

However, in this context, Born has gone from being the beloved uncle of the heir Windchief, to being a real threat to the new heir, Windpeace II. Born intrinsically has more familiar ties to the priesthood, more political connections than the new heir, and he had been officially adopted by a pharaoh's daughter, something even the young Windpeace himself could not claim.

Obviously, Born has to be neutralized. So, reasonably, Born is sent away, probably to Fort Tjaru. Now, one thing I didn't mention about Fort Tjaru is the fact that despite its military significance, Egyptians viewed it as a hellhole. It sat just outside the green belt of the easternmost river, at the extreme northern edge of a hot, rocky desert. Sending a noble to Fort Tjaru was the Egyptian court's equivalent of being sent to Siberia. Assignment to Tjaru is even officially listed as a punishment for nobles who get in trouble.

Now, undoubtedly, given Born's status at the court, once Windpeace gained a secure foothold, Born would have been invited back to court as if nothing had happened. But, a complication sets in. It is likely Born may never have seen the working conditions of the Hebrews up close before. And likely, part of the logic of sending Born to Fort Tjaru was to not-so-subtly remind him of his roots, to prompt him to not get any big ideas.

However, we know how the rest of the story plays out. Outraged at the behavior of an overseer, Born gets in a fight. And, given his advanced martial-arts training growing up in court, intentionally or not, he kills the Medjay.

Born knows that Lawborn has to respond. And so, he packs his things and gets out of Dodge. Likely, with Born gone, Lawborn III would have hushed the matter up, trying to avoid any undue disturbance during this time of insecurity. Many could testify that Born had just walked out of Fort Tjaru and into the desert under his own foot power. "Who knows where, and who knows why?"

Fleeing to Canaan was actually a fairly common and well-known option for inconvenient Egyptian princes. Archeologists have even found a short autobiography that they call *The Adventures of Sanehat*, written by one Egyptian prince who had done just that.[73]

Twelve years later, when Lawborn III's health begins to fade, Windpeace ascends to co-regency with his father, securing his peaceful transition to power when his father dies two years later. During those two years, Windpeace goes through every public monument he can find, franticly chiseling out any mention of the Lady Noblest and her court, banning even the mention of the name Lady Noblest. He wants no mention of the fact that, only a few years earlier, there had been a royal bloodline that now has vanished.

At the same time, he elevates the original Windpeace of eighty years earlier to the status of a full god, complete with temples. He is Windpeace the Second, and he dares anyone to say he is not the direct blood descendant of the original "Windpeace the Divine."[74] One final note: According to some rabbinical traditions, over the forty years of Born's absence, the aging team of Bitteress (Miriam) and Concept (Aaron) function as the moral leaders of the oppressed Hebrews. Bitteress leads by virtue of her great learning and wisdom, gained as she sat at the feet of the famous Uncle next to her mistress,

73. Petrie, 1899
74. http://en.wikipedia.org/wiki/Hatshepsut, accessed July 25, 2007.

Sunbeauty. Concept leads by his ability as a stirring public speaker and storyteller, generally as a mouthpiece for Bitteress. The older they get, the more influence they wield over all Egyptians though their connections with the royal court of the still-remembered and beloved (whisper it) Lady Noblest.

FORTY YEARS OF WINDPEACE II: In the historical record, the teenage Windpeace leaves pompous trophies bragging about his physical accomplishments. For instance, he single-handedly "outrowed a hundred of Pharaoh's soldiers!" This, of course, makes you wonder how brave a hundred soldiers would have to be to even think of beating the self-important little prince at anything at all.

As a young man, his father puts him in charge of finishing the building of Peru-nefer ("Bon Voyage"), the new port next to the Avaris summer palace. He takes great pride in the speed with which he is able to get work to proceed. You can just hear the thunderous applause of cracking whips in the background.

Also, in his monuments he makes it clear that he has nothing but contempt for non-Egyptians, especially that miserable Asiatic slime. In the same vein, during his reign he's not going to let himself be dominated by any woman the way his father had been. Noble women are no longer allowed to play key roles in religious ceremony or public life. There is no longer any talk of a "Pharaoh's daughter," and he leaves no record of even the names of his own wives. He even attempts to take credit for the monument-building accomplishments of his deceased great-aunt/step-grandmother (not that anybody is fooled.)[75]

Windpeace has ruled for twenty-six years and was himself about fifty-five years old. Forty years have passed since the death of the first heir, Windchief. Abruptly, the eighty-year-old Born reappears as if from the dead. Tradition and public opinion would demand that as an old man, a prince of the court, and especially as an uncle, Windpeace must treat Born with respect.

75. http://en.wikipedia.org/wiki/Amenhotep_II, accessed July 31, 2009.

If anyone else had shown up with Born's outrageous demands, they would never have escaped with their lives, let alone have been given regular access to the court. But, as an elderly member of the royal family, and given Windpeace's past record of posturing for public adulation, Born has unfettered access to the court. Born may be humored and ignored as a senile old man, but never disrespected. All of this fits the *story* so well. Windpeace has just the kind of pompous ego that fits him so well to be the villain of the Exodus.

A STUBBORN PHARAOH AND THE GLORY OF GOD: According to the story, God says he intends to "harden Pharaoh's heart" to get "glory" for himself. Now, a lot of people think that this means God is some kind of insecure egomaniac who lies awake at night worrying that we might not know how wonderful he is.

But "glory" serves a very different purpose. The word "glory" means "with an open display of status and authority." When a police officer confronts a bad guy, he prefers to do so in full uniform with a show of overwhelming force and a very stern demeanor. This makes it much less likely the suspect will try something stupid and get himself and possible bystanders filled with holes. When God is glorified, miscreants tend to behave themselves, and thus God avoids unnecessary violence.

If you remember that Lawborn III had already conquered and claimed Canaan for Egypt a generation before, this makes much more sense. At the time of the Exodus, and for the next couple of centuries, Egypt will hold Canaan's walled cities firmly in its grip, exacting exorbitant taxes. If God had actually wiped out the Egyptians, then this would have only strengthened and encouraged the Canaanites, making the task of giving the Hebrew's the land of Canaan more difficult and much bloodier.

By frightening the Egyptians instead of destroying them, God insures that for the next century Egypt continues to tax and weaken the Canaanite cities, but tacitly and strictly leaves the Hebrews at

Gilgal, and then in the surrounding hill country alone, pretending they don't even exist.

This unspoken memory of the Exodus so haunts the pharaohs that follow Windpeace that they abandon Avaris/Peru-Nefer. Despite its prime location, beautiful palace, and wonderful marina, nobody sailing down the Nile wants to even set foot on the cursed soil for the next 120 years.

It's in this interim that Akhenaten and his father ignore the trespasses of the "Habiru" in the Egyptian territory of Canaan, and Akhenaten even tries to emulate the Hebrews in his attempt to establish monotheism in Egypt.

Only when the Egyptian memory of the Exodus fades away does a new dynasty under Rameses the Great dare to rebuild at Avaris/Peru-Nefer, and it is another seventy-five years before Rameses' seventy-year-old son, the mighty Pharaoh Merenptah, dares to stand up to little Israel in battle.

13

Conclusion:
Blood on the Doorposts

Here we are in the last chapter. We've sailed our way through an overview of a whole sea of material, skimming the wave tops of many subjects, not diving very deep into any. By now you are aware of some of the storms that have battered against the Word of God over the last century, and you've had a chance to inspect the hull and assure yourself that it hasn't popped one seam, nor sprung a single leak. Regrettably, quite a few of the traditions we had stacked on its deck have swept overboard, but they weren't tied down very well, and weren't worth much anyway.

Hopefully, now that you have seen how well the Bible has weathered past storms, you won't worry every time you see a few rain clouds on the horizon, or some blowhard begins to spout off.

In this chapter we will begin by looking at the question we raised in chapter nine of who actually penned the Law. Next, we will look at some of the philosophical challenges and implications of tying the creation story so closely to the tenth plague, and of viewing its revelation as such a concrete and objective event. Finally, we will close by visualizing that first presentation of the creation story just for fun (at least for me).

SO WHO DID WRITE GENESIS?: In chapter nine, we touched on the complexity and genius of the Book of Law, made even more so when we remember it is one of the world's oldest works of great literature.

Furthermore, the Law is the seemingly impossible book. We look at the creation story and see science impossibly ahead of its day. We look at its details and see a book that could only have been written by contemporaries of the events, bridging at least two lifespans. Yet, when we consider its structure and unity, it would seem that only a single author held control of the text.

Furthermore, when we consider much of the Law, we see a formality and education that could only have been gained in an Egyptian royal court. But, while we can plausibly claim such training for Moses, Aaron, or Miriam, none of them lived long enough to record many of the events.

Possible candidates for authorship are scarce. Some have suggested one of the prophets, from Deborah to Nathan, as the possible final editor of the book of Joshua. Yet, how would they have had access to training like that? In fact, while plainly the Law was finished at least two generations after the Exodus, it's difficult to imagine anyone at all after the Exodus who could have possibly had access to such training.

And from here we launch into speculation. Personally, I *have* heard of one plausible candidate as the actual author of the Law. However, keep in mind that I have not heard a whole universe of things. And furthermore, just because an explanation is plausible doesn't mean it's true. And, new evidence may pop up in the archaeological record and suggest an even better answer.

THE CANDIDATE: Let's begin by relooking at that incident in Number's 12:1:

> And Miriam and Aaron spake against Moses because of the Ethiopian woman whom he had married: for he had married an Ethiopian woman. And they said, Hath the Lord indeed spoken only by Moses? Hath he not spoken also by us?

Notice something here that most people overlook. Miriam asserts with confidence that the Lord also has spoken by her. Neither Moses nor God himself denies it. We should remember this before we dismiss her as simply the bossy older sister, or perhaps as the senile old lady.

When we consider the pair of Aaron and Miriam, notice that God spanks Miriam, not Aaron. We get the impression that from force of personality and a long-standing family dynamic, the dominant personality here is not Aaron's, but rather Miriam's. Also, note that in the next verse, Numbers 12:2, all of Israel waits for Miriam to return before they are willing to move forward.

Notice also, that when Miriam dies, Numbers 20:1–12, the waters of Kadesh immediately dry up, leading to the infamous double striking of the rock that gets Moses and Aaron both barred from entering the Promised Land. Finally, hundreds of years later, Micah 6:4 mentions Miriam as an implied equal to Moses and Aaron in leading Israel out of Egypt.

This then raises a question. Moses is busy being the leader of Israel. And Aaron is busy doing all that priestly stuff. What is the prophetess Miriam—the one who thinks she ranks equal to Moses and Aaron—doing all this time?

In the book of Exodus, Miriam only figures prominently as the girl who watches the baby Moses and after Pharaoh's army is drowned in the Red Sea: "And Miriam the prophetess, the sister of

Aaron, took a timbrel in her hand; and all the women went out after her with timbrels and with dances" (Exodus 15:20).

Given the Egyptian background of this story, we shouldn't think gypsy campfire dancing here; instead, we should think Egyptian high-ceremonial dancing. You should know that in the Egyptian court in which Moses was raised, to lead a ceremony with a timbrel was one of the functions of the women of the upper nobility. The highest and noblest of the women always led the dance, and often was the one who had actually instructed the younger, less noble women. Tie this with the fact that Miriam's title of prophetess did not just imply visionary, it also implied teacher.

This in turn leads to the question, whom did she teach? Given the paternalistic nature of Hebrew society, it is unlikely that she taught anyone other than women. According to a few rabbinic traditions, Miriam played a much more active role in the birth and childhood of Moses, and for decades prior to the Exodus she taught a school of prophetesses and was Israel's spiritual leader. Furthermore, this school continued its work after Miriam died. Eventually, as the role of women declined over the next few centuries, some think that this school for women morphed into the school of prophets we hear mentioned throughout the book of Kings.[76] The Old Testament only mentions, besides Miriam, two other prophetesses of the Lord: Deborah and Huldah. (A fourth prophetess is mentioned as a false prophet.)

If you don't already know the story of Deborah (Bee), then take a moment to read it in Judges Chapters 4 and 5. In the context of our discussion, this story raises the question—if all women did at this time was keep house, have babies, and cook, how could any woman possibly have gained such a position of prominence? Here we see Deborah introduced as the first major judge, an expert on

---

76. http://jwa.org/encyclopedia/article/puah-midrash-and-aggadah, accessed September 9, 2009; http://vbm-torah.org/archive/intparsha66/39-66chukat.htm, accessed September 9, 2009.

the law, and a respected prophetess. However, while virtually all the other Judges have some great accomplishment listed to explain why they were Judge, the story leaves Deborah's credentials strangely unstated. Yet, we see the macho Hebrew military leaders not only listen to her, but actually go along with her plan against their better judgment.

Furthermore, notice that chapter five retells chapter four in the form a poem, apparently composed by Deborah herself. In this case we see that the prophetess is also a poet. This strongly implies that some institution in place at that time provided a literary training for at least some women, and that it offered them a public forum to air their achievements.

Finally, if we accept the traditional date for the Exodus, then the reign of Rameses the Great most likely occurred during Deborah's lifetime. Remember, that both Genesis and Exodus refer to the land of Goshen and the city of Aravis, with the apposition of "Rameses." This would indicate that the Law may have gone though its final edit during the lifetime of Deborah, making the prophetess/poet Deborah the prime candidate for the Law's final editor. This may explain why all of Israel came to view her as Judge.

We only hear of the next prophetess, Huldah, briefly, in a passage recorded in both 2 Kings 22:14 and 2 Chronicles 34:22. "[They] went unto Huldah the prophetess . . . [who] dwelt in Jerusalem in the college." This word translated as college, *mishneh*—Strong's 4932, implies a doubling or copying. It probably refers to a school where the scrolls of the Law were copied and memorized.

Here we see the only mention in the Bible of the body likely responsible for the early transmission of the written Bible. And, it apparently rests under the hand of a woman. Here again, as in the case of Deborah, the prophetess is tied to a literary tradition.

(Later, the earliest legal opinions of the Jews were gathered into a volume also named the Mishna. This later forms part of the Talmud, which we see referred to in the Gospels as the "Traditions of the Elders.")

When we look at the law, we see a vast, unified work written by eyewitnesses, yet spanning two lifespans. This strongly implies that the written Law of Moses was the work of a committee that functioned contemporary to the events described.

Furthermore, at the risk of sounding sexist, those kinds of tight-knit intergenerational committees tend to be committees of women. Leading men tend to be more wrapped up in politics and war and careers. Even today, we men would tend to dismiss such an academic, long-lasting literary group as an "old ladies' tea club."

Such a tight-knit small group could work together spending their entire adult lives immersed in the message and structure of a unified final work, and yet have the work itself span several generations.

It is possible, but certainly not proven, that the book of the Law was actually penned by a small committee of prophetesses, all close intimates of the leaders of Israel, acting as in-house scribes to take dictation from their husbands, fathers, sons, and nephews, before, during, and after the Exodus.

This would also explain why Genesis has generally more sophisticated literary passages than its counterparts in Joshua. Miriam would have probably written the story of Joseph while she was at the height of her ability and skills, possibly decades before the Exodus itself. So, while her successor(s) a century later could follow the structural outline laid out in Genesis to finish the work, reasonably we would not expect her to necessarily live up to the prophetess Miriam's literary stature.

So, we have to consider the possibility—and at this point *only* the possibility—that the original unifying editor/author/scribe of the creation story and particularly Genesis is not Moses himself, but rather his elder sister, Miriam. And, *if* that was the case, it was likely a committee, or the prophetesses' school founded by Miriam and finally led by Deborah, that finishes the work in the two generations after her death.

This is one more support for the traditional view of the Exodus that sees Hatshepsut—Lady Noblest—as the Pharaoh's daughter who raises Moses. In that whole millennium, she was the most likely to have provided such a high-level education for girls in her court, and only a girl raised in such a court would have had the training and sheer confidence and nerve to do what we think Miriam may have done.

Also, this would explain why Miriam, who has such a major implied role, gets short shrift in the actual text. Often, authors of biblical texts minimize their own role in events, recording only derogatory stories about themselves. For instance, of all the Gospels, Mark has the most negative portrayal of Peter, yet most agree Peter himself is the primary source for the text.

This is not as radical or as original a proposal as you may think. Scholars have long noted that much of the Law has a feminine perspective. While the stories are about the men, we often see them through the eyes of the women. If you think about it for a moment, I'm sure you could easily list at least five scenes that we see and conversations we hear through the eyes of a woman.

This is all the more remarkable when we consider that this was an age that barely considered women human. In that day, most men would no more think with a woman's perspective than they would with a dog's perspective. Yet there it is, story after story told from the women's POV.

Just something for male chauvinist pigs like me to think about. . . .

THE PROBLEM WITH THE TENTH PLAGUE: Tying the creation story to the tenth plague has some weighty implications. In Exodus, the tenth plague stands out as the most unpalatable event to modern tastes. Even evangelicals who say they believe in the miraculous actually have a hard time with the death of the firstborn.

Most of us could have faced seeing the tidal wave that had destroyed Pharaoh's army sweep inland and kill a hundred thousand civilians easier than we can face the tenth plague. After all, just a few years ago a tidal wave swept into Indonesia killing hundreds of thousands of people. Most of us just shook our heads over the sadness of this world, but few of us thought to implicate God.

The problem with the tenth plague is not that we can't believe in the miraculous, the problem is that many of us have a hard time believing that God would ever do anything so *monstrous*. Our modern mindset just can't accept that God would ever *curse*. God only does *good things*. If bad things happen, it's because God just stood back and let *Satan* do it. To get modern people to wrap their minds around God actually directly *killing* people—worse yet, killing innocent *little children* by the thousands—is too monstrous to accept.

Worse than even that, in killing all those children, God frees the Hebrews with the express purpose to launch them at Canaan with an explicit command to kill every man, woman, child, and goat in their path—to commit *genocide*, the most monstrous crime our modern minds can imagine.

This seems so antithetical to the "good news" of the gospel, that it seems to many like the Bible has two Gods—the good God of the New Testament and the evil God of the Old Testament.

It was this tension that drove Wellhausen to devise his JED-P nonsense in an attempt to devalue and minimize the Old Testament.

This same tension drove the Gnostics of the second and third centuries to say that the Old Testament God was actually Satan.

And we see in the book of Isaiah that many in Israel itself before the Babylonian captivity had begun criticizing God over the same issues. It had become fashionable to sit in judgment on such an out-of-control God, and to deplore his acts.

Have you ever heard the phrase *holier than thou*? Today we use the phrase to describe some self-righteous person looking down their nose at someone else's socially unacceptable conduct. However, this phrase comes to us from the book of Isaiah just before Isaiah pronounces God's judgment on Israel, condemning many thousands of them to death, and sending the remainder off to captivity in Babylon:

> I [God] have spread out my hands all the day unto a
> rebellious people, which walketh in a way that was not
> good, after their own thoughts; A people that provoketh
> me to anger continually to my face; . . . Which remain
> among the graves . . . which eat swine's flesh, and broth
> of abominable things is in their vessels; *Which say, Stand
> by thyself, come not near to me; for I am holier than thou.*
> These are a smoke in my nose, a fire that burneth all
> the day. . . . Your iniquities, and the iniquities of your
> fathers together, saith the Lord, which have burned in-
> cense upon the mountains, and blasphemed me upon
> the hills: therefore will I measure their former work into
> their bosom. (Isaiah 65:2–7, emphasis added)

Here you see that the phrase *holier than thou* refers to ungodly
people who cover up their failures by making up and then keeping
some arbitrary rule that God never established. They then go on to
look down their noses at God himself, since he doesn't live up to
their arbitrary rule.

For instance, are you a liar, a thief, a violent drug dealer? Have
you betrayed your spouse and abandoned your children? Then the
solution is simple! Don't repent; instead join People for the Ethical
Treatment of Animals (PETA)! Refuse to wear leather or eat a ham-
burger. Then you too can enjoy the pleasure of looking down your
nose at all those self-righteous Christian hypocrites traipsing into
McDonalds! It's not an accident that vegetarianism is so popular in
our nation's prisons.[77]

Now, I have no problem with people who chose vegetarianism.
And I'm definitely not saying that vegetarianism is evil. What I am
saying is that I have met a lot of holier-than-thou vegetarians who
gasp in disbelief that God could be so monstrous and cruel as to tell
Peter to "kill and eat" (Acts 10:13).

77, http://blog.peta.org/archives/2007/12/top_10_vegetari.php;, http://www.news-week.com/id/74327

The truth is that if we find ourselves forced to accept the concept of a personal God, we would much prefer that he never stepped off the set of "My Little Pony." A God who wades through blood and death, who is quite willing to break lots and lots of eggs to make his omelets—this kind of God is just too harsh for most of us to face.

Philosophically, this brings us to the old question of "How can a good God allow bad things to happen?"

The movie, *The Hiding Place*, narrates the autobiography of Cory Ten Boom, who recorded her family's ordeal in a Nazi death camp, which only she survived. In one scene Cory's sister Betsy leads a devotional with some of the inmates, talking about the love of God, when another inmate interrupts:

"To the mindless these words sound so comforting. In this place it's mockery!"

Betsy responds, "God didn't make this place; man did."

"But he has power? Surely he could stop them, unless of course he's a sadist!"

"Oh no, he is love, all love!"

"Then he is impotent, you can't have it both ways. . . . It's enough to know that we are so much dung, moving from nothing to nothing. But, you must believe that your God smells the stench from those chimneys and refuses to do anything."

Betsy is silent in the face of the inmate's pain, but Cory steps in, "We cannot answer. All I can say is that the same God you are accusing came and lived in the midst of our world. He was beaten, and he was mocked, and he died on a cross, and he did it for love, for us."

Given the circumstances, I cannot imagine a better answer.

However, while this answer met the immediate need for comfort in a horrendous situation, it doesn't actually deal with the question itself. It basically says "I don't know, *but . . .*"

However, I think many of us actually know the straight answer but are afraid to say it. The straight harsh answer to the harsh question is, "Of course God is monstrous! Godzilla has nothing on God. Get over it. Like Job, come to terms with the monster or curse God and die—your choice."

As a young man, when it first dawned on me that there might actually be a real personal God, my first reaction was rage. My first real prayer, if you can call it that, was at least an hour of ranting obscenities and futile hatred. Of course, it didn't even dent one scale on God-zilla's hide.

Fortunately for me, I waited for a response. And then I began to find out that this particular God-zilla had a plan, and that plan had made provision for me and for you. And now, because God-zilla has adopted me as one of his sheep, I have everything I need. Too bad if you're not one of his sheep; if I were you, I would do something about that as soon as possible.

Does this seem too harsh? This is the problem with a real God and the tenth plague. A real God, a God who has shepherded this real universe for the last thirteen billion years, just might not be as impressed with us, and as eager to please us, as we would like. A God like that might even be a bit critical, might insist that we approach him on his terms and not ours. A God like that might not care in the least about our opinions and assumptions about who he *should* be. Like it or not, to paraphrase Exodus 3:14, he is who he is.

Yes, God destroys. But in the tenth plague, he only destroys what he himself first created. God blessed Egypt through Joseph, saving the people from the consequences of a temporary climate shift and resultant famine. Through the plagues, God took back his gift, reducing the population to where it would have been if he had not intervened, (an object lesson that God-blessed-America may want to keep in mind.)

THE CREATION STORY AND THE ANGEL OF DEATH: Down through the ages, pessimists who have considered the possibility of a real God have often raised the same question: "Why would a real God, a God powerful enough to have created this incomprehensibly vast universe billions of years ago, even notice us at all? And, if he did notice us, why would he not simply wipe us all out, cleansing the earth of an infestation of vile scum?"

To answer that, we turn to the creation story, first given at the very moment that the angel of death ravaged its way through Egypt, slaughtering thousands of children by night in their beds. If the creation story tells us anything, it tells us that God has directly intervened to create humanity, and to preserve human culture. He has stamped his image on us—without our permission, by the way—and values our humanity.

Not only that, the creation story implies that God has a plan; he is doing something very specific, working toward an end that he values. This is the grace of God. He chooses to love us; he chooses to offer us life, on his terms, but life nonetheless.

THE FIERY CLOUD AND THE TENTH PLAGUE: Now, let's close with a narrative, visualizing the giving of the creation story. This story translates many of the Egyptian names. Rather than break up the story with definitions as we go along, here is a name list:

Bitteress	=	Miriam
Borderland	=	the land of Goshen
Born	=	Moses
Bon Voyage	=	Peru-Nefer, the port/palace built on the ruins of Avaris.
Bowlander	=	Nubian
Concept	=	Aaron
Great House	=	Pharaoh
Middle-earth	=	Mediterranean
Strongholds	=	Egypt

The Ward	=	the remnants of the city of Avaris, the old Hyksos civil administration ward.
Wanders	=	Hebrews, a euphemism for their Warder epithet.
Warders	=	H'Avaru, the descendants of the Hyksos civil service ward of Avaris, an insulting epithet.
Windpeace	=	Amenhotep

AS THE RED-EYED SUN makes its first timid appearance in nearly three days, fear hangs like its own dust cloud over the near-choked Strongholds, from the vast Delta's northern edge at the Middle-earth Sea, and southward to where the river begins its climb into the southern Kingdom.

Cautiously, with fearful glances skyward, the Stronghold's people creep from their muffled homes, to leave trails in the dust and huddle in whispering groups, high mingling with low, like a thousand small menageries of half-drowned wildlife huddled on reed rafts to escape a flood. They moan over the year's nine disasters. They stutter of the gods' humiliations. Some shake their heads quietly over the mad stubbornness of the Great House Windpeace the Second. And all whisper of the mighty Born, with left hand on their heads, and the right making signs to ward off evil.

In contrast, from atop the watchtowers and the five-paces-thick wall that surrounds the palace garrison at Port Bon Voyage, a thousand ebony Medjay archers watch with impassive faces. The Bowlanders show no emotion—standing solidly erect with ankle-deep gray powder around their sandals and their polished wooden bows hanging at their left sides. The rising sun gleams off their large brass earrings, which they somehow have kept gleaming in spite of the dust.

The Bowlanders had watched unflinchingly as Born rained down curse after curse on the land. They had watched as many of their own number died of plague. Even when the sky had rained burning stones on the northern fortress, forcing them to quick-march into shelter, they had maintained the well-ordered ranks of military disciple, scooping up their comrades' broken bodies as they went.

And from those towers, each guard had watched the warm dust cloud sweep in off the northeastern Middle-earth Sea three days earlier. Ironically, the storm had left the land immediately east of the palace and river entirely untouched—the Ward and Borderland of the muddy Warders was now the only clean land in the Strongholds.

From the tower tops, the Medjay watchmen glower at the Ward, the six hundred Warder slave compounds randomly crowded over the mile south of the palace in the river's bend.

Each compound much resembled the next: a ten-foot-high brick wall laid out in a large rectangle, with an interior wall across the rear to enclose the family elder's living space. Two rows of bundled-reed posts and lintels ran from the front to the rear apartment, dividing the court into thirds. The families of sons and son's sons lived under simple, six-foot-deep palm-thatched lean-tos between the right and left walls and the interior posts. Five rows of reed rails ran between the posts, turning the center space into a livestock corral in the compound's middle.

The ground sloped gently down from both walls, creating a trough to channel urine and manure out the single, narrow, chest-high eastern gate into a muddy trench that surrounded each compound's exposed sides. The stench was the price paid for denying desert lions footing to leap the walls at night. Even then, a pair of skinny, bad-tempered dogs usually patrolled the wall tops, watching for marauders.

In particular, the guards watched the two southernmost and largest compounds, the compounds of the ancient brother and sister, the Herald Concept and Maid Bitteress. Alone of all the compounds, instead of gates of leather-bound un-planed branches, these two had solid carved doors on brass hinges.

The larger inland compound housed the family of the famous orator, Concept. Instead of lean-tos, his sons all had walled rooms.

Rich from entertaining two generations of the court, Concept had retired and spent his time telling folk tales to scruffy mobs of Warder brats. However, the late troubles had drawn him out of retirement to act as herald for the miraculously returned Prince Born.

While not as large, the interior of Bitteress's compound nearest the river had paving of clean baked-bricks and two entrances. One entrance led to a series of bright airy rooms with clean mats to tend broken bones and wounds. The other entrance led into a courtyard with fresco-painted walls lined with potted plants and benches. Instead of a muddy corral, foot baths and a small lotus pond with fish and frogs decorated the entrance way. A low raised platform fronted the rear apartment, facing an open arena where for four decades young Wander women had sat to learn the healing crafts, the short letters, song, dance, and their people's history at the feet of the ancient Maid Bitteress and her attendants.

But such luxury in the middle of Wander poverty raised no envious voices. For, the only charge for healing had been need, and the only charge for education had been a willing heart and some hint of talent. Since she shared her compound's healing skills and beauty so freely, the lowest of the Wanders took as much pride in it as if it had been their own.

Indeed, often a Medjay captain had grumbled about allowing slaves such a source of pride. But this same Bitteress had cleaned the bottoms of three generations of Great House princes, had sung them to sleep on her lap, and was rumored to be the prophetess of the Warder God. So when the Great House Lady Noblest, whose very name the jealous Windpeace had banned, left the Maid Bitteress riches, not even Windpeace had challenged the will.

Never wholly reconciled to such elevated Warders, the Medjay now had even more reason to watch those compounds. For the ancient Prince Born, who had plagued the Strongholds like a god of chaos for most of the last year, Prince Born insanely claimed both Bitteress and Concept as siblings, and lodged in Bitteress's compound.

Whenever Born's guard loaded onto a barge at Bitteress's dock and then drifted downriver toward the palace, all along the western riverbank increasing numbers of the Stronghold's people would rush shoreward throwing dust in the air, pounding the tops of their heads with their palms.

Today, they even stumbled to their knees at reeds' edge to throw pleading hands in the air as they bowed their foreheads in and out of the mud. By the time the barge had docked in front of the palace, the mob on the western bank was so thick that the guards could hear their pleading even from the tops of their towers.

Then, an hour later, the guards watched grimly as the Great House descended into impotent and undignified shouting—the Great House impiously banishing his own ancient uncle, Born, from court, and that same uncle ominously vowing to not return.

Then the contest fell silent. Over the next week, no more delegations visited the palace, and no decree passed through its gates. As each day passed, the Medjay readied for inevitable combat. For every day that the Great House sat in pouting silence, the impudence of the Warder slaves mounted. Bands of them even wandered throughout the eastern Delta, demanding and receiving tribute from the terrorized populous of gold, silver, spices, fine linen garments, and beasts of burden to carry it all.

Then, on the eve of the full moon, the slaves made obvious preparations to leave, in defiance of the Great House's command. All day long flocks have been driven in from the grasslands to the north and east, all sequestered in one or another of the slave compounds.

The Medjay could see bloodshed impending. While armed only with slings and staves, the Warders knew well how to use them, and so outnumbered the Great House's forces that even though certain of victory, the Bowlanders knew they would suffer heavy losses. In a strange way, this prospect came as something of a relief. Death in battle they could at least understand and even take pride in.

By that evening, the palace and marina of Bon Voyage stood virtually deserted. However, the river a mile to the south swarmed with rafts of the Stronghold's civilian men, who leapt to the slave docks, to hurry toward the slave quarters. Each bore a woman's empty water jar; each dropped to kneel outside one or another of the slave compounds—heads to the ground, water jars thrust out in supplicant hands.

The guards watched them with dark eyes, wondering what treachery this signaled.

Then, as the sun began to set, fifteen thousand slaves filed out of their compounds' eastern gates and along the ditch-mounds, to stand facing the lowering sun. Rank after rank, rows of families stood on the western mounds of the muddy trenches that surrounded each of their family compounds. All had freshly scrubbed faces; all impudently wore travel robes and gear.

As the sun leaned into the western horizon, the heads of each Wander household knelt with their right knees to the ground, pinning a male lamb to their left thighs with their elbow. As they did this, a younger man, sometimes even a child, stood in front, raising the lamb's chin high with their left hand, and placing their right hand on the lamb's forehead.

As the sun rippled and puffed toward the horizon, thousands of flint knives rose. Then, as the sun's edge flattened on the earth, signally the official beginning of twilight, myriad knife points carefully sought the hollow behind each lamb's right jaw and plunged in to exit under the opposite jaw. While the lambs' back legs frantically pranced under restraining arms, a quick saw motion forward released gushes of blood into waiting bowls.

At this the Stronghold's supplicant citizens began the beggar's wail, holding up their jars. With a condescending air, the man-slaves stepped forward and carefully sloshed a small splash of blood into each jar. At receiving their dole, each citizen frantically bowed and re-bowed before turning to race back toward their homes across the river.

Meanwhile, the slave-women hurried to take each undressed carcass by hock and foreleg, and then headed back and around the compound wall to duck under each gate's low lintel to lead their extended families in procession back inside their respective compounds.

Once the last of the supplicants had fled, the man-slaves who had slaughtered the lambs gathered up small bunches of leafy thyme twigs in their right hands while the younger men bore the bowls of remaining blood.

These they carried back to each compound's low, narrow entrance. The Bowlander archers watched uneasily as the Warder men paused to use the thyme to paint their gates' posts and lintels with glistening blood, before ducking inside and firmly slamming their gates shut behind them. Across the river, in the gathering dusk, many of the Stronghold's homes received a similar gruesome painting, using the begged blood.

Then suddenly, ululating guards on the palace's northern wall broke the silence, pointing upward to the northeast. In the dim twilight, a strange cloud sailed in from the northeastern sea with a belly that flickered with lights—possibly another rain of fire? Captains yelped their troops into rows, ready to duck behind covering walls if needed. As it loomed near, their dread grew as they could see that the dark cloud was smooth and square-cornered like a speaking platform with an underbelly of fire. Then it sailed by the eastern wall, dwarfing the fortress. It passed so low and near that one foolhardy bowman actually loosed an arrow at it, only to be instantly slapped down by his own captain.

But the strange cloud sailed on without inflicting any apparent damage. The Bowlanders all turned to stare openmouthed as it slowed to stop and then to hover about a mile to the southeast, ignoring the wind, lighting a patch on the far side of the slaves' compounds. As dreadful night crouched lower over the land, the guards realized that the distant light's northern edge framed the compound of the Maid Bitteress and the Prince Born.

On a brazier in Bitteress's courtyard, a lamb roasted whole on the open fire—wool, hooves, entrails, and all. Two women tended it, but now they stood openmouthed, staring skyward, with tongs hanging limply at their sides. About twenty young guards stood at the northern wall, duties also forgotten as they too gazed at the sky. On the compound's platform in front of about twenty Wander elders, Born, Concept, and Bitteress stood with their faces raised to the bathing light. Bitteress called to her attendants, and three of Bitteress's skilled women knelt at the platform's edge with styluses and waxed boards.

Then, all eyes stared upward, as the glory of the Messenger of the I-Am-That-I-Am flickered in the belly of the cloud, so bright that it had even begun to warm the cool spring evening.

Then suddenly, the light quenched, plunging the compound into a long pause of eye-straining darkness. Slowly, a globe of whirling orange liquid swelled in the belly of the cloud, and Born, Concept, and Bitteress raised their voices in unison:

"*Bree'shiyt baaraa' Elohiym!*" ("In the beginning God created!")

One mile north, the whole palace gathered on the walls and watched in awe as lights and images flashed incomprehensibly in the belly of the cloud hovering in the south. Vague rumblings, like a voice of thunder, shook the air as the night thickened. Then finally, the strange cloud dimmed again into absolute darkness and prolonged silence.

Back in the compound, in the dark, in the silence, nobody moved. Then Bitteress gathered her attendants, stepped off the platform, and strode to the roasting lamb. Soon tongs picked thin shreds of meat off the still-roasting carcass and used them to garnish sheets of warm flat bread along with spicy herbs and honey.

The women then gravely distributed these morsels to the standing crowd. But, for many, it took some shoulder tapping and pointed stares before they could recover the presence of mind to look down, place food in their mouths, and chew. Thus the sacred meal began.

A gust of bitter cold swept by the palace walls with the sound of beating wings. Abruptly, in the torch-lit darkness all along the fortress's parapet, about a quarter of the crowd began to stagger and groan; a few even sank to their knees, as if gut-shot with arrows. All up and down the river, in thousands of households, except those whose doorposts gleamed with the blood they had begged off the Wanders, the groans of adults and crying of children shivered the silence, chilling the heart.

For long minutes, the air trembled with pain; then abruptly, silence fell again. Then, out of that silence a thin cry wavered and rose in a sea swell of wailing that built and spread up and down the river, a wail for the dead.

Two hours later, in Bitteress's compound as the feast began to wind down, a guard over the door shouted that torches approached at a run. As if this was the cue he had long awaited, Born strode through the opening gate, gathering a train of guards as he stepped out to meet the arrival of panting, torch-bearing palace messengers. Without slowing, he strode past them, while they bowed so low that their gasping message would have been incomprehensible if he hadn't already known what they had to say.

In the early morning's first dim light, Born strode back to the compound. At his raised arms, all twenty of his guards begin sprinting off in all directions, to pre-assigned sections of the Ward.

Abruptly, an unnaturally deep voice bellowed from the cloud above, shaking even the palm branches.

"Let there be light!"

And, with a blaze to startle the eyes and quail the hearts on the palace grounds a mile away . . . there was light!

Bibliography

Bakker, Robert T., PH.D., *The Dinosaur Heresies*, 1986, Morrow, New York, NY.

Barton, David, *The Myth of Separation*, 1992, WallBuilder Press, P. O. Box 397, Aledo, TX 76008, CD version, "Original Intent."

Begley, Sharon, "The Handwriting of God," *Newsweek*, May 4, 1992, p. 76, 444 Madison Av e. New York NY 10022.

Bower, Bruce, "New gene study enters human origins debate," *Science News*, September 25, 1993, Science Services Inc., 1719 M Street, NW Washington DC 20036.

Bronner, Leah, *From Eve to Esther, Rabbinic Reconstructions of Biblical Women*, 1994, Westminster John Knox Press, Louisville, Kentucky.

Budiansky, Stephen, *The Covenant of the wild: Why animals chose domestication*. 1992, W. Morrow, New York NY.

Budyko, M. I., *History of the Earth's Atmosphere*, 1987, Springer-Verlag Berlin Heidelberg, Germany.

Cornfield, Gaalyah, *Archaeology of the Bible: Book by Book*, 1976, Harper & Row, Publishers, Inc., 10 East 53rd St., New York NY 10022.

Davis, Bernard D., ed., *The Genetic Revolution, Scientific Prospects and Public Perceptions*, 1991, The John Hopkins University Press, 701 West 40th Street, Baltimore, Maryland 21211-2190.

Dorsey, David A., *The Literary Structure of the Old Testament*, 1999, Baker Academic, P. O. Box 6287, Grand Rapids MI 49516.

Drake, Stillman, translation and commentary on *Galileo Gallilei's Dialogue Concerning the Two Chief World Systems—Ptolemaic and Copernican*, 1970, University of California Press, Berkley and Los Angeles California.

Eiseley, Loren, *Darwin's Century* (1958), 1961, Anchor Book, Doubleday & Company, Inc., Garden City NY.

Ellis Enterprises, *The Bible Library* (CD): *Transliterated (Romanized) Hebrew and Greek Bible, and the Literal English Translation Bible,* 1988, Ellis Enterprises, 4205 McAuley Blvd, Suite 385, Oklahoma City OK 73120.

Encyclopedia Britannica, *The New Encyclopedia Britannica*, 1988, Encyclopedia Britannica, Inc., Chicago, Illinois.

Encyclopedia Britannica, *The New Encyclopedia Britannica 15th Ed.,* 2007, Encyclopedia Britannica, Inc., Chicago, Illinois.

Endy, Melvin B., Jr, *William Penn and Early Quakerism*, 1973, Princeton University Press.

Harpending, *Current Anthropology*, (periodical), Aug.-Oct. 1993, University of Chicago Press, 5720 S. Woodland Avenue, Chicago, Illinois 60637.

Hawkings, Stephen W., *A Brief History of Time*, 1988, Bantam Book, Toronto NY.

Hoffmeier, James K., 2005, *Ancient Israel in Sinai: The Evidence for the Authenticity of the Wilderness Tradition*, Oxford University Press Inc., 198 Madison Avenue, New York NY 10016.

Jones, H., ed., *Science Before Darwin: A Nineteenth Century Anthology*, 1963, Andre Deutsch, 105 great Kessell Street, London WC1.

Kerr, Richard A., "Did Darwin Get It All Right?", *Science,* (periodical), 10 March 1995, American Association for the Advancement of Science, 1333 H Street, NW Washington DC 20005, pp. 1422–23.

Larkin, Clarence, *Dispensational Truth*, 7th Edition, 1918, Rev Clarence Larkin Est., 2802 N Park Ave., Philadelphia PA.

Lewin, Roger, "Debate over Emergence of Human Tooth Pattern," *Science* (periodical), vol. 235, February 13, 1987, American Association for the Advancement of Science, 1333 H Street, NW Washington DC 20005.

McGraw-Hill, *McGraw-Hill Encyclopedia of Science and technology*, 1987, McGraw-Hill Book Company, San Francisco CA.

Magill, Frank N., ed., *Magill's Survey of Science,* vol. 1 190, Salem Press, Inc, P.O. Box 50062, Pasadena CA 91105.

Morris, Henry M., *The Genesis Record,* 1976, Baker Book House, Grand Rapids, Michigan.

Morris, Henry M., *Scientific Creationism,* 1974, Creation-Life Publishers, San Diego CA 92115.

Newsweek, "The Search for Adam and Eve," Newsweek (periodical), January 11, 1988, Newsweek, 444 Madison Ave, New York NY 10022.

The Oxford Encyclopedia of Ancient Egypt, 2001, Oxford University Press, Inc., 198 Madison Ave. New York NY 10016.

Peare, Catherine Owens, *William Penn* (1956), 1966, Ann Arbor Paperbacks, The University of Michigan Press.

Ronan, Colin A., *Galileo,* 1974, G. P. Putnam's Sons, New York NY.

Petrie, W. M. Flinders, London 1899, 2nd Edition, Gutenberg.com, Title: *Egyptian Tales,* First Series Release Date: January, 2005.

Ronan, Colin A., *Galileo,* 1974, G. P. Putnam's Sons, New York NY.

Ross, Hugh, *The Fingerprint of God,* Second Edition, 1991, Promise Publishing Co., Orange CA 92667.

Schaeffer, Francis A., *The Complete Works of Francis A. Schaeffer,* vol. 2, No Final Conflict, 1982, Crossway Books Co., Orange CA 92667, 9825 West Roosevelt Rd., Westchester, Illinois 60153.

Schaeffer, Francis A., *Genesis in Space and Time,* 1972, Intervarsity Press, Downers Grove, Illinois 60515.

Schaeffer, Francis A., *How Should We Then Live,* 1976, Fleming H. Revell Company, Old Tappan, New Jersey.

Science, "Origins and Extinctions, Paleontology in Chicago, (Fifth North American Paleontological Convention)," *Science* (periodical), vol.257, July 24, 1992, American Association for the Advancement of Science, 1333 H Street, NW Washington DC 20005.

Scofield, Rev. C. I., D.D., *The Scofield Reference Bible* (1906), Oxford University Press, New York NY, 1945.

Shackley, Myra, *Neanderthal Man*, 1980, Gerald Duckworth & Co. Ltd., the Old Piano Factory, 43 Gloucester Crescent, London NW1.

Showers, William J. & Reese E Barrick, "Thermophysiology of Tyrannosaurus Rex: Evidence from Oxygen Isotopes," *Science* (periodical), Vol. 265, June 1994, The American Association for the Advancement of Science, 1333 H Street, NW, Washington DC 20005.

Spencer Wells, Deep Ancestry, 2006, *National Geographic*, Washington DC.

Stock, Christina, "Flying in the Face of Tradition," *Scientific American*, June 1995, p.22.

Stringer, Christopher, "The Dates of Eden," *Nature* (periodical) vol. 331, Feb. 18, 1988, MacMillan Magazines Ltd., 4 Little Essex Street, London WC2R 3LF.

Stringer, Christopher and Clive Gamble, *In Search of the Neanderthals*, 1993, Thames and Hudson Inc., 500 fifth Avenue, New York NY 10110.

Strong, James, S.T.D., L.L.D., *Strong's Exhaustive Concordance*, 1967, Abingdon Press, New York NY.

Svitil, Kathy A., "Hurricane from Hell," *Discover* (periodical), April 1995, p. 26.

Taylor, Gordon, *The Great Evolution Mystery*, 1983, Harper and Row Publishers, Inc., 10 East 53rd Street, New York NY 10020-1393.

Time, "Echoes from the Big Bang," *Time* (periodical), may 4, 1992, Time Inc., Time & Life Building, Rockefeller Center, New York NY.

Trinkaus, Erik, (Department of Anthropology, Harvard University, Cambridge, Massachusetts), *The Shanidar Neandertals*, 1983, Academic Press of Harcourt, Brace, & Jovanovich, New York NY.

Trinkaus, Erik and Pat Shipman, *The Neandertals: changing the Image of Mankind*, 1993, Alfred A Knopf, New York NY.

Turner, Ronald C., *The New Genesis: Theology and the Genetic Revolution,* 1993, Westminster/John Know Press, Louisville, Kentucky.

Valladas, H., and L. L. Reyss, L. L. Joron, G. Valladas, O Bar-Yosef & B. Vandermeersch, "Thermoluminescence Dating of Mousterian 'Proto-Cro Magnon' Remains from Israel and the Origin of Modern Man," *Nature* (periodical) vol.331, Feb. 18, 1988, MacMillan Magazines Ltd., 4 Little Essex Street, London WC2R 3LF.

Walker, James C. G., *Evolution of the Atmosphere,* 1977, MacMillan Publishing Co., Inc., 866 Third Avenue, New York NY 10022.

Wellhausen, Julius, *Prolegomena,* 1883, accessed October 26, 2009; http://www.gutenberg.org/etext/4732.

Whipple, Fred L., *The Mystery of Comets,* 1985, Smithsonian Institution Press, Washington DC.

Willcocks, Sir William, *From the Garden of Eden to the Crossing of the Jordan,* 1919, Spon & Chamberlain, 120 Liberty Street, New York NY. 2nd Edition.

World Wide Pictures, *The Hiding Place,* (Film) 1975.

P. J. Wiseman, *Creation Revealed in Six Days,* London, Marshall, Morgan, & Scott, 1949.

Zimmer, Carl, "The Ocean Within," *Discover* (periodical) October, 1994.

Zimmerman, Burke K., *Biofuture, Confronting the Genetic Era,* 1984, Plenum Publishing corporation, 233 Spring Street, New York NY 10013.